KINGSHIP AND TYRANNY IN THE THEATER OF GUILLEN DE CASTRO

JAMES CRAPOTTA

KINGSHIP AND TYRANNY IN THE THEATER OF GUILLEN DE CASTRO

TAMESIS BOOKS LIMITED
LONDON

Colección Támesis
SERIE A - MONOGRAFIAS, C

© Copyright by Tamesis Books Limited
London, 1984
ISBN 0 7293 0163 X

The publication of this study was made possible,
in part, by a grant from Barnard College.

Depósito legal: M. 30427-1984

Printed in Spain by Talleres Gráficos de SELECCIONES GRÁFICAS
Carretera de Irún, km. 11,500 - Madrid-34

for
TAMESIS BOOKS LIMITED
LONDON

For the Bear

ACKNOWLEDGMENTS

This study would never have seen the light of day had it not been for the generosity and encouragement of many friends and colleagues.

I should especially like to express my gratitude to Stephen Gilman for sharing with me his invaluable insights and his passionate enthusiasm for the *comedia*. He has been a constant source of inspiration throughout the years. I am also indebted to Francisco Márquez Villanueva for his many constructive suggestions and sound advice. I extend special thanks to Ronald Surtz and Nora Weinerth, not only for their careful reading of the manuscript, but for so much more.

Finally, to my parents, I should like to acknowledge with deep appreciation their continued love and support.

CONTENTS

	PAGE
INTRODUCTION	11
CHAPTER I.—*The Unjust King in Dramatic and Didactic Literature of the Late Sixteenth and Early Seventeenth Centuries*	21
The Tyrant King in the Valencian Theater Prior to Guillén de Castro: Cristóbal de Virués	21
The King in the «Comedia»	32
Political Theory in Sixteenth-Century Spain	39
Aragonese Opposition to Royal Authority	46
CHAPTER II.—*El amor constante*	49
CHAPTER III.—*El Conde Alarcos*	85
CHAPTER IV.—*El nacimiento de Montesinos*	103
CHAPTER V.—*El perfecto caballero*	125
CHAPTER VI.—*Las mocedades del Cid: comedia segunda*	147
CONCLUSION	179
BIBLIOGRAPHY	183

INTRODUCTION

The problem of the abuse of power by the unjust or tyrannical monarch stands out as an important dramatic motif in the theater of the Valencian dramatist Guillén de Castro y Bellvis. It is the central theme of what may well be Castro's first dramatic effort, *El amor constante,* and recurs in at least four other plays, the last of which were written some fifteen to twenty years later, that is, close to the date of composition of his most famous play, *Las mocedades del Cid.*[1] Castro's preoccupation with royal injustice and his repeated portrayal of the king as the source of social disorder contrast sharply with the glorification of monarchy found in the *comedias* of Lope de Vega. The Valencian's personal view of royal power was decisively shaped not by Lope, whose prestige had not yet peaked at the time Castro began writing his works, but by the neo-Senecan tragedy, cultivated in Valencia by Cristóbal de Virués, and by the natural law philosophy of sixteenth-century Spanish theorists. These influences are most strongly manifest in the open condemnation of the tyrannical king found in the first two plays of this study, *El amor constante* and *El Conde Alarcos.* The latter three plays —*El nacimiento de Montesinos, El perfecto caballero* and *Las hazañas del Cid*— seem to draw closer to Lope's works in their apparent respect for kingly authority. However, Castro never fully abandoned his earlier, more critical orientation, and what appears to be a celebration of the principle of absolute loyalty to the king is actually an ambivalent, and even ironic, undercutting of the values and solutions of the Lopean *comedia.*

---

[1] The dating of Castro's plays has been more a matter of speculation than of certainty. Publication dates offer little help (*El amor constante* was published in Valencia in 1609 in a miscellaneous collection of plays entitled *Doze comedias famosas de quatro poetas naturales de la insigne y coronada ciudad de Valencia,* while the other plays we shall discuss were published in 1618 along with eight other plays in the *Primera parte de las comedias de don Guillém* [sic] *de Castro*) since Castro's plays were printed only after he was an established playwright. Courtney Bruerton has attempted to date the *comedias* of Castro employing a method similar to that established by him and Morley for the dating of Lope's works. According to his dating, the plays under discussion probably were written between 1596 and 1615. Datings of each play will be given in later corresponding chapters. See COURTNEY BRUERTON, «The Chronology of the *comedias* of Guillén de Castro», *Hispanic Review,* 12 (1944), pp. 89-151.

At the center of Castro's dramatic cosmos is the conflict between arbitrary power (and the social codes that support that power) and natural and Christian law. Stated in other terms, there exists a tension between a social code that relates personal honor to submission to the king and a moral code that is outraged when the king's actions are manifestly unjust. Whereas the former code demands that the king be obeyed, the latter recognizes that the monarch may not always merit the respect due his office. In the presentation and resolution of this conflict Castro gives far more validity than is usually found in the *comedia* to the principles and claims of Christian morality and natural law. Indeed, in all five of these plays he not only condemns the unjust king but also portrays defiance of royal authority as a morally licit, although a socially and personally problematic, means towards the restoration of order. In the cases of *El amor constante* and *El perfecto caballero* this defiance is carried out to the point of regicide, and in *Las hazañas del Cid,* an assassination traditionally considered an act of treason, Bellido Dolfos's murder of King Sancho, is reinterpreted as an act of divine justice. The presence of such works in a genre usually characterized by the celebration of the subject's unquestioning reverence for the monarch, even when the conduct of the latter proves to be morally questionable, is a phenomenon that has received scant attention.

The first critic to comment on this unorthodox presentation of the king-subject relationship was Eduardo Juliá Martínez in the study accompanying his 1925 edition of Castro's works. Juliá Martínez notes in passing that the king does not obtain unquestioning submission in Castro's theater:

> ... la sociedad tiene como fundamento el poder real y la autoridad que de él dimana. Este poder debe ser paternal, y cuando se manifiesta de otra forma el vasallo no tiene el deber de la obediencia ciega y resignada.[2]

In examining the regicide of *El amor constante* Juliá finds Castro backing away from boldly supporting a theory of defiance:

> Lógica consecuencia de tales ideas es que se haga eco de la teoría de que el Rey, siendo tirano, puede ser muerto, aunque nunca la ponga en práctica, pues en la comedia citada [*El amor constante*], que es de su primer período, y esto debe tenerse muy en cuenta, el regicidio se comete por permisión del mismo monarca, y no sin que produzca protesta violenta entre los cortesanos.[3]

In contrast to Juliá's reservations as to Castro's defiant spirit José María Roca Franquesa proclaimed in an article published in 1944 that

---

[2] Eduardo Juliá Martínez, «Observaciones preliminares» to his edition of *Obras de Don Guillén de Castro y Bellvis* (Madrid: Imprenta de la Revista de Archivos, Bibliotecas y Museos, 1925), I, xliii.
[3] Juliá Martínez, «Observaciones», I, xliv.

Castro's dramatization of the tyrant king was original, daring and revolutionary. He states:

> Un estudio minucioso del teatro de Guillén de Castro nos permite afirmar que fue el dramaturgo valenciano el más revolucionario de nuestros poetas, entendiendo por revolucionario el hecho de solucionar los temas presentados de una manera opuesta al sentir general de la época.[4]

Roca, however, does not undertake an «estudio minucioso». His generalization is based on a study of the ending of *El amor constante* and, to a lesser degree, on that of *El perfecto caballero*. Roca's viewpoint on the ending of Castro's first play differs significantly from that of Juliá. Whereas the latter interprets as most important the king's call for his own assassination, Roca stresses the fact that the king's assassin is proclaimed the new ruler:

> Si alguna vez los dramaturgos de nuestro Siglo de Oro se atreven a discutir la autoridad real, nunca llegan a los extremos del poeta valenciano. Guillén de Castro no sólo la discute, sino que la autoriza, y lo que es más, presenta en escena al regicidio y premia al asesino con la mayor distinción... lo que no se da ni antes ni después de Guillén de Castro es el hecho de considerar al regicida como un ser enviado por Dios para libertar al pueblo de las veleidades de un tirano y, por tanto, digno de ocupar la dignidad del mismo.[5]

Although Roca states that Castro resolves his themes «de una manera opuesta al sentir general de la época», he goes on to show how the regicide of *El amor constante* reflects the sixteenth-century political ideology of thinkers such as Juan de Mariana. This would presumably place the play very much within the ideological currents of its time. This apparent contradiction stems from the questionable assumption made by Roca and by many critics that when Castro began writing *comedias* the «sentir general de la época» was that embodied in the plays of Lope de Vega.

Juliá Martínez, in an article responding to Roca Franquesa, denies the connection between *El amor constante* and contemporary political theory. He suggests instead that Castro, far from striking an original note in dramatizing regicide, merely imitates a stock dramatic device of the pseudo-classical tragedies of the sixteenth-century Valencian dramatist Cristóbal de Virués. In these tragedies regicide is conceived of not in political but in moral terms: «Más que por tema filosófico-político, cultivó Guillén de Castro el regicidio como tema dramático, y en esto fue su modelo inmediato Cristóbal de Virués.»[6]

---

[4] José María Roca Franquesa, «Un dramaturgo de la edad de oro: Guillén de Castro. Notas a un sector de su teatro», *Revista de Filología Española*, 28 (1944), p. 397.
[5] Roca Franquesa, pp. 390-391 and pp. 394-395.
[6] Eduardo Juliá Martínez, «Sobre *El amor constante* de Guillén de Castro», *Revista de Filología Española*, 30 (1946), p. 123.

John G. Weiger also disagrees with Roca's evaluation of Castro's dramas as daring and revolutionary, but for reasons quite different from those of Juliá Martínez. For Weiger, Castro closely follows Lope's dramatic formula and his plays exhibit little real originality or independence of conception:

> ... donde reside la grandeza del valenciano es en su habilidad de tomar situaciones (de la historia, de la épica, del Romancero, de la novela) y adaptarlas a lo que es, a fin de cuentas, el *arte nuevo* de su época, o sea, la «comedia nueva» de Lope.[7]

Thus, Weiger sees *El amor constante* as merely one more elaboration of the theme of honor found time and again in the Lopean *comedia*:

> *El amor constante* no me parece obra revolucionaria. El rey debería ser el protector del honor de sus vasallos. Al no cumplir con este deber, se convierte en tirano, y, por consiguiente, deja de ser rey. Guillén de Castro, pues, se mantiene fiel a la convención lopesca según la cual el honor es el móvil dramático de mayor importancia.[8]

Weiger goes on to comment that Roman law concedes validity and legality to an act of tyrannicide and that Castro's play draws on the authority of that law. However, in an effort to link Castro with Lope, he makes the ungrounded assumption that Lope, too, turns to Roman law to support the concept of regicide.[9] Finally, Weiger concedes that if the ending of *El amor constante* is not «revolucionario» it is at least «atrevido».[10]

Robert R. La Du, in a study devoted to the relationship between honor and the king in the theater of Castro, finds nothing at all unorthodox in Castro's handling of the problem of the unjust king. Rather, he is «... impressed by the loyalty and familiarity which is so often stressed in the relations between monarch and subject».[11] La Du regards anything contrary to this loyalty as an exception:

> It was admitted, however, that if the king sought to injure the honor of a woman, the male who was morally responsible for her could defend

---

[7] JOHN G. WEIGER, «Sobre la originalidad e independencia de Guillén de Castro», *Hispanófila*, 31 (septiembre, 1967), p. 15.

[8] WEIGER, «Sobre la originalidad», p. 8.

[9] WEIGER, «Sobre la originalidad», pp. 7-8.

[10] WEIGER, «Sobre la originalidad», p. 8. Weiger repeats his analysis of *El amor constante* in his book *Hacia la comedia: De los valencianos a Lope* (Madrid: Cupsa Editorial, 1978), pp. 214-218. Although in this later study Weiger continues to deny Castro any real originality or independence, he no longer implies, as he seemed to do in the earlier article, that Castro is a follower of Lope. Instead, he shows how Castro, along with many of the other Valencian dramatists, points towards Lope. However, Weiger does not clarify how Castro differs from Lope, particularly with regard to his treatment of kingship and tyranny.

[11] ROBERT R. LA DU, «Honor and the King in the *Comedias* of Guillén de Castro», *Hispania*, 45 (1962), p. 216.

her from the king even to the extent of using arms to do so. The action occurs at various times throughout Castro's theater... [but] Only in extreme cases is this action taken against the king.[12]

However, he does not examine the dramatic context or nature of such «extreme cases». Later, noting George T. Northup's observation that in the *comedia* natural law allowed for self-defense against an offending king, La Du comments that:

> There is no case in Castro's theater which would bear out Northup's observation. In only one instance does a subject think of attacking the king because the latter threatened his life [the instance occurs in *El amor constante*] but the action is never realized.[13]

At times La Du is inaccurate, as when he states that «... in none of the cases in Castro's theater does the subject ever go so far as to attack the king».[14] But even when objectively accurate La Du's study is misleading for it fails to examine the question of loyalty within its dramatic context. Though many of Castro's characters do strive to remain loyal, others call into question the validity of absolute loyalty and yet others are celebrated for taking action against an unjust king. As a dramatist Castro concerns himself not with the mere *existence* of loyalty but with the anguished problems and ironies of maintaining loyalty in moments of personal and political crisis.

William E. Wilson, far from stressing the loyalty of Castro's characters, finds that the Valencian stands apart from other Golden Age playwrights precisely in his willingness to dramatize openly acts of defiance against the king. Noting that in the typical *comedia* subjects generally find an «ingenious solution» to avoid confronting the offending monarch, Wilson declares:

> Seeking an ingenious solution may be true in the case of Calderón and some other dramatists of the Golden Age, but it is not true of Guillén de Castro, some of whose characters resort to drastic action in such a situation... There are in Castro's plays suggestions that a tyrannical king can be repudiated by his subjects... It is evident that Castro does not follow slavishly the doctrine of the divine right of kings.[15]

In his important study, *El teatro de Guillén de Castro*, Luciano García Lorenzo takes exception to Weiger's denial of Castro's originality and independence from Lope:

---

[12] LA DU, p. 215.
[13] LA DU, p. 215.
[14] LA DU, p. 215.
[15] WILLIAM E. WILSON, *Guillén de Castro* (New York: Twayne Publishers, 1973), pp. 51-52.

> ... lo que nos parece también indiscutible es que nuestro autor tampoco está exento de originalidad y de una cierta independencia... originalidad que es manifiesta... en el tratamiento y sobre todo en el desenlace de alguna de sus obras que desarrollan el tema del rey tirano...[16]

In a chapter devoted to the figure of the tyrant in Castro's works, García Lorenzo reaffirms Roca's claim that the dramas of this author reflect the sixteenth-century natural law theorists' concern with the questions of resistance and tyrannicide. For this critic, the mere fact that Castro dramatizes this doctrine is demonstration of his originality. Although an important contribution to *comedia* studies, García Lorenzo's book does not analyze the dramatic conflicts that result when a kingdom is forced to make a decision as to how it will deal with a king who has turned against his people. However, García Lorenzo does sense a certain ambivalence towards social laws in Castro's theater; he notes «Reticencias, ligerezas e ideas acerca del honor y de sus leyes... que, aun siendo de una ortodoxia indiscutible, destacan por la fuerza de sus afirmaciones».[17] He suggests that in at least one play, *El perfecto caballero,* one can detect this ironic ambivalence hovering over the issue of absolute loyalty:

> ... hay cierta ambigüedad en esta pieza, pues si bien es cierto que al matar al Rey y premiar con el trono a Ludovico está Guillén defendiendo el tiranicidio —decisión aprobada por todos, incluso por don Miguel Centellas— también es verdad que este último personaje, verdadero protagonista... declara en más de una ocasión, la imposibilidad del tiranicidio. ... Si frente a esto ponemos los calificativos continuos de tirano... y, lo que resulta más significativo, la evidente antipatía con que [the king] es reflejado por Guillén, la ambigüedad resultante puede hacernos dudar de la sinceridad del valenciano e incluso del propio título de la obra que define a don Miguel Centellas... Quizá el autor, para comprender a su personaje don Miguel Centellas —caballero español, valeroso, leal, honrado y etc.— nos aconsejaría acercarnos a Centellas con cierta ironía, no exenta de leve sorna...[18]

In general, then, there has been no critical consensus as to Castro's treatment of the problem of royal injustice. Critics have tended to overlook the dramatic integrity of the works by stressing individual statements or scenes taken out of their dramatic context. The results have been a series of diametrically opposed interpretations. For some, Castro supports a doctrine of defiance, while for others he rejects that doctrine. Similarly, his *comedias* are regarded either as original and revolutionary or as merely conforming to Lope's dramatic formula.

---

[16] LUCIANO GARCÍA LORENZO, *El teatro de Guillén de Castro* (Barcelona: Editorial Planeta, 1976), p. 43.
[17] GARCÍA LORENZO, p. 43.
[18] GARCÍA LORENZO, pp. 63-64

To a certain extent the plays themselves invite these contradictory readings. If these works seem to support both submission and resistance it is because Castro repeatedly plays off opposite stances of loyalty and defiance in such a way as to make the audience feel that each holds a just claim. Within each of these structurally-related plays the playwright presents a society of loyal subjects forced, in spite of itself, to acknowledge the monarch's betrayal of his own kingdom and to come to terms with those who seek to rescue that kingdom by active resistance. While largely sympathetic to those who would remain loyal to their king, Castro suggests in these plays that loyalty must, at times, be put aside and that defiance, and even regicide, are morally defensible under certain circumstances.

Castro's highly personal vision of these issues can be placed in its proper perspective only if it is seen as, in part, emerging from a dramatic tradition that predates the triumph of the Lopean *comedia*. The pre-Lope orientation of Guillén de Castro's early theater has been noted by a number of scholars, although most of their observations have been of a very generalized nature. Juliá Martínez was the first to note three discrete periods in Castro's dramatic craftsmanship:

> ... se observa en Castro un momento inicial dependiente de la escuela valenciana de aquellos días, y especialmente influido por Virués... Después vuelve los ojos hacia la realidad en ocasiones, y otras veces hacia sus lecturas, y produce comedias como *Los mal casados de Valencia*, y dramas llenos del épico sabor del Romancero como *Las mocedades del Cid*. Por último, en lo que podemos considerar como su tercer período, idea intrigas con las que ya intenta renovar los aplausos alcanzados en la primera manera de construir... o forja, ya conflictos tratados de una manera enérgica y rápida..., ya situaciones semejantes a las de otras obras anteriores, pero tratadas con mayor maestría y destreza escénicas...[19]

Rinaldo Froldi reduces these periods to two, the first growing out of local theatrical forms and the second reflecting the influence of Lope:

> Cuando más tarde volvió [Lope] a Valencia, en 1599, ya seguro dominador de la escena española, encontró en Guillén de Castro al que, siendo aún joven, tras sus primeros intentos llevados a cabo en la órbita de la tradición local, tenía genio y capacidad para desarrollarla en formas más decididamente innovadoras y en consonancia con la conciencia de la época.
>
> Es justo distinguir, como hace Juliá Martínez, dos épocas en la producción de Guillén de Castro, porque la segunda llegada de Lope extingue las características de la tradición local; ésta ingresa en la órbita lopesca casi espontáneamente, dado que no presentaba elementos irreductibles con aquella *comedia* de la que, por el contrario, había sido un fundamental esbozo precursor.[20]

[19] Juliá Martínez, «Observaciones», I, xxxvii.
[20] Rinaldo Froldi, *Lope de Vega y la formación de la comedia* (Madrid: Anaya, 1973), pp. 157-158.

García Lorenzo agrees with Juliá's division and adds that Castro's assimilation of Lope's art occurs naturally and gradually:

> Es suficiente una lectura del teatro de Guillén... para observar que el camino no se trunca de una forma violenta con el fin de dar paso a la nueva fórmula. En el teatro de Guillén de Castro existen, desde las primeras obras, unos rasgos, unos elementos, que, si no están coherentemente sistematizados, facilitan la práctica definitiva de la nueva fórmula dramática.[21]

However, he adds, if certain aspects of Castro's early craft anticipate Lope's system there exist still others that distinguish Castro from Lope throughout his dramatic production:

> ... parte de la dramaturgia valenciana, y la de Guillén de Castro más concretamente, posee... unas particularidades desde el principio y hasta el final de su carrera que no lo hacen mero discípulo siguiendo fielmente al maestro.[22]

What scant chronological data we have at our disposal corroborates the critical notion that Lope began to influence Guillén de Castro only after the Valencian had been in contact with earlier dramatic currents. Born in 1569, Castro showed the first public evidence of his literary inclinations in 1592 when, at the age of twenty-three, he joined the prestigious Valencian literary group the *Academia de los Nocturnos*. There Castro found himself in direct contact with some of the leading dramatists of that city — Rey de Artieda, Francisco Tárrega (known as «el canónigo Tárrega») and Gaspar de Aguilar. If, as Froldi has lucidly argued, these dramatists were exploring new theatrical possibilities, investigating new elements that were to have a decisive influence on the *comedia* as fixed by Lope, they had not totally abandoned elements of an earlier dramatic moment, the school of neo-Senecan tragedy. Certain plays of these authors —Tárrega's *La duquesa constante* and *El esposo fingido*, for example— reveal a still-present «predilección por el senequismo».[23]

Neo-senequism had found its greatest Valencian exponent in Cristóbal de Virués. While his constant travels away from Valencia prevented him from actively participating in the *Academia de los Nocturnos*, his plays greatly influenced the dramatists of that group.[24] This influence is particularly evident in the early dramatic vision of Guillén de Castro.

---

[21] García Lorenzo, p. 51.
[22] García Lorenzo, pp. 51-52.
[23] Eduardo Juliá Martínez, «Observaciones preliminares» to his edition of *Poetas dramáticos valencianos* (Madrid: Tipografía de la Revista de Archivos, 1929), I, vii.
[24] After noting the direct imitation of Virués in the works of some of these dramatists Juliá comments that «fue de los que mayor influencia ejercieron sobre sus contemporáneos», Juliá Martínez, *Poetas dramáticos valencianos*, I, xlvi.

Lope's influence on the Valencian theater was not to be felt until his second, more triumphant, visit to that city in 1599, that is, after Guillén de Castro had already written a number of works, according to the chronologies established by both Bruerton[25] and Juliá Martínez.[26] An earlier visit in 1588 occurred before Lope had fully formulated his own *arte nuevo*. According to Froldi, in this year Lope was to learn much from the Valencian dramatists:

> No es posible... seguir creyendo... en una «escuela valenciana» formada por Lope: la verdad es que Lope, con su llegada a Valencia en 1588, aprendió más que enseñó... En Valencia, además, Lope de Vega tuvo ocasión de discutir sobre teatro, valiéndose de la tradición, crítica y académica local, que de allí a poco se manifestaría en la Academia de los Nocturnos; debió así de madurar en él una conciencia crítica más precisa de lo que el teatro representaba en la cultura del tiempo.[27]

Before proceeding to Guillén de Castro's plays of unjust power it will be necessary to examine the portrayal of king and subject in both the theater of Virués and the *comedia* of Lope. We shall also study the problem of tyranny as it appears in sixteenth-century Spanish political philosophy since, as Roca has suggested, these ideas are integrated as well into Castro's theater.

---

[25] Bruerton dates six plays as possibly having been written before 1599: *El amor constante, El desengaño dichoso, El nacimiento de Montesinos, Los mal casados de Valencia, El caballero bobo* and *La humildad soberbia*. BRUERTON, p. 150.
[26] Juliá Martínez dates what he considers to be Castro's first play, *El amor constante*, as 1593. JULIÁ MARTÍNEZ, «Observaciones», I, lii.
[27] FROLDI, pp. 156-157.

CHAPTER 1

THE UNJUST KING IN DRAMATIC AND DIDACTIC LITERATURE OF THE LATE SIXTEENTH AND EARLY SEVENTEENTH CENTURIES

THE TYRANT KING IN THE VALENCIAN THEATER PRIOR
TO GUILLÉN DE CASTRO: CRISTÓBAL DE VIRUÉS

In Valencia the figure of the tyrant king first appears as an important theatrical element in the tragedies of Cristóbal de Virués, written roughly between 1580 and 1586.[1] Though certain elements of his works —his adaptation of varied meters to conform to plot situation, the first use of *romance* meter in the theater, the free use of novelistic elements, the reduction of the number of acts to three, the use of subplots, and the use of Spanish settings in the later plays— anticipate Lope de Vega's *comedia* formula,[2] the theater of Virués gets its fundamental orientation from the Italian neo-Senecan school of tragedy.[3]

The neo-Senecan Renaissance drama had its origins in Italy and can be said to have taken root with the *Orbecche* of Giraldo Cinthio, a drama first performed in 1541. At that time it was Seneca more than the Greek tragedians whose works were considered the model of a generic Greco-Latin tragedy. Seneca was both more accessible to the Humanists, because he had written in Latin, and more appealing because of the closeness of his Stoic vision to the Christian ethic. Also, Roman drama, having lost the religious and ritualistic orientation of the Greek theater,

---

[1] This tentative dating is established by HENRI MÉRIMÉE, *L'Art dramatique à Valencia, depuis les origines jusqu'au commencement du XVIIe siècle* (Toulouse: Edouard Privat, Editeur, 1913), p. 331.

[2] For Lope's dept to Virués see W. C. ATKINSON, «Seneca, Virués, Lope de Vega», in *Homenatge a Antoni Rubió i Lluch. Miscellània d'estudis literaris, històrics i lingüistics* (Barcelona: 1936), I, 111-131; and FROLDI, pp. 110-115.

[3] For a general overview of the Spanish neo-Senecans consult ALFREDO HERMENEGILDO, *La tragedia en el renacimiento español* (Barcelona: Editorial Planeta, 1973). For a psycho-historical interpretation of the neo-Senecan vogue in Spain see ERBERT E. ISAR, «La cuestión del llamado 'senequismo' español», *Hispanófila*, 2 (enero, 1958), pp. 11-30.

emphasized a more superficial «humanness», more comprehensible to the Renaissance mentality than the mythological cosmos of the Greeks:

> Nominally, Seneca's themes are the same as those of Greek drama; but the terror they there inspired was controlled by the religious awe which was its basis; and that dissolved, they became in Seneca not terrible but horrible. It is precisely this horror which Seneca emphasizes. The doers of terrible deeds, no longer comprehended as elements of an all-embracing divine dispensation, become just the villains of the piece: virtually the theme of Personal Revenge is superseding that of Divine Retribution.[4]

Early Italian Humanist dramas of the late fourteenth and early fifteenth centuries were often dramas intended for reading and were based on Senecan sources. These works tended to place emphasis on the already abundant rhetorical devices of the Latin dramatist.[5] They also tended to exploit Seneca's most melodramatic vein, turning to lust, love intrigues and cruelty for plot material and as sources of horror. Favorite models were *Thyestes,* a play dealing with the cruelties of a tyrant, and *Medea,* centering on the revenge of a wronged woman. According to Charlton:

> The Senecan model becomes the Senecan tradition by diversion of all efforts to the production of horror; the accumulation of gruesome deeds is even greater than in Seneca; the hero is a still blacker villain than Seneca's. As the straining for effect increases, the romantic impulse becomes more marked in the Senecan tradition than in Seneca himself.[6]

Humanists of the later half of the fifteenth century sponsored actual performances of Seneca's plays. At this time there was also an established tradition of performing comedies written in the vernacular. It was Giraldo Cinthio who brought together the Italian comic tradition and Seneca; by doing so he «made classical tragedy modern».[7] Beginning with the *Orbecche* Cinthio fused the classic and the romanesque by applying Senecan technique to a novelistic source, in this case the second novel of his own *Hecatommithi*. According to Cecilia V. Sargent, Cinthio's innovation:

> ... not only pioneered greater variety of plot but changed its whole character. It sanctioned the modification of history, and the use of fiction; this in turn permitted an element of suspense due to interest in the unforeseen, impossible in drama on strictly mythological or traditional subjects; it also tended to multiply characters and complicate the action. The classical atmosphere was quite lost; regardless of date or setting, the

---

[4] H. B. CHARLTON, *The Senecan Tradition in Renaissance Tragedy* (1921; rpt. Manchester: Manchester University Press, 1946), pp. xxii.

[5] CHARLTON, p. xxii, notes that Seneca «diverts tragedy to rhetorical opportunity» by filling his works with proverbs, moralizations, etc. Seneca maintains many of the formal conventions of the Greeks: the chorus, the unities, etc.

[6] CHARLTON, pp. lxvii-lxviii.

[7] CHARLTON, p. lxxix.

life depicted was that of sixteenth-century Italy, and the contemporary court with its overbearing tyrants and perfidious courtiers replaced the royal personages of classical tragedy. To this modern or popular material Giraldi applied the methods of Seneca... that is, he made abundant use of narration replete with bloody detail, bombastic declamation and philosophic aphorisms. In fact he adopted the moral lesson as a definite principle of tragic drama, stressing the punishment of evil in a way calculated to appeal to the popular sense of justice.[8]

Thus, the evocation of horror and pathos (*orrore* and *conmizeratione* as Cinthio called them) through unmitigated violence, a heavy dosage of «uplifting» moralization, particularly in the punishment of the evil figure, and novelistic invention form the foundation of the theater of Cinthio and of his followers.

The tyrant is a stock figure in this school of tragedy. Charlton adduces the following reasons:

A favorite character is the tyrannous king, and the reason is obvious. The office of kingship provides a maximum of the *maestà* and *decoro* which the dignity of tragedy demanded, and the prerogative of kingship a maximum of power for the provision of unmitigated cruelty and horror. Furthermore, a character in the most exalted station offers by this fall the most striking type of *peripeteia*. Almost inevitably the tyrant tends to become not only the main figure because the most potent worker of horror, but also a sheer villain, because through villainy he is most horrible.[9]

The tyrant king appears in two tragedies of Cristóbal de Virués: *Atila furioso* and *La gran Semíramis*. As in the neo-Senecan tradition, Virués' tyrant stands as a «universal» moral example (or anti-example) and is not a truly political figure. By setting his plays in remote epochs and places Virués can focus on moral issues rather than on contemporary political concerns.

Briefly, the plot of the *Atila furioso* is the following. Atila the Hun is enamored of Flaminia, whom he disguises as a page in order to keep her at his side. The Queen lusts after this supposedly male page, now called Flaminio, and she is in turn desired by the courtier Gerardo. Flaminia, hoping to eliminate the Queen, tricks Atila into believing that his wife is carrying on an affair with Gerardo. The king, so deceived, kills the two «lovers» in order to defend his honor. Atila later falls in love with the slave girl Celia and marries her. Flaminia, enraged that Atila has

[8] CECILIA VENNARD SARGENT, *A Study of the Dramatic Works of Cristóbal de Virués* (New York: Hispanic Institute in the United States, 1930), pp. 136-137.
[9] CHARLTON, p. xc. On the same page Charlton includes some interesting passages from contemporary dramatic theorists. The Italian DENORES in his *Poetica* (1588) includes as a specific function of tragedy, «fargli abhorrir la vita de'tiranni & de'piu potenti». The Englishman HARRINGTON in his *Preface to Ariosto* (1591) sees tragedy as «representing onely [sic] the cruell & lawless proceedings of Princes, moving nothing but pitie or detestation».

not made her Queen of Hungary, poisons the tyrant. In his madness Atila kills Celia and Flaminia and finally dies himself after a lengthy mad scene. Other characters end the play commenting on the moral lesson of his fall.

The *Atila furioso* is loosely based on a combination of historical fact and legend. Sargent[10] believes that Virués probably drew his basic facts from the *Suma de todas las crónicas,* published in Spain in 1510, or from its Italian translation or from the original Latin manuscript. However, Virués supplied the plot and most of the bloody details. Only the death of Atila is drawn from history and although various sources claimed that he died on his wedding night, there was disagreement as to how he met his death.[11] Virués turned to Seneca for inspiration for the mad scene in Act III, borrowing heavily from *Hercules Oetaeus* and *Hercules Furens*.[12] Though nominally a tragedy, Virués's play, with its intricate plot intrigues, is reminiscent of sixteenth-century romantic comedy.

The prologue of the play serves to orient the spectator to the moral intent of its tragedy. In describing Cupid as a monstruous offspring begotten of an illicit union between savage Mars and lascivious Venus, Virués calls attention to the two vices that dominate the action — cruelty and lust:

> De Marte tan furioso i tan sangriento,
> i de Venus, tan fuerte i tan molesta,
> por un adulterino ajuntamiento,
>   nació un gigante; ya veréis si desta
> mezcla tan buena, el ser el hijo bueno
> tiene dificultad bien manifiesta.
>   El padre de rigor i saña lleno,
> de rebueltas, de bravas dissensiones,
> cevado en muerte el iracundo seno,
>   i de la torpe madre los blasones
> son viles apetitos sensuales,
> infortunios, miserias, sinrazones.   (92a) [13]

We soon see that Atila with his furor and lasciviousness is a mirror image of the grotesquely gigantic Cupid Virués presents in his prologue.

In keeping with this overtly moral tone, Virués' characters are less human beings than incarnations of vice. Thus, when one courtier calls Atila a *fiero,* another corrects him, saying:

> Nombre de fiero le das;
> llámale el mismo furor.   (113b)

---

[10] SARGENT, pp. 89-90.
[11] For details see SARGENT, pp. 92-93.
[12] SARGENT, p. 93.
[13] All citations from the plays of Virués are from the edition of EDUARDO JULIÁ MARTÍNEZ, *Poetas dramáticos valencianos*, I.

As a king Atila has at his disposal limitless power which he exercises in an arbitrarily cruel manner for the gratification of his ego. In his eyes the king must command the total respect of his subjects and that respect is earned only by quickly avenging the slightest offense to his personal honor:

> A quien la injuria el ánimo no ofende
> no le den entre [h]ombres de [h]ombre nombre;
> quien sin vengarse de la injuria entiende
> no deve ser llamado entre [h]ombres [h]ombre;
> quien sin vengarse de la injuria entiende
> entre los [h]ombres alcançar renombre,
> no tiene frente digna de corona,
> no merece respeto su persona.
> Yo siento tanto una pequeña injuria,
> que estoi, hasta vengarme, ardiendo en fuego. (95a-95b)

This exaggerated sense of honor is offended by any hint of defiance to his royal authority, as is revealed in the following passage:

> A un tiempo, como veis, me [h]an ofendido
> el Rei de Esclavonía i la insolente
> Reina del Epidauro; [h]aviendo sido
> cada cual a mi edito inobediente,
> no me dan el tributo que [h]e pedido,
> antes hazen comigo del valiente;
> ¿assí se menosprecia i se aniquila
> el Rei de Reyes y de [H]ungría, Atila? (95b)

He demands absolute submission to his will and punishes with death those who disobey. In the course of the play he orders the execution of countless «enemies». In one specific case Atila demands that submission to the monarch supersede filial devotion; when one of his servants asks Atila how he is to dispose of:

> Los tres [h]ermanos que a su padre dieron
> escapo [sic] de la cárcel de la vaina
> adonde estava preso [h]avía seis años
> porque, sin los poder pagar, devía
> dos mil ducados a la real Cámara... (96b)

the king responds:

> Háganlos cuartos a essos tres [h]ermanos
> i pónganlos en palos esparzidos
> todos a la redonda de la cárcel. (96b)

All this boosts Atila's sense of *hombría*:

> Aborrézcame el mundo, i aborrezcan
> mi nombre a mi presencia mis vassallos,

> i sea aborrecible a cielo i tierra,
> como me tema el mundo, i como teman
> mi saña i mi castigo mis vassallos,
> que es cosa de mugeres ser amables,
> i de varones es el ser temidos. (97a)

In designating himself «el Rei de Reyes» (95b) Atila implicitly compares himself to God and as such demands adoration and obedience. Yet when he states that he feels himself «ardiendo en fuego» (95b) whenever he senses an offense to his honor he reminds the spectator that his actions ally him closer to Satan.

By the third act Atila is fully identified with the forces of Hell. The equation of his court with Hell is established at the very beginning of the act as the courtier Ricardo comments in awe:

> ¿Qué furia [h]orrible del abismo eterno
> anda por esta triste casa suelta?
> ¿Quién causa en ella este espantoso infierno,
> esta terrible i áspera rebuelta? (108a)

Present-day readers can only imagine the hellish, deathlike sounds which must have filled the theater when Flaminia asks:

> Ricardo, ¿qué rumor este este i llanto? [sic]
> ¿Quién causa este alboroto i alarido? (108b)

What was presented as pure plot intrigue in the first two acts assumes a moral significance in the third as what began as an act of vengeance of an ambitious woman is transformed into an act of divine retribution. Flaminia, awakened to the sinful nature of her life, experiences a conversion and decides to kill Atila in order to liberate herself spiritually. Through the assassination of Atila Flaminia seeks to put an end to both spiritual corruption and political tyranny:

> Muere, pérfido in[h]umano;
> muere, cruel, in[h]umana;
> salga essa alma tan tirana
> de esse cuerpo tan tirano.
> Acábesse ya tu imperio
> i essa alma encruelecida
> salga de su libre vida
> i yo de mi cautiverio. (110a)

She sees the murder in terms of divine retribution:

> ... que sé, sin duda,
> que es justicia justísima del cielo
> executada por la débil mano
> de una débil muger mui ofendida. (111b)

Atila's mad scene is filled with references to Hell as he feels his entrails burning and being devoured by snakes and lizards. Upon the death of the tyrant, Ricardo comments on the justice of the regicide and exhorts the spectator to see the act as sanctioned by Heaven:

> ¡O[h], justa paga i castigo,
> i justo infierno al que vas,
> pues fuiste de Satanás
> tan gran secuaz i amigo!
> ¡O[h], Rei, que el mundo goviernas
> solamente con mirar;
> haz, Señor, considerar
> estas justicias eternas! (116a)

Many of these same elements can be found in *La gran Semíramis,* a tragedy whose stated moral purpose is to reveal the instability of worldly Fortune by dramatizing the rise and fall of various noble characters. Like *Atila,* it offers Castro a strong precedent for the figure of the tyrant and the presentation of regicide as an act that partakes of both vengeance and divine justice. Furthermore, the principal character of the first act of *Semíramis,* Menón, seems to be the model for the type of central protagonist found in Castro's earliest plays: the loyal but passionate male subject betrayed by his king and ultimately destroyed by his inability to come to terms with that betrayal.

Virués presents himself in the prologue as a dramatic innovator. Each of the three acts (this in itself is a novelty) is announced as an individual tragedy:

> ... advierto
> que esta tragedia, con estilo nuevo
> que ella introduze, viene en tres jornadas
> que suceden en tiempos diferentes:
> en el sitio de Batra la primera,
> en Nínive famosa la segunda,
> la tercera y final en Babilonia.
> Formando en cada cual una tragedia
> con que podrá toda la de [h]oi tenerse
> por tres tragedias, no sin arte escritas.
> Ni es menor novedad que la que dixe
> de ser primera en ser de tres jornadas. (25b-26a)

Thus, Act I can be considered the tragedy of Menón, a soldier who entrusts himself to worldly values and is destroyed by Fortune personified in King Nino.

In this act Menón, a ranking general in the army of the Assyrian king Nino, attempts to capture the enemy city of Bactra. His wife, Semíramis, disguised as a man and tired of the separation from her husband caused by the war, meets him on the battlefield. She suggest a successful strategy for taking the city. King Nino, then, falls passionately in love with Semíramis and offers Menón his own daughter in exchange for the general's wife. When Menón refuses, Nino abducts Semíramis. Menón hangs himself in despair.

Menón, like Guillén de Castro's earliest protagonists, allows his human emotions to take precedence over any strict sense of duty. In his opening lines he shows a disdain for honor by placing greater value on his love for his wife. He risks his reputation by leaving the battlefield in order to be at her side:

> Arremetía ya el abierto muro,
> puestos los ojos en la gloria i fama;
> pero sabiendo que llegastes, juro
> que me traxo volando a vos mi llama,
> i aunque el [h]onor viniendo me aventuro,
> verá quien me juzgare, si me infama,
> que importa más gozar de vos, mi cielo,
> que quanta gloria puede darme el suelo. (26a)

King Nino is presented not as a pathologically cruel king, as was Atila, but as one who will exploit his royal prerogative for his own immoral ends. Thus, when he finds himself wavering as to whether he should attempt to abduct Semíramis, the realization that as a king his will can be translated into law spurs him to action:

> Mas ¡qué poco coraçón!
> Si a serlo me determino,
> ¿quién hará contradición? (30b)

Later, responding to Semíramis' protests, he adds:

> No curéis de adelgazar
> tanto lo que haze un rei,
> pues es de considerar
> que su voluntad es lei
> i cual lei se ha de guardar. (31a)

He tells Menón that he expects no resistance from his general but rather gracious submission:

> pues siendo yo tu rey te pido aquello
> que de potencia puedo yo tenello.
> ... ...
> haz por tu Rei este amoroso hecho
> con voluntad, pues eres tan discreto. (32a-b)

The response of the passionate Menón is not that of a submissive vassal but that of an angry, offended man. He instinctively and vociferously revolts, clamoring that the king is attempting to impose a decision on him:

> Aunque suspenso, atónito i pasmado
> me tiene tu demanda, señor mío,
> i si es o no de veras lo tratado
> no sepa ni distinga mi alvedrío,
> i aunque en confusas dudas engolfado
> de acertar a salvarme desconfío,
> en vez del sí, que pides por tal gusto,
> a darte un no me fuerça el amor justo.
>   I digo que aunque el Cielo me atormente
> con sus mayores fuerças y tormentos
> ... ...
> no podrá dar tal sí jamás mi lengua. (32b)

Unlike the heroes of Lope's *comedias,* Menón allows love to take precedence over a blind submission to the king's will.

Angered at his disobedience, Nino commands Menón to choose between self-exile and a horrible death at the hands of the king. Alone, the general invokes Jupiter's wrath upon the tyrant:

> ¡O[h], bárbaro in[h]umano,
> ingrato a mis servicios,
> cruel, tirano, inico, injusto i fiero!
> Con rigurosa mano
> en medio de tus vicios
> mostrándose el gran Júpiter severo
> te ponga en este miserable trago
> i me dé con tu muerte justo pago. (33a)

In spite of his moral outrage Menón makes no physical attempt to defy the king. This fails to occur not because social strictures keep him from rebelling against his ruler (as will later be the case with the protagonists of Lope's *comedia*), but because he feels overwhelmed by the king's brute power. He despairs of successfully wresting his wife from the clutches of the powerful Nino. In his mind, the abduction of Semíramis is as irreversible as death; in a delirium he envisions his beloved as already inhabiting the Heavens and calls on her to carry him with her:

> Ya voi, ya parto, espera,
> señora, no te allexes;
> Semíramis, no huyas de tu esposo,
> i a la luziente esfera,
> sobre los altos exes
> donde tienes tu trono suntuoso
> pues con tan grande fe te llamo i sigo,
> llévame, mi Semíramis, contigo. (34a-b)

In his despair he turns to death as a means of deliverance from his suffering and disillusion. At the moment he is about to take his own life, Menón believes he has learned a moral truth: he sees Nino as the embodiment of inconstant Fortune, and prays that courtiers, soldiers, and all those who «seguís estos tiranos» (34a) for the purpose of rising in Fortune will learn from his example the transient nature of worldly glory.[14]

Virués makes use of the king-vassal relationship, then, to demonstrate the folly of depending on the world for certainty. He shows the fall from Fortune of Menón, who, glorying in human love and earthly favors, is deprived of both and must turn to death for consolation. He dies at his own hands because the values upon which he had built his life are shattered by a *golpe de Fortuna* in the guise of a tyrant's arbitrary power.

Guillén de Castro seems to have amply borrowed from this act for certain scenes included in *El amor constante* and *El Conde Alarcos*. But Castro's treatment differs in two important ways from that of his model. First, he refrains from drawing any moral conclusion. And second, and of utmost importance, he adds a dimension of interiority barely suggested in the theater of Virués, creating characters who struggle to come to terms with the inner conflict between their human passions and their sense of social obligation.

Act II introduces another motif that will be further developed in Castro's theater: the equation of the king's submission to illicit passion with the abdication of his social role. King Nino is so enamored of Semíramis that he cedes his throne to her:

>Sentaos, Reina i señora, en este asiento
>que es dedicado a la Real persona;
>tomá este cetro, i seaos ornamento
>de verdadera Reina esta corona;
>con ecesivo amor, gozo i contento
>de su mano el gran Nino aquí os corona. (37a)

---

[14] In spite of the apparent wisdom of his words, Menón is not the innocent victim he pretends to be. His message of *desengaño* fits his situation, but it is only part of the story. Although the king is the immediate cause of Menón's misfortune, the latter helps contribute to his own fall. In allowing his wife to assume his role as general and to win the battle for him, Menón both relinquishes his duties and unwittingly brings his wife to the attention of his monarch. For her part, Semíramis is not the devoted wife her husband believes her to be; she hardly protests her abduction by the king. It is significant that Menón, though provoked by Nino, takes his own life. This is a symbolically fitting end for a man who willingly hands over his social role and responsibilities and, therefore, his very being, to his wife. For a lengthier analysis see JAMES CRAPOTTA, «The Unity of *La gran Semíramis* of Cristóbal de Virués», in *Creation and Re-creation: Experiments in Literary Form in Early Modern Spain*, ed. Ronald E. Surtz and Nora Weinerth (Newark, Delaware: «Juan de la Cuesta» Hispanic Monographs, 1983), pp. 49-60. See also JOHN G. WEIGER, *The Valencian Dramatists of Spain's Golden Age* (Boston: Twayne Publishers, 1976), pp. 35-39; and WEIGER, *Hacia la comedia*, pp. 81-86.

This action underscores the king's moral weakness and his vulnerability to lust. As he transfers the symbols of royal power to Semíramis he also surrenders his identity, just as Menón had in the first act. Fittingly, no longer who nor what he was, Nino falls victim to Semíramis and is destroyed by her. The King in Castro's *El amor constante* expresses a similar desire to give up the throne so as to be able to follow his amorous impulses. In Castro's play the monarch's refusal to accept his royal responsibilities is a sign that he no longer merits the respect due his office. Hence, he must be punished for his violation of the social contract. What is simply a moral tale in the hands of Virués takes on political overtones when taken over by Castro.

The death of Queen Semíramis, like that of King Atila, is couched in terms of divine justice. Having won the throne by murdering Nino, Semíramis, disguised as her son Ninias, attempts to subjugate the Assyrians to her ambitious rule by claiming that Ninias' ascendence to the throne is divinely willed. She publicly proclaims that Nino was assumed into Heaven by the gods and that they had ordered Semíramis to retire from public life and cede the throne to her son. She appeals to the people to follow an order ordained by Heaven and quotes the god Belo in the following passage:

«La voluntad del grande Dios i mía,
de mi Iuno i tu Nino, es que govierne,
que sea universal Rei i Monarca
el moço Zameis Ninias, tu buen hijo.» (43b)

This cynical view of the doctrine of the divine right of kings as an instrument used to persuade subjects into submission is worlds removed from Lope. It also prefigures the ironic juxtaposition of markedly un-Godlike behavior on the part of the king and the claim that the king is the image of God that we find in Castro's theater, notably in *El nacimiento de Montesinos*.

In spite of Semíramis' acknowledged prowess as a military leader she has not been able to dominate her own vices and appetites:

[h]a sido rei i capitán famoso,
alcançando vitorias i trofeos
de todos sus contrarios, sino solo
de aquellos que consigo el [h]ombre trae,
que son los viles apetitos ciegos,
de quien [h]a sido siempre avassallada. (55a)

As a licentious monarch she has also corrupted the kingdom from within. In a long monologue the courtier Zelabo, functioning as a chorus-like commentator, laments the loss of freedom the kingdom suffers under her rule. The rotting of the state, where now self-seeking is rewarded and loyalty punished, has occurred not from any exterior enemy but from a weakening of its most interior values:

> sirvo en la guerra i en la Corte, donde
> la fiel lealtad corrida el rostro esconde.
> ... ...
> ... tentadora [h]ipócrita in[h]umana
> paz i quietud, vida i [h]onor destruye,
> i ambiciosa, insolente i temeraria
> es de virtud, sacrílega falsaria. (50b)

The real Ninias is morally outraged not only by the incestuous lust his mother has for him but by her whole immoral rule. He sees her as a diabolical presence:

> Daré fin con su muerte a sus marañas,
> acabarán sus vicios i maldades,
> sus diabólicas artes i sus mañas. (48b)

In disgust, he kills his own mother. His act of matricide is applauded by the kingdom as «justicias del eterno cielo» (53b).

But for all Ninias' righteousness he too promises to follow in the footsteps of his mother. His first act as king is to lie to the people, as his mother did, by propagating the myth that Semíramis assumed the form of a dove and ascended into Heaven. The courtier Diarco predicts the continued decline of the kingdom as he comments «En cuerpo i alma todo es cual su madre» (57a). Thus Virués ironically undercuts the pattern, later to be that of the *comedia,* of order restored.

THE KING IN THE «COMEDIA»

The dramatic formula of the neo-Senecan movement was to have a short life in Spain, roughly spanning the period between 1575 and 1590. What Lope instinctively understood and what Cervantes would finally, though reluctantly, accept was that a public immersed in the heroic medieval world of the *romancero* and the *libros de caballerías* and which, as Stephen Gilman has shown, experienced its medieval past not as dead history but as a living present,[15] wanted to see the heroic values of that world mirrored and celebrated on stage. Virués and his contemporaries offered their public not only settings distant in time and place, a false classical world that would fail to spark the imagination and stir the emotions of the theatergoer, but a dramatic world devoid of heroes and

---

[15] STEPHEN GILMAN, «The Problem of the Spanish Renaissance», *Folio,* 10 («Studies in the Literature of Spain of the Sixteenth and Seventeenth Centuries», Michael J. Ruggerio, ed., 1977), pp. 37-54.

positive values. Valor, honor and virtue are scarcely to be found in this school of drama where evil is magnified, multiplied, and finally punished. If the later *comedia* celebrates order restored, the earlier dramatic moment preaches disorder destroyed.[16]

What emerged as the triumphant theatrical form in Spain replaced the morally chaotic vision of the neo-Senecans with an idealized and heroic medieval society founded on «la restauración, en plena monarquía absoluta, de los ideales heroico-caballerescos de la Edad Media».[17] Order in this society is ultimately guaranteed by the existence of a strictly defined social (and vertical) hierarchy which assigns each member to a social station with corresponding honors and obligations. As Arnold G. Reichenberger has explained:

> One could almost say that there is only one protagonist in the Spanish *comedia*, the Spanish people. From king to peasant, each person exists primarily as a member of his community, to whom are assigned definite duties. The king has to act as a king —to dispense justice; the nobleman as a nobleman— to be a faithful vassal, or a reliable friend, or a passionate lover; the peasant as a peasant— to be proud, independent, and at the same time loyal to the king.[18]

In this system each member defines himself and his worth in terms of his social role. Thus, in the oft-repeated and revealing formula «soy quien soy», the noble character sees himself not in terms of a discrete individual personality with the freedom to determine his own course of action but as a member of society whose conduct is virtually prescribed by hallowed tradition. According to Leo Spitzer:

> un hombre, noble de nacimiento o de carácter... en el momento de escoger el curso de su acción se representa el ideal a que su personalidad *debe aspirar*, dada su naturaleza congénita... El noble que *es quien es*... es «lo que debe ser» dada su particular tradición... Parece aceptar la variedad de la vida, pero al mismo tiempo afirma la existencia de un molde, que ha configurado a su propio linaje.[19]

In the *comedia*, then, the noble character represses his individual impulses when they run contrary to the sacred laws of society. A basic characteristic of the heroic protagonist of this genre, and one that alienates him from twentieth-century sensibilities, is his conformity to

---

[16] In neither *Atila furioso* nor *La gran Semíramis* is there any promise of order returning to the state. It seems to happen at the end of the second play but comments on how Ninias will repeat his mother's sins warn us otherwise.

[17] VICENTE LLORÉNS, «La intención del *Quijote*», in *Literatura, historia, política* (Madrid: Revista de Occidente, 1967), p. 213.

[18] ARNOLD G. REICHENBERGER, «The Uniqueness of the *Comedia*», *Hispanic Review*, 27 (1959), p. 305.

[19] LEO SPITZER, «'Soy quien soy'», *Nueva Revista de Filología Hispánica*, 1 (1947), pp. 124-125.

the demands of society. Individual self-expression is not exalted as a positive value, for, as Américo Castro has pointed out, «la discordancia del individuo con la sociedad ... producía la infamia».[20]

The *comedia* repeatedly demonstrates the axiom that personal integrity and, ultimately, true spiritual fulfillment can only be realized by carrying out the responsibilities of one's social role:

> el teatro español se hace cuestión de los comportamientos y acciones de los hombres y de los grupos, tratando de demostrar que, obrando de una manera o de otra manera, pueden alcanzar o no a vivir felices, según su inserción en, el sistema social en que se encuentran. Sistema social en el cual las posibilidades de la felicidad están garantizadas por el respeto recíproco a ese orden de la sociedad y al puesto que a unos y a otros corresponde y que lleva tras sí el mecanismo coactivo de la autoridad suprema que lo restablece en caso de violación.[21]

On a theoretical level, then, the social system espoused by the *comedia* functions as a perfectly harmonious unit when each member fulfills his social obligations.

But this closed system becomes problematic when juxtaposed to other ethical systems. A good number of *comedias* —the anonymous *La Estrella de Sevilla*, Lope's *El Duque de Viseo*, Calderón's *El médico de su honra*, to mention a few widely-read examples— create a strong dramatic tension by setting in opposition the demands of the social code with the laws of natural justice and Christian morality. When faced with the problem of choosing between committing an injustice or violating his social duties, the honorable character may bitterly complain about the injustice of the social code, but he invariably accedes to its demands, thereby affirming his nobility. As Maravall explains:

> la comedia hace un doble juego: poniendo bien claro lo que en, él [i.e. the honor code] hay de problemático para hacer resaltar su impresionante condición dramática y servirse de la fuerza psicológica que por esa misma condición ofrece, mantiene, sin embargo, a rajatabla el principio del honor, y trata de inculcar en el público, al que hace enfrentarse con tales tensiones, la creencia de que hay que asumir su condición, conflictiva, hay que vivir sin escapatoria su dolorosa tensión. En el dominio que uno alcance de sus sentimientos personales, en el acatamiento a esa moral social, está la grandeza nobiliaria del individuo. Llegar a ese dominio es el grado más alto, por más costoso, de participación en los valores aristocráticos.[22]

---

[20] AMÉRICO CASTRO, «Algunas observaciones acerca del concepto del honor en los siglos XVI y XVII», *Revista de Filología Española*, 3 (1916); rpt. in his *Semblanzas y estudios españoles* (Princeton: Princeton University Press, 1956), p. 358.

[21] JOSÉ ANTONIO MARAVALL, *Teatro y literatura en la sociedad barroca* (Madrid: Seminarios y Ediciones, S. A., 1972), pp. 34-35.

[22] MARAVALL, *Teatro*, pp. 94-95.

In such works, though the honor code may be shown to be unjust and un-Christian, its precepts are never violated.

These same principles and problems come into play in the *comedia*'s treatment of the king and of the vertical relationship between king and subject. The theory of kingship reflected in Lope's *comedia* is that of seventeenth-century Europe, the doctrine of absolutism and of the divine right of kings.[23] According to this principle, the king's power proceeds directly from God and consequently can be withdrawn only by Him. As God's representative on earth the king merits his subjects' absolute submission and obedience. This unquestioning loyalty constitutes one of the main obligations of the noble *caballero* and compliance with it is essential for him to be able to affirm «soy quien soy». Thus statements such as the following abound in the *comedia*:

> Que no hay más honra, vida ni mas leyes
> que el gusto y la obediencia de los reyes.[24]

The *rey justiciero* exemplifies the best aspects of the *comedia*'s hierarchical order. He displays generosity, magnanimity and concern for the well-being of the state and of his vassals.[25] As seen in *Fuenteovejuna, Peribáñez, El mejor alcalde, el rey* and many other plays, the king often acts to restore order and justice to a disordered society. But the king may also be the cause of disorder in the *comedia* when he himself places his *gusto* over *lo justo*. When this occurs, the loyal male subject does not look upon the king as a tyrant, but rather considers him a legitimate ruler who, in spite of his human fallibilities, merits absolute respect by virtue of his office.[26] The code of honorable behavior demands that the noble *caballero* who finds his personal feelings to be at odds with the will of the king cede to the authority of his monarch.

In cases where the king's will and the noble's honor seem to conflict, the subject resolves the problem by affirming that the king, the bestower of all honor, cannot offend the honor of his subject and that therefore no vengeance is required. According to Américo Castro this special privilege of the king:

---

[23] For a discussion of this political doctrine in Spain see José Antonio Maravall, *La Philosophie politique espagnole au XVIIe siècle,* translation of his *La teoría española del estado en el siglo XVII* (Madrid: 1944), by Louis Cazes and Pierre Mesnard (Paris: Librairie Philosophique J. Vrin, 1955).

[24] Lope de Vega, *Amor, pleito y desafío,* Act III.

[25] For a typology of the king in the *comedia* see Carlos Ortigoza Vieyra, *Los móviles de la comedia* (México: 1954); and Juana de José Prades, *Teoría sobre los personajes de la comedia nueva* (Madrid: CSIC, 1963).

[26] In this the *comedia* proves itself to be even more «conservative» than the seventeenth-century political theorists, who admitted the existence of tyrants, claiming that once a king becomes a tyrant he ceases to be king. Nonetheless these theorists, in contrast to the natural law theorists of the sixteenth century, declared that in such cases the subject is morally bound to tolerate the tyrant until God sees fit to punish him. Consult Maravall, *La Philosophie,* pp. 315-322.

es fundamento de la sociedad vivificada por el honor. En esquema podría decirse que no hay honor fuera de la nobleza, ni nobleza sin que el rey cree y corrobore la calidad de noble... el noble se negaría a sí mismo si tomase una actitud superior a la del rey, como lo haría si lo castigase; las reglas formales sobre que descansa la comedia se invalidarían. Dicho con otras palabras, el honor expresa la relación del individuo con la sociedad, cuya esencia y representación condensa el rey. Así comprendemos por qué los conflictos entre el rey y el noble no tienen solución posible...[27]

Even in the one case where the king could theoretically offend the honor of his subject, the latter backs away from seeking vengeance:

> While a king cannot wrong a male subject directly, he can dishonor a female subject by seducing her, and thereby offend her male relatives. Theoretically these have the right to erase the wrong by shedding the royal blood, but this situation (it occurs in *La vida es sueño*) is never courageously met in the *comedia*. Instead of taking drastic action, the offended one battles with his wits and finds an ingenious solution.[28]

A classic example occurs in Rojas Zorrilla's *Del rey abajo, ninguno* in which García, believing that the king has dishonored him by making advances to his wife, resolves to avenge his offense by killing the innocent woman rather than by taking action against the king. But when he discovers that the true offender is Don Mendo, he spares his wife and kills Don Mendo instead, since:

> No he de permitir me agravie,
> del rey abajo, ninguno. (Act III)

In cases not concerning affronts to his honor the loyal subject must obey the will of the king even if that obedience results in a morally reprehensible act. The subject in such a case refuses to judge the king's actions, for the king is responsible to God alone:

> Es soberana justica
> el Rey, y aunque yerre, vos
> no lo habéis de remediar,
> porque nadie ha de juzgar
> a los Reyes sino Dios.[29]

---

[27] AMÉRICO CASTRO, p. 346. Menéndez Pidal offers a less metaphysical reason: «Todos los móviles humanos debían subordinarse al honor, mientras el honor sólo cedía ante la persona del rey. En multitud de comedias trágicas se expone la doctrina de que los agravios que proceden del rey no se vengan, aunque atropellen la honra del vasallo... [The principle reason] es la expuesta por JERÓNIMO DE CARRANZA en su *Destreza de armas* (1571): el ofendido no puede matar al ofensor cuando éste es una 'persona universal, necesaria a la comunidad o ejército, como el rey o el capitán'. Esta subordinación de la dignidad individual al bien común... nos compruebe el carácter social del sentimiento del honor.» RAMÓN MENÉNDEZ PIDAL, «Del honor en el teatro español», *De Cervantes y Lope de Vega* (Madrid: Espasa-Calpe, S. A., 1940), pp. 153-154.

[28] GEORGE TYLER NORTHUP, «Introduction» to *Three Plays by Calderón* (New York: D. C. Heath & Co., 1926), pp. xvii-xviii.

[29] CALDERÓN DE LA BARCA, *Saber del mal y del bien*, Act I.

Thus in *La Estrella de Sevilla,* for example, Don Sancho, ordered by the king to kill his best friend and future brother-in-law, fights to repress his human emotions and resolves to obey the king, trusting that God will punish the monarch if he is unjust:

> Mas soy caballero,
> y no he de hacer lo que quiero,
> sino lo que debo hacer.
> Pues ¿qué debo obedecer?
> La ley que fuere primero.
> Mas no hay ley que a aquesto obligue.
> Mas sí hay; que aunque injusto el Rey,
> debo obedecer su ley;
> a él después Dios le castigue. (Act II)[30]

Plays such as the *Estrella* demonstrate an important principle of the *comedia*: while bad kings could be portrayed and criticism of the social system implied, defiance, disobedience or rebellion against the king, even on moral grounds, could not be presented even if it meant that the play would end on a tragic note. If certain characters prove themselves to be morally superior to the king, they never translate that quality into material resistance:

> Y así encontramos en el teatro de Lope con frecuencia esta figura del vasallo amargado en su corazón y justificado en su conciencia, que siente que toda esta máquina de conceptos reposa en algo falso y no sabe ni quiere saber qué es. Sólo su propia amargura es el contraste y el criterio de la inmoralidad del sistema. Pero más vale no pensar en ello, y su voluntad, sin más resistencia, se dobla como un junco al soplo poderoso de la pasión desenfrenada del monarca.[31]

In Lope's plays, the problem of the abuse of royal power is generally resolved by the king himself. A subject never need take corrective measures against his king, even in cases where the monarch's actions threaten a vassal's honor or the welfare of the kingdom, simply because the king invariably realizes his errors and corrects his own behavior. This, ac-

---

[30] A similar sentiment is expressed in SHAKESPEARE's *King Henry V.* In Act IV, scene 1, King Henry is disguised as a common soldier and tries to inspire valor in his followers. The following is an interchange between the disguised monarch and two of his soldiers, Michael Williams and John Bates:

> KING HENRY: Methinks I could not die any where [sic] so contented as in the king's company, his cause being just and his quarrel honourable.
> WILLIAMS: That's more than we know.
> BATES: Ay, or more than we should seek after; for we know enough if we know we are the king's subjects. If his cause be wrong, our obedience to the king wipes the crime of it out of us. (vv. 130-140).

[31] JOSÉ F. MONTESINOS, «Observaciones y notas», to *Lope de Vega, La corona merecida* (Madrid: Teatro Antiguo Español, textos y estudios, V, 1923), p. 169.

cording to José María Díez Borque, is but one more example of the way in which Lope glorifies kingship:

> Llegamos al desenlace que presentará una solución del conflicto, totalmente de acuerdo con la exaltación, del Rey y la monarquía. El Rey es superior a todos... porque *pudiendo* se vence, limita, voluntariamente, su acción en favor de un vasallo suyo, con lo que al carisma de la autoridad se suma el de la bondad y respeto a su pueblo, que lo alejan de la tiranía.[32]

Castro's plays of the unjust use of royal power are quite another matter. The Valencian playwright is reluctant neither to have his characters openly accuse the king of tyranny nor to show human defiance to the king's authority as justified and even as divinely sanctioned. In all but *Las hazañas del Cid,* a character who takes a decisive stand against the king's abuse of power —a stand that may even include killing the king— is acquitted of the charge of treason and in most cases is hailed by the people as their new ruler, or promised the throne in the future. In the case of the *Hazañas,* while Castro is virtually bound by tradition to condemn Bellido Dolfos as a traitor, he places that particular act of regicide in such a light as to make the audience feel that it is less an act of treason than a divinely inspired act of justice and retribution.

Yet, if Castro ultimately supports the validity of resistance to misdirected royal authority, he also shows it to be a thorny issue for men of conscience brought up to respect their monarch. Alongside every character who successfully takes a stand against the king is another who, in his desire to remain a loyal subject, cannot fully justify to himself opposition to the king's authority. Like the archetypical vassal of Lope's plays he is too bound to the belief embodied in the phrase «soy quien soy» to conceive of defiance as completely licit. It is this character who is the central, problematic protagonist of Castro's plays. In the earliest plays, modeled to some degree after those of Virués, this *dramatis persona* is torn between resistance and obedience. He can accuse the king of tyranny but his attempts to oppose him are frustrated by both his inner doubts and the king's greater political power. In the later plays, closer to the patterns set by Lope, the code of «perfect» honorable behavior effectively and totally enslaves the subject to the will of the king.

Castro's plays, then, place the opposing views of submission and defiance to the will of the king in a sharp dialectic tension. This tension may be felt both within and between individual characters. Without negating the value of loyalty Castro consistently places the claims of natural and Christian law above those of arbitrary royal power, and he supports as licit the call for resistance against an unjust ruler.

---

[32] JOSÉ MARÍA DÍEZ BORQUE, *Sociología de la comedia española del siglo XVII* (Madrid: Ediciones Cátedra, 1976), p. 81.

Political Theory in Sixteenth-Century Spain

The problem of the unjust king dominates not only dramatic literature but also political theory in the Spain of the sixteenth century. University theologians, both Dominicans and Jesuits, repeatedly turn their attention to the questions of the origins, duties and limitations of sovereign power and of the relationship between a ruler and his subjects. Among the most illustrious names one finds Francisco de Vitoria, Fox Morcillo, Domingo de Soto, Luis de Molina, Francisco Suárez and Juan de Mariana.[33] The concept of law and of the state shared by these theorists derives from and continues the medieval political philosophy of St. Thomas Aquinas, and, by implication, opposes what was to become the doctrine of the modern state, the political theory expounded by Machiavelli:

> Sixteenth-century Spain.... remained basically medieval, and saw a great Thomist revival; its scholasticism was humanized by the literary bent of the Renaissance and directed by nominalist influences to apply morality to political problems. The theory taught in the universities... was that of a Christian state... The influence of Roman law was felt more in a christianized version of the sovereignty of the people than in any idea of the ruler being above the law... Although Machiavelli's *Prince* was widely read and discussed in Spain, political thought continued to be expounded within a framework of morality and law. The writers... all assume an ordered universe; all adopt the Thomist hierarchy of laws: the eternal law, governing all things; the natural law, written in men's minds, through which they participate in the eternal law and distinguish good from evil; the positive divine or revealed law (Scripture) supplementing the natural; and positive human (civil and canon) law.[34]

The theory of kingship espoused by these writers is based on the Roman law doctrine of the sovereignty of the people in a Christian version that «is, and is not, at the same time, a theory of divine right».[35]

---

[33] VITORIA was a famous lecturer of theology at the University of Salamanca from 1526-1546; his ideas are to be found in the manuscripts of his lectures published after his death. Fox MORCILLO's *De regni regisque institutione, libri III* was published in 1556; SOTO's *De justitia et jure, libri X*, in the same year; MOLINA's *De justitia et jure, libri VI*, in 1592; SUÁREZ's *De legibus ac de deo legislatore* was published in 1612 but was basically a transcript of lectures delivered in the last decade of the previous century at Coimbra; and MARIANA's *De rege et regis institutione, libri III*, first appeared in print in 1599.
Mention should also be made here of the Jesuit Pedro de Rivadeneyra whose *Tratado de la Religión y virtudes que debe tener el Príncipe cristiano para gobernar y conservar los Estados. Contra lo que Nicolás de Maquiavelo y los políticos enseñan en este tiempo*, published in 1595, anticipates the type of anti-Machavellian treatise which was to achieve great popularity among seventeenth-century Spanish political theorists. While in theory these tracts place Christian morality over the «razón de estado» they nonetheless cede absolute authority to the king.
[34] BERNICE HAMILTON, *Political Thought in Sixteenth-Century Spain* (Oxford: Clarendon Press, 1963), pp. 4-5.
[35] HAMILTON, p. 38.

Following the ideas of Aristotle, these theorists begin by affirming that man is a social animal and therefore has need of an organized society. Furthermore, this need forms part of the Divine Plan, for, according to Mariana:

> Sabía empero Dios, creador y padre del género humano, que no hay cosa como la amistad y la caridad mutua entre los hombres, y que para excitarlas era preciso reunirlos en un solo lugar y bajo el imperio de unas mismas leyes. Habíales concedido ya la facultad de hablar para que pudiesen asociarse y comunicarse sus pensamientos, cosa que ya de por sí fomenta el amor mutuo; y para más obligarlos a querer lo que estaba ya en sus facultades, les creó sujetos a necesidades y expuestos a muchos males y peligros, para satisfacer y obviar los cuales fuese indispensable la concurrencia de la fuerza y habilidad de muchos.[36]

God, then, created in man an instinct for self-government; Soto goes on to specify:

> But the body politic could not in any way govern itself... unless it chose magistrates, to whom it should give its own power; for otherwise, the whole congregation, being without order or head, would not exhibit itself as one body... Accordingly, for this reason, communities, divinely taught and instructed... set up... forms of government for themselves... Behold how public civil power is an ordinance of God! — not that the community did not set up princes, but that it did so by divine instruction.[37]

This interpretation of the origin of the ruler's power differs in an important way from what would be the strict divine right theory of the following century in that «though the king's power came ultimately from God, it was derived mediately from the people, who determined, or had at one time determined, the form of government and who should exercise it».[38]

Nonetheless, once power has been delegated to a ruler he becomes greater than the community. Suárez writes:

> Once power has been transferred to the king, he is at once the vicar of God and by natural law must be obeyed... he is by that very power made superior even to the kingdom which granted it; for in giving it the kingdom subjected itself and deprived itself of its former liberty... And for the same reason the king cannot be deprived of his power —for he has acquired a true dominion— unless he falls into tyranny, when the kingdom may wage a just war against him...[39]

---

[36] JUAN DE MARIANA, *Del rey y de la institución real,* translated by Humberto Armella Maza (Madrid: Publicaciones Españolas, 1961), I, 32-33.
[37] DOMINGO DE SOTO, *De legibus,* Book IV; English translation in HAMILTON, p. 34.
[38] HAMILTON, p. 41.
[39] SUÁREZ, *De legibus,* Book II; in HAMILTON, p. 39.

In such a system it follows that obedience to a king's *just* laws is not a matter of choice but is morally binding according to the precepts of natural law.

The concept of natural law is evoked not only to support the claim of obedience but also to justify disobedience in cases of injustice. According to the natural law theory, even prior to the establishment of governments God endowed man with a natural reason, or instinct, that allows him to distinguish right from wrong. According to Suárez:

> Because God is the author of nature He gave particular things their own instincts and stimuli through which they act for their own ends. But for man in particular, He placed in his mind a natural norm by which he might govern himself according to reason, which is natural to him. This is the natural law: a knowledge of those principles which are self-evident without the action of discursive human reason... Then he gave men the power to set up by reason, according to time, place and duties, laws which they might judge expedient. These laws are called human laws.[40]

Reduced to its essence, natural law asserts two basic principles: «Do good and avoid evil» and «Do unto others as you would they should do unto you».[41] Natural law holds its claim on all men, whether civilized or barbarian, and whether its precepts are actually codified in writing or not. In the Christian state, however, the principles of natural law coincide with the divine law as revealed in the Decalogue and the Gospels. Beginning with Vitoria, the Spaniards declare that «nada que sea lícito por ley natural es prohibido por el Evangelio».[42] Hence, in these treatises human laws are seen as subject to a double scrutiny since «the laws of the community are constantly referred to and judged by the laws of nature and of God».[43] Unjust human laws stand in violation of both.

In the case of an unjust law, natural law sanctifies the rights of the individual conscience. Laws that command an evil action do not bind in conscience since they are not laws at all; hence, disobedience is not only morally legitimate but the only morally appropriate response. Suárez explains it thus:

> ... if he [i.e. the king] practices injustice and evil by ordering some wicked action, then he does not produce any binding effect by it. For an iniquitous law is not a law, nor is royal power conferred for the making of such laws. So if an order is really wicked subjects can and ought to disobey the king, but they cannot absolutely deny obedience to him in matters which are just.[44]

---

[40] Suárez, *De legibus*, Book I; in Hamilton, p. 15.
[41] Hamilton, pp. 13-14.
[42] Luis Sánchez Agesta, *El concepto del estado en el pensamiento español del siglo XVI* (Madrid: Marisal, 1959), p. 107.
[43] Hamilton, p. 30.
[44] Suárez, *De legibus*, Book III; in Hamilton, pp. 60-61.

However, in cases that border on the evil the theorists generally caution the subject to exercise discretion before deciding to disobey. In cases of doubt, they prescribe obedience as better for the well-being of the community. Soto states that:

> Those laws which are only in opposition to human good, although they are not of themselves binding in conscience, may sometimes bind for fear of scandal... for in things which are manifestly tyrannical it is impossible to resist those in power without causing scandal, and so one must put up with them until such time as they are brought by leniency to a more healthy frame of mind.[45]

Suárez agrees and elaborates further:

> All the Doctors point out that it is necessary for the injustice of the law to be such as to constitute a moral certainty. If there is any doubt, a presumption must be made in the legislator's favour, partly because he has and possesses a superior right, partly, too, because he is moved by higher advice and may be prompted by general reasons unknown to his subjects; and partly because otherwise his subjects would assume too great a license to disobey the laws; for laws cannot be so utterly just as to make it impossible for some people to find plausible reasons for treating them as dubious.[46]

The theorists, then, admit the existence of ambiguous cases in which the burden of choosing a course of action resides with the individual. In such situations the natural law theory does not absolve the subject from moral responsibility, as will the theory of divine right, but rather makes his responsibility that much greater by forcing him to make a moral choice. The problems of living with the uncertainties concommitant with choosing to oppose the king are, as we shall see, strongly dramatized in Guillén de Castro's *El amor constante*.

Similar uncertainties and reservations arise concerning the question of resistance to the tyrant king. In the tradition of medieval political ideology, the sixteenth-century Spanish theorists distinguish two types of tyrants: the ruler who has illegally usurped his power and the legitimately appointed monarch who rules tyrannically. Mariana, who sees tyranny as the antithesis of monarchy and as the worst form of government, describes the difference between the tyrant (of either type) and the true king in the following graphic manner:

> Es propio de un buen rey defender la inocencia, reprimir la maldad, salvar a los que peligran, procurar a la república la felicidad y todo género de bienes; mas no del tirano, que hace consistir su mayor poder en poder entregarse desenfrenadamente a sus pasiones, que no cree indecorosa maldad alguna, que comete todo género de crímenes, destruye la hacienda de

---

[45] Soto, *De justitia*, Book I; in Hamilton, pp. 46-47.
[46] Suárez, *De legibus*, Book I; in Hamilton, p. 49.

> los poderosos, viola la castidad, mata a los buenos y llega al fin de su vida sin que haya una sola acción vil a que no se haya entregado. Es además el rey humilde, tratable, accesible, amigo de vivir bajo el mismo derecho que sus conciudadanos; y el tirano, desconfiado, medroso, amigo de aterrar con el aparato de su fuerza y su fortuna, con la severencia de las costumbres, con la crueldad de los juicios dictados por sus sangrientos tribunales.[47]

He goes on to add that while the king unites the kingdom in harmony, the tyrant works towards the destruction of the kingdom.

How is the kingdom to deal with the tyrannical ruler? The theorists find the issue a thorny one, for what may be in accordance with the precepts of natural law may run contrary to the welfare of the state. Tyrannicide is admitted as a legitimate means of defeating tyranny but one which should be avoided if possible for the good of the kingdom. Natural law may have to forgo its claims at times, as in the case of the right of self-defense against a king; in his *Defensio Fidei*, published in 1613, Suárez states that although natural law permits the killing of the king when necessary in cases of self-defense, «if that death would leave the country in a perilous state, the man would be bound —but in charity alone and not by natural law— to refrain».[48]

Of the two types of tyranny, the case of the tyrant/usurper poses fewer problems. The consensus among Spanish writers is that as the usurper used violence to seize the throne for himself, the state may resort to violence to overthrow him:

> En primer lugar, tanto los filósofos como los teólogos están de acuerdo en que si un príncipe se apoderó de la república a fuerza de armas, sin razón, sin derecho alguno, sin el consentimiento del pueblo, puede ser despojado por cualquiera de la corona, del gobierno, de la vida; que siendo un enemigo público y provocando todo género de males a la patria y haciéndose verdaderamente acreedor por su carácter al nombre de tirano, no sólo puede ser destronado, sino que puede serlo con la misma violencia con que él arrebató un poder que no pertenece sino a la sociedad que oprime y esclaviza.[49]

All agree with Mariana in affirming that any individual may kill the tyrant/usurper without seeking explicit public approval:

> He acts with the authority of the tacitly consenting community, and with the authority of God, who has given everyone by natural law the right to defend himself, and his country, from the violence done by such a tyrant...[50]

But certain theorists, notably Soto and Suárez, express reservations about killing a usurping tyrant after he has been allowed to rule for a length

---

[47] MARIANA, I, 92.
[48] HAMILTON, p. 62.
[49] MARIANA, I, 109-110.
[50] SUÁREZ, *Defensio fidei*, Book VI; in HAMILTON, p. 63.

of time, for in not immediately opposing him the community has tacitly assented to his rule. In such cases the tyrant must exhibit a consistent pattern of injustice for assassination to be licit, and even then it must be:

> essential for the liberty of the realm, because if there is any less drastic means for removing him it is not lawful to kill him forthwith without the approval of a superior and an investigation. This includes the proviso that no treaty, truce or pact ratified under oath has been made between the tyrant and the people... We must add still another restriction: always provided that there is no danger of the same or worse evils falling on the community as a result of the tyrant's death as it already suffers under his rule. And, finally, the community must not openly oppose it.[51]

The case of the legitimate king ruling tyrannically elicits warnings for greater caution. Soto is the most reluctant of the theorists in affirming the right of armed defiance; he admits the use of arms as a last resort but prefers that «supplication... be made to God, in whose hand is the heart of the king; and God sometimes because of the sins of the people suffers a hypocrite to reign».[52] Suárez states that natural law allows for the deposition of a lawful king only after other measures have proven inadequate:

> It resides in the people only as a necessary means of defense, for self-preservation... so that, if a legitimate prince governs tyrannically and no other means of self-defense can be found than the expulsion and deposition of the king, the people, acting as a whole, in conformity with the public and general councils of its communities and magnates, may depose him. This is allowed by natural law, which says that force may be met with force...[53]

Before counseling armed opposition, Mariana outlines a number of intermediate steps aimed at giving the king the opportunity to amend his ways:

> No hemos de mudar fácilmente de reyes, si no queremos incurrir en mayores males y provocar disturbios... Se les ha de sufrir lo más posible, pero no ya cuando trastornen la república... Entonces es ya preciso pensar en la manera cómo podría destronársele, a fin de que no se agraven los males ni se vengue una maldad con otra. Si están aún permitidas las reuniones públicas, conviene principalmente consultar el parecer de todos, dando por lo más fijo y acertado lo que se estableciere de común acuerdo. Se ha de amonestar ante todo al príncipe y llamarle a razón y a derecho... si se mostrare dispuesto a corregir sus faltas, no hay para qué pasar más allá... si empero rechazare todo género de observaciones... debe empezarse por declarar públicamente que no se le reconoce como rey, que se dan por nulos todos sus actos posteriores... [A war will almost necessarily result from this] y si así lo exigieren las circunstancias, sin que de otro modo fuese

---

[51] Suárez, *Defensio fidei*, Book VI; in Hamilton, p. 62.
[52] Soto, *De justitia*, Book V; in Hamilton, p. 62.
[53] Suárez, *Defensio fidei*, Book VI; in Hamilton, pp. 63-64.

> posible salvar la patria, matar a hierro al príncipe como enemigo público, y matarle por el mismo derecho de defensa, por la autoridad propia del pueblo...[54]

All agree that in such cases the voiced approval of the community must be obtained prior to the assassination but that once that consent is publicly declared, any member of the community may carry out the public will. Mariana declares:

> Dado este caso, no sólo reside esta facultad en el pueblo, reside hasta en cualquier particular que, abandonando toda especie de impunidad y despreciando su propia vida, quiera empeñarse en ayudar de esta suerte la república.[55]

But in cases where public assembly is not possible Mariana assumes that tacit assent has been given for an individual to punish the king:

> No por no poderse reunir los ciudadanos debe faltar en ellos el natural ardor por derribar la servidumbre... Nunca podré creer que haya obrado mal el que secundando los deseos públicos haya atentado en tales circunstancias contra la vida de su príncipe.[56]

The political theory of the aforementioned writers, and not the theory of the divine right of kings, was the most widespread and influential political ideology current in Spain during the years that Guillén de Castro began his theatrical career.[57] It is not surprising, therefore, that such ideas should find their way, in modified form, into plays concerned with the tyrannical king just as the theory of divine right of kings, the «official» seventeenth-century ideology, would find its echo in Lope and later writers of *comedias*. Three major points of this doctrine infiltrate Castro's dramas: (1) the idea that natural law stands above the will of the king; (2) that disobedience, resistance and tyrannicide are valid and legitimate measures against an unjust king; (3) that although these measures may be taken, there also exists pressure to keep rebellion in check, however morally grounded it may be, for the good of the state.

---

[54] MARIANA, I, 110-111.
[55] MARIANA, I, 111.
[56] MARIANA, I, 111.
[57] «It is not absolutely certain that this 'official' church and university political theory —written in medieval Latin and reasoned in the scholastic manner— represents the main currents of the time... But the influence of the university philosophers must certainly have been great: e.g. several thousand students, lay and clerical, passed through the classrooms of Francisco de Vitoria, and many of his pupils later occupied prominent positions in church, university or administration in Old and New Spain» (HAMILTON, p. 2).

ARAGONESE OPPOSITION TO ROYAL AUTHORITY

In his study of Juan de la Cueva,[58] Anthony Watson advances the hypothesis that the plays of the Sevillian dramatist, with their emphasis on royal tyranny, are not merely vehicles for anti-Machiavellian propaganda but, rather, are veiled criticisms of Philip II's aggressive and absolutist position towards the annexation of Portugal. In other words, they are not plays of abstract political ideology but responses to a specific historical circumstance.

Although the present study examines Castro's plays of tyranny and royal injustice in the light of their literary precedents and as literary incarnations of the natural law theory of sovereignty, we cannot ignore the possibility that, as in the case of Cueva, the anti-monarchical sentiments repeatedly expressed in these plays may to some degree reflect Castro's own feelings regarding a major contemporary political issue. Here we are speaking not of Portugal but of the threat posed to the political autonomy of the kingdom of Aragon —of which Valencia was one of three states— by Philip II, a problem that reached its peak with the incident of Antonio Pérez in the years 1590-1592, years in which Guillén de Castro was beginning to reveal his literary talents and inclinations to his native city.

According to the historian María Soledad Carrasco Urgoiti:

> ... la historia aragonesa del siglo XVI puede interpretarse como una larga contienda entre un régimen parlamentario de signo medieval y la tendencia absolutista que en esa época se impone en Europa y que los aragoneses identificaban con la política castellana.[59]

Although Castile and Aragon had been united under one crown by the Catholic Monarchs, Spain's peculiarly federalist system of government gave Aragon a great deal of political autonomy. Under the Habsburgs, while Castile was ruled directly by the king, Aragon retained its own *fueros,* or charter rights, with its own legislative body, or *cortes.* The king was represented by a viceroy who was, traditionally, a native of Aragon. The *fueros* were most jealously prized by the nobles, for they allowed them almost unlimited power over their vassals. On the other hand, the peasants, resenting the tyranny of the nobles fostered by the *fueros,* sought to be placed under direct royal jurisdiction. Philip II, seeking to strengthen his power in Aragon, began undermining the position of the Aragonese nobles by:

---

[58] ANTHONY WATSON, *Juan de la Cueva and the Portuguese Succession* (London: Tamesis Books Ltd., 1971).
[59] MARÍA SOLEDAD CARRASCO URGOITI, *El problema morisco en Aragón al comienzo del reinado de Felipe II* (Madrid: Castalia, Estudios de Hispanófila, 11, 1969), p. 15.

> ... encouraging the efforts of the rural populations to transfer themselves from seigneurial to royal jurisdiction and encouraging inter-marriage between Aragonese nobility and that of Castile in order to further the process of integration.[60]

In 1588 King Philip further disturbed the nobles by breaking with tradition in appointing a Castilian viceroy to Aragon.

The breaking point came with the flight of Antonio Pérez from Castilian justice to Aragon in 1590. There he had hoped to take advantage of the protection offered him by Aragon's autonomous legal system. According to John Lynch:

> He had chosen his moment well. In Aragon, defence of the *fueros* was then the leading issue and regionalist sentiment was ready for any pretext to resist the crown... in Aragon Pérez was in a country hostile to Castile...[61]

When King Philip attempted to have Pérez removed from the prison of the Aragonese *Justicia,* where the *fueros* protected him from the king, to that of the Inquisition, a move that would have placed Pérez once again under direct Castilian jurisdiction, a virtual civil war erupted between Aragonese rebels, led by the nobility, and the invading Castilian army of the king.[62] The invaders quickly claimed victory and a dangerous precedent was set:

> [The king]... had already used the Inquisition as a political weapon against Pérez and against the rebels; now he used it as a means of royal control afterwards.[63]

Although Valencia refused to respond to the call of the Aragonese nobles for support against the king, it is probably safe to assume that the Valencians, and particularly the nobles, could not fail to be alarmed by the threat of an ever-expanding Castilian hegemony. How could they not fear that their own legal prerogatives would soon fall victim to the will of a «foreign» king? Indeed, they would soon have reason to resent the power of the central government: in 1609, against the will of the Valencian nobles, the *moriscos* were exiled from Spain, bringing financial ruin to Valencia.

Whether Castro's plays were written in direct response to the Castilian threat to Aragonese autonomy remains a question. However, his plays of royal power, with their insistence on the problem of royal injustice,

---

[60] JOHN LYNCH, *Spain Under the Habsburgs* (Oxford: Basil Blackwell, 1964), I, 339.
[61] LYNCH, p. 341.
[62] For details see GREGORIO MARAÑÓN, *Antonio Pérez,* 2 vols. (Madrid: Espasa-Calpe, S. A., 1958) and in particular Chapter XIX.
[63] LYNCH, p. 344.

may well reflect the general anti-Castilian, anti-Habsburg sentiment dominant in the kingdom of Aragon in the late sixteenth and early seventeenth centuries. This may help to explain why Castro never fully accepted Lope's view of kingship, bound as it was to an absolutist and utterly Castilian reverence for kingly authority.

CHAPTER II

«EL AMOR CONSTANTE»

The problem of tyranny is the central concern of what may well be Castro's first play, *El amor constante*. In it Castro explores the problems that an unjust king poses to the individual subject and to the kingdom he betrays, and he defends throughout the work the right to oppose and depose the tyrannical ruler. *El amor constante* is in part a natural outgrowth of sixteenth-century literature and thought; in it may be seen the influence not only of the theater of Virués and of the doctrines of the university theologians but also that of heroic literature of the epoch, namely the *libros de caballerías* and the *romancero*. Yet in the exploration of the inner psychological turmoil of some of his characters Castro strikes a strongly original note that sets him apart from his literary predecessors.

While the exact dating of *El amor constante* has not been firmly established, both Bruerton and Juliá Martínez have speculated that the *comedia* in question represents either Castro's first work or, at the very least, one of his earliest. Basing his hypothesis on internal metric evidence, Bruerton dates the play between 1596 and 1599.[1] Juliá Martínez, noting that the name of the play's female protagonist, Nísida, appears repeatedly in Castro's lyric poetry of 1593, believes the play to have been written around that year.[2]

Set in the royal palace of Hungary, the play opens on a scene of domestic discord. The King has tired of his wife[3] and fallen madly in love with the young lady-in-waiting, Nísida. Nísida, in turn, is in love with the King's brother Celauro who, we soon learn, has been imprisoned

---

[1] BRUERTON, p. 115. The tendency to judge Castro as dependent on Lope forms, at least in part, a basis for Bruerton's choice of date: «... there is also a passage of *dec.* [i.e. *décimas*] in the play. Lope's earliest use of *dec.* is probably not before 1596» (p. 114).

[2] EDUARDO JULIÁ MARTÍNEZ, «Observaciones», p. lii.

[3] The problem of the unhappy marriage appears repeatedly throughout Castro's plays and has led some critics to speculate that it is a reflection of Castro's own marital problems. For a brief discussion see JOHN G. WEIGER, «Matrimony in the Theater of Guillén de Castro», *Bulletin of the Comediantes*, 10 (Fall, 1958), pp. 1-3.

by the King for unknown reasons. In the opening scene Castro portrays a king desperately trying to avoid coming to terms with the moral implications of his illicit passion. Throughout the scene the King repeatedly voices a wish to free himself from the responsibilities imposed by his roles as king and husband, and hurl himself headlong into the darker regions of blind passion.

In the first verses of the drama the King bristles at the Queen's attempts to calm his unrest. He rejects any consolation that would force him to accept the reality of his marriage:

> REINA: Deja el pesar.
> REY: Con dejarme
> menor le harás.
> REINA: Señor,
> que algún consuelo...
> REY: El mayor
> para mí es no consolarme. (I, 3b)[4]

For him marriage has become a slavery:

> ¡ah, matrimonio,
> cautiverio el más pesado! (I, 4a)

He would even inflict violence on himself to be able to be free of his wife. When the Queen asks for his hand, he answers in an aside:

> Cortada te la daría
> por no verte. (I, 4a)

Merely the sight of the Queen represents an obligation he no longer wishes to acknowledge. Soon, his desire to rid himself of his wife will become a desire to shut himself off from all responsibility, both moral and political. His refusal to examine his behavior is equated to a self-inflicted blindness in the following passage:

> REINA: Vuelve a mirarte en mis ojos,
> y verás tu mal.
> REY: No quiero
> velle ni miralle.
> ... ...
> REINA: ¡Ah, Rey! ¿Que no has de acabar
> de andar en tan ciego error? (I, 3b)

But the King cannot shut out reality as completely as he would like. His wish to live irresponsibly clashes with an inner awareness of

---

[4] All citations from Castro's plays are from the edition of EDUARDO JULIÁ MARTÍNEZ, *Obras de don Guillén de Castro y Bellvis*, 3 vols. (Madrid: Imprenta de la Revista de Archivos, Bibliotecas y Museos, 1925-1927). Roman numerals in parentheses refer to volume number, Arabic numerals to page number, and letters to column.

the sinfulness of his passion. In various passages the King acknowledges a conflict between duty and passion:

> que yo quisiera adorarte,
> porque sé que fuera justo. (I, 4a)
> y sabe Dios que me pesa
> de no quererte. (I, 4b)
> sería muy mal efeto
> perder a Dios el respeto
> y perderte a ti el decoro. (I, 5a)

He is also aware at some level of consciousness that he is acting dishonorably:

> ¿Que haya un hombre de mentir
> para parecer honrado? [*Aparte*] (I, 4a)

To appease his guilty conscience the King develops a convenient philosophy: he cannot exercise his free will because Fate prevents him from conquering his passion:

> Llegado a considerar,
> culpado no puedo ser;
> sin amor ¿puedo querer?
> Sin gusto ¿puedo gustar?
> A Nísida quiero, y muero
> porque el alma no la quiera;
> y a ti quererte quisiera,
> y por eso no te quiero.
> Mas el rigor de mi estrella
> es tan infelice y fuerte,
> que ni me deja quererte
> ni que deje de querella.
> Con esto, debes pensar,
> porque mi mal no te asombre,
> que no está en mano del hombre
> el querer y el olvidar. (I, 4a)

The King's appeal to the pagan concept of Fate stands in direct opposition to the Christian doctrine of free will and constitutes the first indication, later to be developed extensively in the play, that the King's private actions, unless halted, will lead to an erosion of the Christian values of the kingdom. Thus, the Queen counters his argument by declaring that the King's notion of Fate is nothing more than self-deceit and could be used to justify any immoral desire:

> Hacéis siempre a vuestro modo
> siguiendo injustas querellas,
> y después a las estrellas
> echáis la culpa de todo;
> y hacéis al saber agravio,

> pues vence su inclinación.
> ... ...
> Pues desa suerte, Señor,
> el hombre que amor tuviere,
> disculpará cuanto hiciere
> con decir que tiene amor. (I, 5a-b)

Her remarks serve to defuse the King's view of himself as a tragic figure and place emphasis on his moral weakness.

The King's desire to abdicate his moral responsibilities is further underlined in his many allusions to a metaphoric love-death. Courtly love poetry since the time of the medieval troubadours had long associated unfulfilled love with suffering and death,[5] and the King expresses his longing in the imagery of this conventional love language. Mortally suffering out of love for Nísida, the King yearns for death as a deliverance from pain:

> y que estoy de pena loco,
> llamando la muerta a apriesa. (I, 4a)

Like any true courtly lover the King is enamored of his own «sweet suffering» and refuses to abandon the love which causes his pain. Thus the King rejects the rational cure offered by his wife; to her pleas that he save himself and reject his passion the King retorts, «Déjame morir...» (I, 4b).[6] Ironically, his death-wish will be fulfilled at the end of the play not as a culmination and glorification of his passion, as he would have it, but as a punishment for having allowed that passion to get out of control.

The King's appropriation of this courtly love rhetoric carries with it greater moral implications than it would in a purely lyrical setting. The world of *El amor constante* is not the morally indifferent one of the lyric poem, where passionate sentiments may be celebrated in a pure poetic form. Rather, it judges passion in the light of Christian moral values. Moreover (and here Castro seems to be anticipating Lope) it is a world in which characters are conceived of not as mere individuals but as members of a social structure in which personal and social conduct are inseparably bound to each other. In this system the King's willful surrender of personal responsibility necessarily leads to political irresponsibility. This interdependence of the personal and the socio-political

---

[5] See DENIS DE ROUGEMONT, *Love in the Western World* (1940; rpt. New York: Harper and Row, 1956); for courtly love rhetoric in Spain see OTIS H. GREEN, *Spain and the Western Tradition* (Madison: University of Wisconsin Press, 1964), I, 171-173.

[6] LEON HEBREO writes of this refined love: «The greatest wonder is that, since love is intolerable and extreme in cruelty and tribulations, the mind does not seek to be free of it, but regards as a mortal enemy him who comes offering advice or proffering relief.» Quoted and translated in GREEN, I, 171.

becomes apparent early in the play when the King tells his wife that she may dispose of the kingdom as she wishes:

> gobierna mi reino todo,
> gasta hacienda y haz mercedes.
> Todo de ti lo confío,
> y cuanto es mío te doy,
> sino a mí, que tal estoy,
> que es cierto que no soy mío. (I, 4b)

Similar cases may be found in the theater of Lope. A familiar example is that of *Las paces de los reyes y judía de Toledo* in which King Alfonso's amorous adventures with the Jewess Raquel severely undermine his effectiveness as ruler and almost lead to the political defeat of Castile. But if both Lope and Castro see the ruler's private conduct as influencing his ability to rule effectively, in *El amor constante* Castro goes further than Lope in establishing an absolute identification of the king *qua* private individual and the king *qua* ruler. In plays such as *Las paces...* the king who violates his mandate to rule judiciously is considered a derelict king but a king nonetheless who *ex officio* continues to merit respect and obedience. In Castro's play the King's claim that he is no longer himself (vid. above: «que es cierto que no soy mío») will be countered at various times with the declaration that he is also, therefore, no longer king. Instead he is a tyrant who, by definition, is not a king:

> El rey, en siendo tirano,
> luego lo deja de ser. (I, 29b)

The King describes his passion for Nísida in terms of another common metaphor of courtly love rhetoric: that of love as a burning fire. Early on he cries: «abrasar me siento» (I, 5b) and

> ... que me siento arder
> deste fuego que me toca. (I, 6a)

But as in the case of the language of death Castro concedes a moral dimension to a morally indifferent poetic image. Gradually the fire of love becomes associated with the fire of Hell and the King soon sees his condition as an «infierno de amor» (I, 7a). As the play develops, this internal Hell of lustful and illicit passion explodes into an external Hell of tyranny and political oppression. The King is repeatedly associated with the devil as he turns against Christian law.

Conversely, the imagery of Heaven and Redemption becomes associated with Nísida, her son Leonido and, to a lesser degree, the problematic character of Celauro. The development of these positive images also grows out of a conventional love language: the King calls Nísida an «ángel» (I, 5b) whose intervention can rescue him from his suffering.

As both of these spheres of imagery develop, the struggle between the King and his subjects assumes dimensions of a clash between Hell and Heaven, bringing the play close to what Northrop Frye sees as the pattern of «romance». Frye's conception of this pattern involves the conflict between hero and villain, each of whom is endowed with special and opposite attributes:

> The enemy may be an ordinary human being, but the nearer the romance is to myth, the more attributes of divinity will cling to the hero and the more the enemy will take on demonic mythical qualities... Hence the hero of romance is analogous to the mythical Messiah or deliverer who comes from an upper world, and his enemy is analogous to the demonic powers of a lower world.[7]

In this private world of contained passion the King attempts to control himself and his outbursts. Torn between duty and passion he manages in the first scenes of the play to remain in contact with his obligations, although he desires to discard them. But the explosion of fury into the public sphere is imminent, as can be sensed in the second scene of the first act, with its playing-off of asides, alouds, side glances and word plays. Castro repeatedly uses such devices throughout his works to create scenes in which characters attempt to hide their true feelings. The result is a moment of high tension on stage, where the slightest move could set off an explosion of violent emotions. In this case the King is trying to communicate secretly his feelings to Nísida in the presence of the Queen. All three of the characters understand his true intention, but no one will talk about it openly. Cross-communications and veiled meanings understood by all but acknowledged by none contribute to the highly-charged scene. Nísida and the Infanta enter the room. The Queen wants her daughter to dance for the King so as to perhaps distract him, but the King cannot take his eyes off Nísida. The King and Nísida talk about their situation in veiled language based on the double meaning of *mudanza* (a step of a dance and a change). The King hints that he wants Nísida, but the noblewoman rejects him. The use of words that carry a double meaning allow them to voice publicly their most intimate thoughts:

<pre>
REY: ¿no os ocupáis en danzar? [Alto]
NÍSIDA: No, señor, por no mudar
         con los pies el pensamiento.
REY: No perdáis las esperanzas
         de mudallo.
NÍSIDA: ¿Cómo?
</pre>

---

[7] NORTHROP FRYE, *Anatomy of Criticism* (New York: Atheneum Press, 1970), p. 187.

> REY: Pues
> el tiempo os enseña que es
> maestro de hacer mudanzas.
> REINA: Daría alguno por vellas
> mucho a fe, yo soy testigo.
> NÍSIDA: Hartas ha hecho comigo [sic],
> pero yo no pienso hacellas. (I, 5b-6a)

The King then falls into a revery, communicating to the audience through asides that his thoughts are fixed on Nísida alone. The Queen quietly observes her husband. She then awakens him from his daze by rebuking him with a comment that seems to be directed to their daughter, but which is really intended for the King:

> ¡Qué mal danzarás,
> si no guardas más compás
> que le han guardado sus ojos! (I, 6a)

The King catches the inference and promises the Queen he will control himself and be on guard. But he cannot keep his word. As the Infanta dances, his attention is again focused on Nísida. Even the servants are aware of what is happening, and they comment on the King's behavior in asides. The Queen tries to dispel her husband's fantasies by declaring aloud that the dance is over.

There immediately follows another scene of veiled communication when the Queen suggests that Nísida enliven the atmosphere by singing. There follows a dialogue based on word plays on *tercera, prima, cuerda* and *cordura,* where the Queen indicates to her husband that she knows what he wants, while he reassures her that he will control his passion in favor of duty:

> REINA: Si falta alguna tercera,
> aquí está quien lo será,
> pues ya para prima yo
> no hago el són acordado.
> REY: Si las cuerdas me han faltado,
> Reina, la cordura no.
> Y así, palabra te doy
> que no hará quel seso pierda
> ninguna tercera cuerda,
> porque yo también lo soy.
> No me tengas en tan poco. (I, 6b)

The precariousness of this controlled situation is upset by the presence of Celauro. Until this point the King has walked the tightrope between holding in his passion and giving free rein to it. With the arrival of Celauro the passion of jealousy disrupts the balance and plunges the King into a Hell of tyranny. The King indicates that he has crossed the border into Hell when he says:

> Pues si fui, puesto en balanza,
> purgatorio en la esperanza,
> ya soy en la pena infierno. (I, 8a)

The King had had Celauro imprisoned for a number of years.[8] Suspecting that Nísida loves his brother, the King has set Celauro free in order to test his theory. When Celauro first appears on stage it is again through asides that Castro transmits the precariousness of a situation where each must dissimulate his true feelings. Celauro and Nísida realize that they must hide their love in front of the King, and the King understands that he must hide his hatred and jealousy.

In the King there occurs a split between his private self and his public, ceremonial self. Asides here serve to undercut the ritual meaning of ceremony, as they will many times in Castro's theater. The asides bring in discordant notes of passions held in abeyance, which threaten to explode and destroy the harmonious social union symbolized in ritual and ceremony. Here, a less striking example of a type of scene often repeated by Castro,[9] the King greets Celauro with warm words and a ceremonial embrace («Y los brazos quiero darte»; I, 8a) only to undercut his feigned joy with a sinister aside («Pues en mejor ocasión / servirán para matarte»; I, 8b).

The corresponded love of Celauro and Nísida is associated with the world of light and Heaven. Having lived in the darkness of prison, a darkness imposed by the infernal King, Celauro greets Nísida as the sun:

> sol hermoso, alegre cielo,
> cuyo divino arrebol,
> como el cielo y como el sol,
> luz ofrece y da consuelo. (I, 8b)

Nísida responds with a calm that verges on the mystic, a calm that contrasts to the tortured emotions of the King:

> ¿cuándo
> se vio más sabrosa calma?
> Mi bien, regalos del alma
> mejor se dicen callando. (I, 9a)

Their exchange is filled with set phrases referring to Heaven and Divine Will that serve to depict their love as willed and protected by God. In attempting to force the lovers' will, then, the King is violating Heaven's law. Thus, Nísida underlines how the King's behavior has erred from the rule of God:

---

[8] There are indications that the imprisonment was unjust. For example, the Queen rejoices that the King has finally come to his senses in this matter: «Pues desengañado estás, / aunque tarde, justo ha sido» (I, 7b).

[9] A prime example occurs in the first scene of the *Mocedades*, where Count Lozano conveys through asides his displeasure at the king's honoring the young Rodrigo.

> ¿Puede un rey...
> ... forzar el libre albedrío,
> que Dios no quiso forzar? (I, 10b)

But if free will cannot be forced, Celauro does not underestimate the political power the King can wield against them in trying to destroy their love («que temo... / lo que un rey podría hacer»; I, 10b). Both vow that the King will be able to separate them only through death and with this there enters the note of martyrdom that characterizes their defense of true love and honor. Their doom is foreshadowed already in the first act when Nísida faints at the mere mention of death, seeing it in an apparition:

> Mi bien, a la muerte vi
> al punto que la nombré. (I, 10b)

From this point on theirs will be a valiant but futile struggle against the superior forces of the King, a struggle to uphold the values that the King has banished from his soul and from the kingdom.

Like King Nino of *La gran Semíramis* the King expects to count on the unquestioning obedience of his vassal to facilitate the realization of his scheme to separate the lovers. He imagines this cooperation to be a less problematic means to achieving his ends than would be a violent confrontation of wills:

> Quisiera hacerte apartar
> de los hombros la cabeza;
>   pero por otro camino
> más llano pienso obligarte. (I, 11a)

Taking Celauro aside he asks him how far he would be willing to go for his king and brother. Celauro's answer, to the King's joy, is that of a perfect subject:

> Cuanto puede hacer un hombre,
> por mi hermano y rey haré;
> sin recelo emprenderé
> imposibles en su nombre. (I, 11a-b)

The King then demands the impossible — not that Celauro not interfere with his plans but that he extinguish all feeling of love for Nísida: «Hermano, dejar de amar / a Nísida» (I, 11b). Celauro refuses to obey, claiming that neither he nor the King, but only Heaven itself, has the power to break the bonds of their constant love:

> Todo lo haré, y eso no;
> que hacer, señor, de manera
> que a mi Nísida no quiera,
> el cielo puede, y yo no. (I, 12a)

Thus the love between Nísida and Celauro is established as inviolable for two complementary reasons: first, it is ordained by God and second, it is an act of free will. Both stand in contrast to the King's passion, which both denies the role of free will and lays the blame on non-Christian Fate. Celauro, unlike Lope's heroes, places divine law over the arbitrary will of the king.

The angered monarch then orders Celauro to leave him alone with Nísida. Celauro, feeling the King will take advantage of his absence, adamantly refuses to cede to the King's will. He even goes so far as to contemplate killing the King, but his sense of loyalty stays his hand:

> ¿Daréle con esta daga [*Aparte*]
> la muerte que me procura?
> Es mi rey. (I, 12a)

These last verses serve to establish the conflictive nature of Celauro, a man torn between instinct and duty. Throughout the *comedia* Celauro will attempt unsuccessfully to resolve the inner battle he feels between what he instinctively senses to be his natural right to oppose tyrannic oppression and his obligation to remain loyal to the king. Although Celauro's case is shown in a sympathetic light, Celauro himself suffers from a flaw of character that will lead to his downfall. His attacks on the king are impulsive and hot-headed and do not grow organically out of a reasoned conviction that he can rightfully oppose him. Unable to convince himself of the absolute righteousness of his opposition, he will be plagued by guilt and finally driven to madness.

It is Nísida who first suggests that regicide is a morally acceptable method of dealing with a tyrant. When the King finds himself alone with her he openly declares his passion and rebukes her for not alleviating his pain:

> que muero de amor y celos.
> ... ...
> Y ¿es razón que muera un rey? (I, 12b)

His question, posed in metaphorical terms, takes on a new moral-political meaning in Nísida's answer:

> Si es tirano, poco importa.
> Tu mal intento corrija
> el cielo, pues tal ordena. (I, 12b)

Her reply echoes the ideas of the sixteenth-century theorists we have examined: when the king violates divine law he ceases to be king and becomes a tyrant whom the kingdom can openly oppose and even kill if necessary. Unlike Celauro, Nísida's conscience is unencumbered by the question of her role as a royal subject. As a woman, her place in society is not defined in terms of political obligations, and hence defiance to royal authority does not precipitate in her the crisis it does for the male, who sees his honor as linked to allegiance to his monarch. As A. A. van Beysterveldt has shown, in the *comedia* a woman's first concern is the defense of her chastity, for that alone assures her honor:

> ... il convient de mettre en relief le caractère essentiellement chrétien que prend la notion de l'honneur féminin, contrairement à l'honneur de l'homme qui est toujours anti-chrétien. Ce contraste est dû au fait que, pour la femme, le souci de sa chasteté était à la fois une vertu chrétienne et un impératif social. Par conséquent, l'exercise de cette vertu constituait pour elle une garantie de participer, en toute conscience, à la communauté spirituelle de l'Eglise et en même temps à la société terrestre.[10]

What distinguishes Nísida from other virtuous women of the *comedia* tradition is that she not only defends her honor against the King but also takes an ideologically aggressive stand against tyranny in general. The ability of women to judge freely the immorality of the king and to call for action against him will also be found in *El Conde Alarcos, El nacimiento de Montesinos* and, in a more ambivalent case, in *Las hazañas del Cid*.

With Nísida's rejection the King's moral confusion heightens. He senses he can no longer translate his will into action and sees himself caught in a web of contradictions:

> siempre yerro con la boca
> lo que acierta el pensamiento.
> ... ...
> soy Alcides en la fuerza,
> y vénceme una mujer.
> ... ...
> es que pienso como cuerdo
> y procedo como loco. (I, 13b)

And he feels that his soul is possessed, in a reference to the devil that goes beyond the conventional courtly love rhetoric:

> Mas ya siento que en el pecho
> se me reviste un demonio. (I, 14b)

In a last attempt short of violence the King expresses a desire for a conspiracy of deception. He asks Nísida to feign love for him in order to «engañar el deseo» (I, 14a), for he wrongly feels that he can live in a dream world. The Queen joins her husband in his request, hoping to calm his passion. Nísida, in her first affirmation of honor as religion,

---

[10] A. A. VAN BEYSTERVELDT, *Répercussions du souci de la pureté de sang sur la conception de l'honneur dans la «Comedia Nueva» espagnole* (Leiden: E. J. Brill, 1966), p. 117.

refuses to compromise. Her reasons are manifold. First, her self-image is bound to her sense of honor:

> ¿Yo he de fingir que soy mala,
> sabiendo que buena soy? (I, 14a)

The analogy between honor and religion is made when Nísida sees the deceit as a occasion of sin which could very well lead to the sin itself:

> que quien finge que lo es,
> de veras lo viene a ser. (I, 14a)

Finally she sees herself a Christian martyr who must not break the faith of honor in any manner:

> Que esta fe que al honor toca
> la de Cristo ha de imitar,
> que no la puede negar
> el corazón ni la boca. (I, 14a-b)

Nísida warns that honor is a value to be placed above the life of a king and that in no way may it be sacrificed to please the whims of a tyrant. The burden of obligation is not on the vassal to cede his honor but on the king to correct his behavior or be deposed:

> que a un rey, en siendo tirano,
> pueden quitalle ese nombre. (I, 14b)

The King can no longer understand the meaning of honor, a further degeneration from the beginning of the act where he was aware of his own honor while trying to come to terms with himself. He scoffs at Nísida for valuing her honor so highly:

> ¿de honra blasonando estás...?
> ... ...
> ¿Honra nos vendes ahora? (I, 14b)

Surrendering all control of himself, he seizes Nísida, referring to himself as a «Tarquino desta Lucrecia» (I, 15a). With this allusion to the pagan ruler Tarquin, Castro indicates to his public that the King no longer upholds the Christian values upon which his kingdom is founded and instead declares himself their enemy. As Nísida's struggle becomes likened to that of a Christian suffering martyrdom for her faith, so does the King's lust for her take on the garb of a pagan ruler's persecution of the faithful Christians. The King's offense against the individual now becomes an offense against God and against the Divine Order as well. Consequently, added to the notion that the individual may oppose the unjust king is the Queen's evocation of the notion of divine punishment:

> ¿Es verdad que sus orejas
> me oyeron, Dios soberano?
> mas, sin duda, de tu mano,
> por castigarle, le dejas. (I, 15a)

From this point on until the play's startling *desenlace* opposition to the king will be seen as both a human and a divine concern.

Nísida's aged father, the Duke, takes yet another stance vis-à-vis the unjust monarch. The old man's reaction centers on the problem of honor. He sees the attempted abduction of his daughter not as a violation of a divine mandate but as an affront to his personal honor. As a result, he must reconcile two conflicting aspects of the honor code: that which demands that a vassal loyally submit to his ruler, and that which demands a confrontation with those who seek to offend one's honor. As a staunch defender of social order the Duke refuses to compromise his honor by revolting against the King, but neither is he able to be a silent witness to his own infamy. Though he stands up to the King he argues the case of his loyalty with a Jesuit-like casuistry, defining at every step the exact intent of his actions. Thus, when the King attempts to abduct Nísida the Duke draws his sword, but when the King protests that this constitutes an act of treason, the old man retorts that he is merely defending his honor:

> No lo está para ofenderte,
> que la rige mano honrada;
> nadie me puede culpar
> que nunca he sido traidor,
> pero defiendo el honor
> que tú me quieres quitar. (I, 15a)

The exactness of his argument becomes evident when the King draws a sword and deals the Duke a blow on the head. The old man does not strike back and refuses to defend his person. As a loyal subject his body is at the disposal of the king, but his honor is not. His attitude prefigures that of Calderón's Pedro Crespo:

> porque si ella [i.e. la cabeza] es tuya y mía,
> el honor es sólo mío. (I, 15a)

Following his logic, the Duke feels free to defend himself physically from the King's servants when the King orders them to kill the old man:

> Eso no, villanos.
> ... ...
> Que para el Rey tengo lengua,
> mas para vosotros manos. (I, 15b)

At this juncture, the Duke believes that the perfect subject may act to frustrate his monarch's evil desires, but must respect both the person and the office of the King. The vassal owes obedience and homage to the king alone and not to his representatives. Thus, while the servants may act on the King's behalf, their blood is less noble than the King's, and to be killed by them, albeit under the King's orders, would be dishonorable.

In his refusal to judge the King on moral grounds the Duke prefigures to some extent the type of loyal vassal that will dominate both the theater of Lope and the later plays of Guillén de Castro. Within a play of defiant attitudes, the Duke, as befitting an old man, takes the most conservative position: although he affirms the right to protect his honor against the King, he does not contest his sovereign's moral or social authority. But even within his ideological prudence the Duke rebukes the King and even breaks the «ley de palacio» by drawing a sword in his presence.

The Duke's restraint seeks to maintain order not only on the social plane but on the personal plane as well. In refusing to carry his defiance beyond the defense of his honor he acts in accordance with what he regards as the time-honored obligations of his station. In his own eyes the Duke «es quien es» and he suffers no remorse for his actions. Yet, ironically, in Castro's plays of unjust power the character who attempts to remain faithful to social laws pays homage to a king who is shown to have clearly ceded his royal privileges and immunity by his tyrannical deeds. In these situations order is restored not by the loyal, and, therefore, impotent subject, but by one who ignores the rigid, abstract strictures of the social code and judges the concrete situation of tyranny.

On the other hand Celauro, younger and more impetuous, rashly allows his contained anger to explode violently. Celauro is a morally ambiguous figure, for while his cause is just, the manner in which he revolts promises not renewed order but a continued state of disorder. That disorder eventually overtakes Celauro himself and leads to his spiritual defeat. When the King continues to assault the Duke, Celauro reacts by drawing his sword against his henchmen. The King orders his brother killed, but no one moves for fear of Celauro's strength. The angered Celauro threatens to lead a revolt against the monarch and to seek the aid of foreign princes. Although he also invokes the aid of Heaven and refers to the «espada de la justicia» (I, 16a), his terms are those of destruction. He threatens to throw the whole kingdom into disorder as he evokes the invasion of a foreign armada:

> porque verás de naves y galeras
> cubierto el mar, y tremolar el viento
> flámulas, gallardetes y banderas.
> ... ...
> pues cuando desembarquen mis soldados,
> dando su acero al sol luciente y puro,

tus campos talen, roben tus ganados,
en tu palacio no estarás seguro. (I, 16a)

Celauro's epic challenge bodes protracted chaos for the kingdom, a chaos that will soon overtake Celauro's conscience as well. Having been educated under the same code of honor and loyalty as the Duke, Celauro will not be able to live with the reality of his rebellion and will be plagued with guilt.

The task of restoring order to the state will be assumed with success by Celauro's son Leonido, a character who, like Nísida, understands his opposition in terms of reason, natural law and divine justice. The phenomenon of a son taking over the obligations and responsibilities of his father will be familiar to readers of *Las mocedades del Cid*. There, the young Rodrigo must seek to avenge the affront dealt to his aged father by Count Lozano. This is a recurrent motif in Castro's theater, appearing in varied guises in all the plays we shall examine. In the play in question, although Celauro is much younger and stronger than his counterpart Diego Laínez, his spiritual vacilation renders him morally impotent to carry out his proposed act of vengeance/justice. This task will befall the younger Leonido. The moral superiority that the son demonstrates in *El amor constante* underscores once again the structural proximity of this play to «romance»; Frye notes that similar father-son relationships are a key pattern of the «romance» that verges on myth:

> The conflict of son and father that we noted in comedy recurs in romance: in the Bible the second Adam comes to the rescue of the first one, and in the Grail cycle the pure son Galahad accomplishes what his impure father Lancelot failed in.[11]

Leonido will act simultaneously as the avenger of his father's dishonor and as the saviour of the troubled kingdom. As in «romance», just as the kingdom's enemy becomes identified with the forces of Hell so its saviour becomes a Messianic deliverer and assumes quasi-divine attributes.

In the incidents surrounding his birth and his youthful exploits, or *mocedades,* Leonido's life follows the pattern of that of the archetypical youthful saviour-hero. Otto Rank describes seven basic characteristics of this archetype: (1) the hero is a child of distinguished parents; (2) his origin is preceded by difficulties, such as continence, prolonged barrenness or secret intercourse of the parents due to external prohibition or obstacles; (3) during or before pregnancy there is a prophecy in the form of a dream or oracle cautioning against his birth and usually threatening danger to the father or his representative; (4) he is sur-

---

[11] NORTHROP FRYE, p. 196. The best-known case in Spanish literature prior to Castro is that found in the ballad cycle of Montesinos, a story Castro himself was to dramatize.

rendered to the water in a box; (5) he is saved by animals or by lowly people —often shepherds— and is suckled by a female animal or by a humble woman; (6) when grown up he finds his parents, takes revenge and is acknowledged for who he really is; (7), finally, he achieves rank and honors.[12] In the first act of *El amor constante* we learn from Nísida that she had conceived a child out of wedlock by Celauro and that, sensing danger, she placed it in a «cesta de mimbres» (I, 9b) and entrusted it to a shepherd. From the beginning the child is associated with Christian symbols: Nísida placed a cross of jewels around the child's neck, and the protecting shepherd was named Crisanto. These are the first indications of Leonido's special relationship with the mandates of divine law.

This young hero is introduced at the beginning of the second act. The first scene is set in the woods. Its natural peace and rusticity offer a striking contrast to the violent and emotionally charged atmosphere of the court in Act I. In the conversation between Leonido and the comic peasant girl Rosela[13] that opens the act we learn that Celauro's

---

[12] OTTO RANK, «The Myth of the Birth of the Hero», 1914; rpt. in *The Myth of the Birth of the Hero and Other Writings*, ed. Philip Freund (New York: Vintage Books, 1959), pp. 1-96. There are many other studies on this mythical archetype, many of which list other salient characteristics of the hero's birth and youth. WILLIAM C. MCCRARY in his review of these studies mentions a number of other features which we will see reflected in *El amor constante*: «... (d) in his late youth or early manhood he enters into a round of adventures, overcomes a hostile and menacing enemy or series of enemies; (e) because of this victory or victories he returns with a magic elixir or some other redemptive symbol without which his people would perish; (f) marries a princess or high-born lady (if the enemy is human, the bride may be either the antagonist's wife... or daughter...); (g) after which he becomes king or exercises a similar function...». WILLIAM C. MCCRARY, «Guillén de Castro and the *Mocedades* of Rodrigo: A Study in Tradition and Innovation», in *Romance Studies in Honor of Edward Billings Ham* (Hayward-California: California State College Publications, no. 2, 1967), p. 99.

After this study was completed I became aware of an article by GEORGIA PAPPANASTOS, «The Heroic Ideal in Guillén de Castro's First Play», *Kentucky Romance Quarterly*, 23 (1976), pp. 421-437.

Professor Pappanastos shows in great detail how Leonido conforms to the mythical hero pattern. Citing Joseph Campbell, she affirms that the archetypal hero «is a synthesizing image, a representative of the dual perspectives of reality. He is the link between the finite and the infinite, the natural order and the supernatural order» (p. 426). This indeed describes Leonido. Although our studies coincide on many points, our analyses are complementary rather than identical. Pappanastos is most interested in showing how *El amor constante* is one more elaboration of a universal mythical pattern. My study gives greater attention to the ways in which the play addresses contemporary political and moral issues, and to the conflictive nature of Castro's characters. To a large degree, Castro is less interested in the unproblematic Leonido than he is in Celauro, the Duke and the King, that is, the human figures who are engaged in internal and external struggle. One could say that Castro both politicizes and humanizes the traditional pattern so as to speak to the Spanish audience of his time.

[13] In Castro's earliest plays the comic is limited to a few remarks by a rustic character. It is only later and gradually that the *gracioso* takes his place among Castro's cast of characters. Even so, in a play of his maturity, *Las mocedades del*

armada suffered defeat at sea by natural elements. The divine and infernal imagery of the first act is pursued as Rosela condemns the King as «este Bercebú / del Rey» (I, 17a), and Leonido, looking at a portrait of Nísida, feels a strange attraction to this «ángel» (I, 17a): «pues como a cosa divina / le tengo amor y respeto» (I, 17b). Leonido's initiation into the world of adult responsibilities and emotions begins as a sexual awakening when the Infanta, having lost track of a hunting party, finds the boy asleep.[14] Finding herself sexually attracted to him she substitutes her portrait for that of Nísida.[15] Leonido's pastoral peace and filial love are exchanged for the confusions of the adult world and sexual yearning:

> Tuve un tierno sentimiento
> sin interés ni disgusto;
> pero ya en el pecho siento
> el interés para el gusto,
> y para el alma el tormento. (I, 18b)

But even these natural feelings are put in a framework of a divine scheme:

> Imaginar es mejor
> que es permisión de los cielos. (I, 18b)

Although bravery and strength will characterize this hero, these are qualities common to the heroic tradition; what makes him a hero of what was to become the *comedia* tradition is his sense of *honor*. When the Infanta returns with her entourage of *caballeros* she provokes them into testing his honor. They deliver him a blow on the head and his reluctance to seek revenge immediately disappoints the Infanta. Her first attraction to him was physical and she now desires to be further aroused by watching his powerful masculinity in action; she would like to see him physically overwhelm the well-dressed, «feminine» courtiers. When Leonido refuses to respond to the challenges the Infanta sees him

---

Cid, Castro reverts back to his original pattern, limiting the comic to the shepherd's humorous description of Rodrigo's defeat of the Moors. The absence of the *gracioso* in these plays is another indication of Castro's independence in certain areas of Lope de Vega, both before Lope's theater was to exercise its influence on his theater and after. For a brief, if incomplete, discussion of the *gracioso* in Castro's theater see GARCÍA LORENZO, pp. 29-39.

[14] This is the first occurrence of a repeated scene in Castro's theater in which the hunt brings the intrusion of the adult world into a pastoral paradise. We shall see it again in the plays *El Conde Alarcos* and *El nacimiento de Montesinos*. In *El perfecto caballero* the hunt is associated with illicit passion. A later reworking of this type of scene may be found in the second act of *Las mocedades del Cid* when Rodrigo, armed for battle, encounters Urraca in her peaceful country retreat.

[15] Castro's women often show an uncontrollable sexual attraction to strong and gallant men and linger over their physique and physical prowess. See the competitive description of Rodrigo by Urraca and Ximena in the first act of the *Mocedades* (vv. 591-ff).

as less of a man but couches her feelings in terms of a more acceptable honor code:

> que no puede ser honrado
> hombre que no es atrevido. (I, 19a)

Leonido, however, is endowed not only with a sense of honor but also with a quality his father lacks — prudence. He submits his natural strength to the power of reason. He delays not out of fear, as the Infanta would have it, but because he sees that the courtiers carry swords and he none. Rather than rash bravura he seeks real victory:

> Pero las venganzas yerra
> el que así las precipita. (I, 19a)
>
> ... ...
> no hay hombre de más juicio.
> No es tan agudo y tan pronto
> el hijo del sacristán. (I, 19b)

He asks to borrow their swords («Si me diesen una espada, / maravillas aquí haría»; I, 19b) and craftily uses them to exact vengeance («veréis... / las maravillas que hago»; I, 19b). This is an incident with a double importance. First, the manner in which the courtiers unknowingly cede their power to Leonido by handing over their swords to him foreshadows the end of the play in which the King, without really understanding the import of his words, will grant Leonido permission to assassinate him. Second, Leonido's judicious, thought-out reactions lead to successful revenge and contrast to Celauro's rash impulses and subsequent failure.

Leonido's valor and strength are tested and proven when he single-handedly saves the courtiers from an attacking lion.[16] Leonido comments that he draws his strength from the earth and his virtues and power are those of uncorrupted man in his natural state:

> Tuve a la tierra por madre,
> y en este valle nascí,
> y el valor que siento en mí
> tengo agora por mi padre. (I, 21a)

Leonido's is a natural physical and moral strength that will later enable him to establish a new order.

Contrasted to this positive assertion of manly values is the moral vacillation that plagues Celauro in this act and continues throughout the

---

[16] This incident, naturally enough, leads to remarks relating the strength of the lion with that of *Leoni*do. According to GEORGIA PAPPANASTOS, «... the young hero's exploit symbolically foreshadows the eventual death of one lion (the King) by the sword of another lion (Leonido)». GEORGIA PAPPANASTOS, «Verbal Subtlety in Castro's *El amor constante*», *Bulletin of the Comediantes*, 28 (1976), p. 21.

drama. In the second act darkness of night accompanies the psychologically confused and doomed Celauro, the external darkness serving as a metaphor for his interior confusion. Like Lope in *El caballero de Olmedo,* Castro exploits the poetic quality of the night and, as with Don Alonso, fear of death eats away at Celauro's manhood. The distraught nobleman is engulfed in ominous forebodings:

>   Agora de horrores vistes [he is addressing the «noche escura»]
> mi afligido corazón.
>   ¡Ay Dios, qué agüeros tan tristes,
> que anuncian mi perdición!
> ... ...
>   Para el ansia con que vengo
> de recelar y temer,
> confieso que he menester
> todo el ánimo que tengo. (I, 21b)

Although in the next verses he rouses himself to face life, throughout the play we witness a wavering of purpose and of courage, a desire to die and give up his cause against the King. Filled with remorse, Celauro cannot face up to the consequences of his actions; the obligations of his station weigh too heavily upon him to allow him to accept his revolt. While he accepts the omens as sure signs of a tragic death it is his own guilt that seals his doom; appropriately he dies not at the hands of the King but as a result of madness. When Celauro meets Nísida in Act II and she tells him of omens of bad luck that have plagued her, Celauro interprets them as punishment for his revolt and blames himself:

>   ¿También
> con esto afligirme quieres?
> Porque pienso que lo eres, [i.e. desdichada]
> pues a mí me quieres bien,
>   que tengo culpa confieso
> en que estés desa manera. (I, 22b)

Celauro's sense of guilt gives a tone of psychological uneasiness to the meeting of the lovers. Celauro offers to kill himself in order to release Nísida from doom; Nísida faints at the sound of approaching men; and both anticipate death not as a joyful deliverance from a hostile world but as a punishment. Theirs is not the conventional lovers' embrace of death but a fear of its powers. If Celauro yearns to die it is because he cannot face life without honor; the failure of his attempted revolt has profoundly shaken his sense of self-worth.

The key scene of the second act puts the question of the deposition of the evil king in an important perspective by bringing together the King, Celauro and Leonido. In the darkness of the evening Celauro and the King meet. Celauro prepares himself to meet the death that he believes awaits him at the hands of his brother's minions:

> Esta gente a mí me espera;
> mas ya en la ocasión estoy. (I, 23b)

When he asks Heaven for help Leonido enters and chases the assassins away and almost kills the King. The King interprets this as divine intervention, for the very earth seems to rise up against him:

> Hasta la tierra me injuria.
> Son del cielo sus rigores. (I, 24a)

Leonido is stopped from killing the King by Celauro's cry to halt. Leonido had judged the King's actions outside of a hierarchical context, that is, as if the King were only a man, seeing the King's execution orders as unnatural and against all laws of honor:

> Y acometer a uno tres
> ¿fue gran prueba de hidalguía?
> ... ... Por su vileza
> ahora matarle quiero. (I, 24a)

This is a double condemnation of the King because not only is it a base act for any man, regardless of his social station, to ambush another, but for a king it is an even greater fall from nobility. Leonido finds this unequal assault to be against natural law; his reaction is spontaneous and objective, making no excuses for the King's social position. And yet when Celauro cries it is the King, Leonido shows respect and withdraws the condemnation, at least for a while:

> ¡El Rey! Perdona,
> a tus pies estoy rendido. (I, 24a)

Celauro, in spite of his revolt, maintains allegiance to the King and to the principle of loyalty by offering his own life in order to save the King from Leonido's blows:

> Antes a tu golpe fiero
> Daré el pecho o la cabeza.
> El Rey es. (I, 24a)

Repentant, unable to live with himself, he asks the King's pardon for his treason:

> No quiero darte disculpa;
> que no hará mi causa buena
> pedir perdón de la pena
> y estar negando la culpa.
> Digo que soy un abismo,
> que es la disculpa mayor;
> ... ...
> y, que así, a pedirlas vengo
> de sus manos generosas
> perdón... (I, 24a-b)

Celauro insists that he still loves Nísida, but his spirit is broken. He now submits to the King's power:

> Y si no ofrece perdones
> tu pecho, de endurecido,
> ... ...
> toma y viértase a porfía
> esta sangre que deseas. (I, 24b)

The King acknowledges his obligation to pardon his brother but refuses to claim control over his anger:

> pues de tu ofensa maldita,
> ese proceder honrado,
> la obligación me ha quitado
> y la rabia no me quita. (I, 24b)

He tells Celauro that he prefers to be known as an infamous king rather than lose the opportunity to kill him. But while on one hand he repudiates *honor* by claiming that he has no concern for his future *fama* nor the *opinión* of others, he asks Leonido to kill Celauro for him so that «será mi honra restaurada» (I, 24b). Clearly true *honor* has taken a subordinate position to blind fury, and the term has a hollow sound when he seeks its restoration.

Leonido's response to the King's order contrasts strongly with what will later be the pattern of Lope's *comedia* formula. While in Lope most subjects show a quasi-religious devotion and unquestioning obedience to the royal mandate, Leonido refuses to obey the King and sets out in objective, rational argument his reasons for not doing so. Leonido, though a subject of the King and bound to him by loyalty, does not feel the direct allegiance of those brought up in the court. He belongs to and yet remains outside the laws that govern the kingdom. This has its source in the circumstances of his upbringing: although born of courtly parents he was nurtured by the earth and obeys a set of moral rules based on natural law and reason. This is why, unlike Celauro, he can take his stand confidently against the King. He instinctively understands the nature of justice and kingship and so tells the King:

> aunque rey te hayan llamado,
> a mí no me lo pareces. (I, 25a)
>
> que a injusto rey no obedezco. (I, 25a)
>
> Contra ti está la razón. (I, 26a)

He even considers killing the King at this point:

> que tu crueldad mereciera
> que a ti la muerte te diera. (I, 25a)

He decides, however, to give the King a warning and offer him a chance to correct himself. Leonido assumes the qualities of a divine messenger,[17] warning the King to repent and spelling out his imminent fall if he refuses:

> ... puedes volver,
> si a lo que es justo se ajusta;
> porque no viniendo justa, [i.e. la corona]
> está cerca de caer. (I, 25a)
>
> El consejo que te doy,
> para tu remedio aplica. (I, 26a)

In his reasoning Leonido echoes words of Nísida in Act I:

> ¿es muy bueno que los reyes
> nos pongan y quiten leyes,
> y no sepan guardar ley? (I, 25a)

Although Leonido leaves no doubt that it is licit to kill a king turned tyrant, he wants to give the King the opportunity to avoid this catastrophe by allowing him to amend his ways. Thus, when Celauro, recovering his sword, impetuously attempts once again to kill the King, Leonido prevents the assassination, seeing himself in this way:

> destas balanzas el fiel.
> Y si alguna sin compás
> más pesada viene a ser,
> a la otra he de valer,
> por que venga a pesar más. (I, 25b)

As the act draws to a close it becomes patent that the King will not benefit from this period of grace. He speaks as if possessed:

> mi reino y el mundo todo
> en mi fuego he de abrasar. (I, 26a)

In sum, regicide is considered in this act as a possible resort against a tyrannical king, although a serious and last resort. Leonido acts as a messenger of divine and natural order who seeks to restore the cohesive social values that the King sets out to destroy. In this natural order moral values and social welfare take precedence over absolute obedience. Leonido judges by reason rather than by social convention.[18] For him, honor does not depend on an absolute loyalty to an evil king. Leonido's freedom resides in his ability to view the situation afresh without the

---

[17] Celauro asserts here in an aside: «El cielo le habrá enviado / a valerme» (I, 25a), and a relationship to Christ as Messiah may be inferred from the King's comment that Leonido was «... entre ovejas nacido» (I, 25a).

[18] He tells Celauro that «La mucha razón que tienes» (I, 26b) caused him to come to his defense.

obligations that so confuse Celauro. In Act I the Duke showed a conventional submission to the royal will while in this act Leonido, two generations younger, feels free to redefine his position. Celauro, however, lives between the two and seeks death as an escape from his dilemma. He cannot disassociate himself from his obligations; he feels that his military defeat is also his dishonor and a punishment for having violated an unwritten code of honorable conduct. Narrating the destruction of his armada, he tells Leonido that:

> que, de mi hermano vencido,
> perdí la opinión en todas.
> ... ...
> Con esta gloria sin gusto,
> con esta vida sin honra,
> espero siempre los fines
> de mi lamentable historia. (I, 27b)

What is of most interest is that no one but Celauro considers his defeat, or even his revolt, dishonorable. Celauro's loss of honor is merely a projection of his own sense of guilt and has no basis in objective reality. Indeed, throughout the play other characters repeatedly call for action against the King and consider their opposition licit. Leonido will reestablish order based on the traditional values of natural and divine law, a task his father can no longer carry out with inner conviction. To accomplish this will require killing the King.

The last act of *El amor constante* returns to the court where a group of grandees, called into special council, discusses the King's aberrant behavior. Their comments serve to put into moral focus the actions of the play, as do the observations of the courtiers in the last act of both *Atila furioso* and *La gran Semíramis*. In this scene Castro is adapting the stock dramatic device of the chorus, a key moralizing element of the neo-Senecan theater.[19] As a chorus the nobles take no active role in the dramatic movement, while at the same time as caretakers of the state they look on their very inaction as a cause for shame and alarm. They unanimously, but secretly, protest the King's continued persecution of Celauro and the subsequent detention of the Duke («por tantos años»;

---

[19] «El uso del coro en la tragedia renacentista española sufrió una seria y profunda codificación... Entre los más clasicistas existe el coro, pero su cometido y forma tradicional... han desaparecido en parte. Suelen presentarse al final de los actos como portavoces de la opinión común...

Por otra parte, en los trágicos alejados de los clásicos, en las tragedias de horror, el coro ha desaparecido. Pero hay ciertos personajes o series de personajes secundarios (los cortesanos de *La gran Semíramis* o los bandidos de *La infelice Marcela*, de Virués, por ejemplo) en los que todavía se encuentran rastros de algunos de los cometidos que tenía el coro de las tragedias clasicistas. Hay que decir, sin embargo, que el coro, como elemento básico de la estructura dramática, ha dejado de existir» (HERMENEGILDO, p. 441).

I, 29b), yet they feel powerless to oppose the King. Their docility is less a question of loyalty than of impotence before what they regard as the seemingly limitless political strength of their monarch:

> GRANDE 2.º: ¿Qué remedio puede haber?
> GRANDE 3.º: Siendo rey, está en su mano
> cuanto quisiere hacer. (I, 29b)

Yet they realize that the whole kingdom opposes the King and interprets the nobles' inertia as morally irresponsible:

> GRANDE 1.º: Y ya de nuestra tibieza
> por las calles se murmura. (I, 29b)

Their comments recall for the audience important ideological concepts expressed in the first act. First is the idea that the manner in which a king conducts his personal life necessarily affects the political life of the state he rules:

> GRANDE 3.º: Algún antojo habrá sido,
> para acabar de perder
> el reino, como el sentido. (I, 29b)
> GRANDE 4.º: Quien no se gobierna a sí,
> mal gobernará su imperio. (I, 29b)

They also concur with Nísida's statement that a tyrant by definition cannot be considered a king:

> GRANDE 4.º: El rey, en siendo tirano,
> luego lo deja de ser. (I, 29b)

Though the rhetoric of the nobles is that of Nísida and Leonido, they have reached the same impasse as Celauro: while acknowledging the injustice of the King they cannot distance themselves sufficiently from the political system to accept fully the validity of their own active intervention in opposing him. Subliminally, this scene serves to enhance the underlying romantic-mythical vision of a kingdom overpowered and laid to waste by its enemy and awaiting a Messianic deliverance.

The political implications of the King's mad passion become even more clearly focused when he announces his intention to divorce the Queen and place Nísida on the throne. Now, in a Christian society divorce is considered a sinful and willful violation of divine law and, as in the case of Henry VIII of England, a case which Castro may well have had in mind, the King's repudiation of this law constitutes an attack on the very legal foundation of the state. In seeking to impose his own will in this matter, the King works towards the destruction of the very Christian kingdom he is to guide. His intention to discard these Christian principles is implicit in the examples he chooses to justify his actions. Looking for historical precedents he cites the cases of pagan rulers, and for religious authority he turns to the Old Testament:

> mas porque no digáis que cito reyes,
> que, por su condición esquiva o brava,
> no tuvieron o no guardaron leyes,
> en la vieja el Señor licencia daba
> que desde el rey hasta el que guarda bueyes
> dejase su mujer honrada y bella,
> con sólo que llegase a aborrecella. (I, 30a)

In returning to paganism and Jewish law the King denies the authority of Christian law as embodied in the New Testament and the Patristic writings. The Duke protests that Christ's death has established a new law that invalidates all previous codes and that the King's divorce stands in direct opposition to the law of Christ:

> Y si él mismo [i.e. Dios] en la [ley] que dió
> en el Sinaí a Moisén
> los repudios aprobó,
> en aquélla estaba bien,
> y en ésta de gracia no;
>   que ahora será violento
> lo que entonces justo trato.
> ¿No advierte tu pensamiento
> que entonces era contrato
> lo que ahora es sacramento? (I, 31a)

It now becomes evident that the intervention of Leonido, associated with Christ and Christianity in Act II, will signify a return not only to natural law but to Christian law as well.

With the decision to divorce the Queen the King fully loses his sense of duty; the passions and angers so carefully held in check in the first act (and communicated dramatically through asides and metaphoric language) finally explode. The King no longer observes his own deeds with a critical and fearful eye. The desire to die from suffering is replaced by a desire to destroy. He now begins to sound like Atila: «Todo lo pienso abrasar» (I, 32a).

In the prison scene that follows, the equation of Nísida's defense of her *honor/virtud* [20] with the Christian martyr's defense of the faith, first suggested in Act I, is developed to its logical conclusion. The King, now more fully associated with pagan rulers, sets out to force Nísida's free will and test the strength of her conviction. He offers her the choice of either a sinful marriage to him or death through a forced suicide.

---

[20] I borrow the term from BEYSTERVELDT who contrasts it to the *honor/opinión* preoccupation of the male in the *comedia*.

This scene brings together the Duke, Nísida and the King. An important change in attitude occurs in the old man, formerly the most staunch defender of his monarch's claims on his vassals. The old man now finds himself in chains and at the mercy of his lord. Seeing that the King threatens both his honor and his daughter's life, he begins to understand his ruler's actions as a violation of Christian law. He no longer feels obligated to respect his monarch. Instead, he accuses the King of tyranny, and he subtly suggests that he may no longer be a legitimate king; speaking of the King's royal blood, he states:

> ... para hacerte honrado,
> harto limpia te la han dado
> tus bien nacidos agüelos;
> mas vence en esta jornada,
> en un tirano homicida,
> una maldad adquirida
> a una nobleza heredada. (I, 33b)

He declares that only death can stop him from cursing the man to whom he once so loyally paid homage:

> ... Dame la muerte;
> que mi lengua ha de ofenderte
> todo el tiempo que la tenga. (I, 33b)

The father commands his daughter to choose death over dishonor in terms that reveal the intrinsically religious nature of female honor:

> Mira, hija, que te ofrece
> lo que imposible ha de ser,
> pues la ley que vive en ti,
> de Cristo, no da lugar. (I, 34a)

He sees her death for honor as a religious martyrdom:

> En tu intento persevera;
> que otra corona te espera
> del martirio a que te ofreces. (I, 34b)

For the Duke honor is holy and must be maintained even in the face of death and grief:

> ¡Ay santo honor, mucho vales,
> pero a mí mucho me cuestas! (I, 36b)

Nísida, after some hesitation, accepts the challenge of her faith/honor; she drinks poison and dies. As befitting a martyr, her glory now radiates in Heaven:

> Ya al cielo te levantas,
> ya sus claras estrellas
> con inmortales pies pisas y mides.
> Ya entre las almas santas
> escuchas mis querellas,
> y a todo el cielo mi consuelo pides. (I, 39a)

Like Atila, the King begins to go mad from the horror of having killed his beloved. His guilt carries him to a desire to punish everyone, including himself, for his foul deed:

> Todo lo pienso acabar,
> pues mi esperanza acabó;
> para al fin morirme yo
> de cansado de matar. (I, 36a-b)

For the conscience-stricken Celauro, Nísida's death only heightens his sense of guilt. He sees himself as personally responsible for what she has suffered:

> Mas ¿es bien empleado
> que pague un ángel lo que yo he pecado? (I, 39b)

Like his brother he seeks to destroy the world for his grief, and he expresses his emotions in language as fiery as that which ended the first act:

> Págueme el Rey y el mundo
> el triste eclipse de mis luces bellas,
> tantas almas sacando,
> que al cielo y al profundo
> le faltará lugar donde ponellas. (I, 39b)

But once again his angry words fail to carry him through his task. Instead, he unheroically goes mad from grief.

The opening of Celauro's mad scene is clearly patterned after that of Atila, and, as in Virués' play, choral-like commentaries alert the audience to his psychological suffering even before his actual appearance on stage. In *El amor constante* three servants commanded by the King to kill Celauro describe the latter in the following manner:

> Sus acciones son de loco:
> ya camina poco a poco,
> ya corre, y ya no camina,
> ya voces y ojos levanta
> al cielo, ya los compone
> y ya en la tierra los pone
> callando. (I, 40b)

Menón's death scene in *La gran Semíramis* seems to be the model for part of this scene as well. Like the shattered and disillusioned Menón, Celauro imagines he sees his beloved fleeing from him to Heaven:[21]

> ¿Huyes? Seguirte no puedo,
> porque ya el pecho desmaya;
> para que a vengarte vaya
> dame valor, y no miedo.
> ¿Qué horror es éste? ¡Ay de mí!
> Que a espantarte no te obligo;
> o llévame allá contigo,
> o no me dejes sin ti.
> Oye, ¿conmigo rigores? (I, 41a)

Still plagued by guilt for his failure, he imagines he sees Death before him. Regarding his rebellion as sinful and his subsequent defeat a sign that he has offended God, he desires to die a Christian death. He wants to confess his wrongs so that he can join Nísida in Heaven:

> Cristiano en efeto soy;
> procuradme allá la palma,
> porque ya, esposa del alma,
> a veros con Cristo voy.
> ... ...
> Soy en efeto cristiano,
> y aunque malo pude ser,
> quisiera ahora tener
> la cruz bendita en la mano.
> ... ...
> que la cruz es la bandera
> de los soldados de Cristo. (I, 41b)

At his moment of death Celauro recognizes Leonido as his son. He passes his sword and a mission to the young hero:

> Tú eres honrado y podrás;
> mas, por ser del cielo amigo,
> que te vengues no te digo,
> sino que ofendido estás. (I, 43a)

Celauro sees vengeance as anti-Christian, and, seeking to die in grace, he cannot counsel his son, whom he sees as sent by Heaven, to avenge his death.

Leonido, however, immediately resolves to exact vengeance, although he knows that the offender is the King. In an epic-like oath he swears not to live a normal life

> hasta que el brazo ahora levantado,
> tan lleno de valor y de osadía,

---

[21] The stage directions emphasize his madness: «Entrase como que vas tras aquella sombra que finge representalle la imaginación...» (I, 41a).

> me saque de ofendido y de obligado;
> hasta poder beber helada y fría,
> enjugando estas lágrimas que bebo,
> del Rey la sangre, injustamente mía;
> para vengar entonces, como debo,
> ofensas hechas al valor altivo
> deste segundo Aquiles... (I, 43b)

As in the plays of Virués, vengeance becomes intimately linked with divine punishment. And although the rhetoric of Leonido's vow is that of a highly-charged emotional reaction, the language and imagery used in his confrontation with the King once again return to the concepts of reason and divine retribution associated with Leonido since his earliest appearance in the play.

As the last scene opens we find the King grieving over the death of Nísida. He blames himself for her death and fears divine punishment:

> Injusta mano mía,
> de ti salió el rigor que me tormenta;
> quité la luz al día,
> y agora en las tinieblas de mi afrenta
> me consume y me asombra
> del muerto sol la imaginada sombra.
> ... ...
> desde la tierra miro
> la espada, a tu justicia, impireo cielo;
> y que la pide aquella
> que fue mi sol, y la eclipsó mi estrella. (I, 43b-44a)

The King's vision turns out to be prophetic, for in the following scene Leonido enters the court brandishing the very sword of justice that the King so dreads and yet so welcomes as a means of deliverance from his inner torment.

Leonido's just defiance of the King is, paradoxically, carried out under the guise of respect for the monarch's authority. This is evident from the opening of the scene, for while Leonido enters the court in a manner that reveals clearly his intention both to deceive the King (he is dressed «en hábito de villano» [I, 44b] and does not reveal his identity) and to punish him (breaking the *ley de palacio,* he makes his entrance «con la espada desnuda» [I, 44b]), he first dutifully asks the King's permission to appear before him. While seeming to pay homage to the King, Leonido actually tricks him into granting him permission to be his assassin, just as the young boy had duped the courtiers in the second act. What on the surface appears to be respect for the King and his authority is, then, just the opposite.

Whereas Celauro's confrontation with the King was impetuous and almost irrational, that of Leonido is cooly calculated and made to appear a natural and rational appeal to law; and while Celauro was paralyzed by the recognition of his obligations to his sovereign lord, Leonido makes a game of those obligations and turns them to his advantage. Leonido tells the King that he seeks to avenge a personal affront, and he asks that either the King punish the wrongdoer or that he grant Leonido permission to do so. Without ever mentioning the name of the offender, Leonido asks that his case be judged strictly in terms of reason and without regard for the social status of those involved:

> hice, Rey, esta jornada,
> con esta desnuda espada
> y este vestido, vestido;
>   porque así se representa
> a la razón, que me ayuda,
> aquí mi verdad desnuda,
> y aquí vestida mi afrenta;
> ... ...
> veas la razón que tengo. (I, 44b)

Leonido's words and syntax are laden with ambiguity. He appears to be appealing to the King's sense of justice when he states:

> y así, pide en la presencia
> de tu corte mi esperanza,
> a tu justicia venganza,
> o para hacella licencia. (I, 44b)

But the words «pide... a tu justicia venganza» also imply that Leonido means to take revenge on the King because of the latter's perversion of justice. Similarly, the following passage, with its playing off of the words *dar* and *tomar,* is both respectful and threatening in tone:

> mas licencia me has de dar,
> porque si echo de ver
> que no lo quieres hacer,
> me la pueda yo tomar. (I, 44b)

Although on the surface Leonido defers to kingly authority in asking for permission to realize his proposed act of vengeance, his language simultaneously suggests that he intends to wrest that authority from the King if necessary. Leonido's ambiguous use of language and his subversion of logic only lightly veil an outright condemnation and defiance of the evil monarch.

The King agrees to let the case rest on its merits, as an offense of one man against another. Without understanding that Leonido is speaking about him, the King grants the boy permission to slay the offender. Stricken with grief, the King also wishes for his own death:

> Sea así; que tal estoy
> y tal me contemplo aquí,

> que aun para matarme a mí
> licencia también te doy. (I, 44b)

The King interprets his death as an act of divine punishment:

> Justo castigo me envía
> el cielo. (I, 45a)

    The King's response to Leonido's request is but one more example of Castro's ambiguous handling of this final confrontation. If the King assents to his own assassination, he does so not in response to Leonido's call for justice but in response to his own suffering. The King wishes to die because he has lost the woman he loves, and his death is the culmination of his appropriation of courtly love rhetoric. By the end of the play the King is nearly mad with grief and he cannot be held responsible for what he says, particularly as he is answering an ambiguously-phrased request. To see the King as truly granting permission for his own slaying and to regard Leonido's appeal to the King simply as respect for the latter's authority is to ignore the linguistic ambiguities and equivocations of the text. Only on the most literal level can it be said that the regicidal act is carried out with the King's assent. Clearly, Castro is not backing away from supporting a doctrine of resistance. Rather, he is attempting to carry off a splendid *coup de théâtre* by harmonizing opposites, that is, by disguising defiance in the clothing of submission.[22]

    The first reaction of the courtiers to the assassination is to cry for Leonido's death, for although they have acknowledged the need to rid the state of the tyrant, their conventional attitude of obedience makes them see the regicide as an act of treason. But when they discover the true identity of Leonido they interpret the deed as divine intercession and see Leonido as the new shepherd who will guide their flock:[23]

> GRANDE 4.°: ¡Gran secreto el alto cielo
> nos descubrió en este día!

---

[22] In addition to the comment of JULIÁ MARTÍNEZ (cited above in the introduction) to the effect that Leonido only kills the King because he has obtained his permission to do so and that therefore Castro backs away from supporting the sixteenth-century theory of regicide, may be added that of ROBERT LA DU who sees it as an example of the following principle of Castro's theater: «The subject had no recourse but to appeal to the king's sense of justice to remedy the affront, for he could not take vengeance upon the king»; LA DU, p. 212. Similar comments may be found in WEIGER, «Sobre la originalidad», p. 8. See also FRANK P. CASA, «Affirmation and Retraction in Golden Age Drama», *Neophilologus*, 61 (1977), pp. 561-562. All fail to consider Leonido's ambiguous use of language and the King's delirious response. Though the king does indeed give his consent it is clear that action against him in no way depends on his approval to be morally legitimate.

[23] The allusion to Christ as the Good Shepherd is obvious.

> GRANDE 2.°: Sin duda el cielo lo envía,
> y ha de ser nuestro consuelo.
> GRANDE 4.°: Pues que vimos sus extremos,
> gobernará nuestra grey;
> ¿queréisle por vuestro rey?
> TODOS: Por nuestro rey le queremos. (I, 45a)

Even the Duke accepts the regicide as a fitting punishment for the King's crimes. The deaths of Nísida and Celauro have awakened in him a moral consciousness that now stands above his loyalty to his monarch. When the courtiers first turn against Leonido, the Duke points to the corpses of the faithful lovers and offers them as proof of the King's misdeeds and of the justice of Leonido's actions:

> ¿Es posible que os altera,
> deudos míos, pueblo amado,
> que quien hizo este pecado
> le pague desta manera? (I, 45a)

But when he believes Leonido is about to accept the crown he accuses him of treason. However, Leonido refuses to accept the change of station from subject to ruler; he takes the crown only to hand it over to the Infanta:

> De mi mano has de gustar
> que esta corona te dé;
> que yo sólo la tomé
> para podértela dar. (I, 45b)

This refusal further establishes Leonido's moral purity, for it proves that he seeks merely to restore order and not to usurp power for himself. Nonetheless, the announced marriage of Leonido and the Infanta assures, in the archetypical pattern, his ascent to the throne. With Leonido as ruler order is restored to a weakened kingdom, as are the values of natural and Christian law.

In *El amor constante,* then, Guillén de Castro dramatizes the case of a kingdom forced to come to terms with a legitimate king turned tyrant. It explores the tension between the demands of a social code which places restraints on defiance, and those of a moral code which admits the legitimacy of the deposition of a tyrant. It is a tension finally resolved with the triumph of the latter in an act of regicide.

Forming the underlying ideological basis of the play is the sixteenth-century political doctrine that asserts the supremacy of natural and Christian law over the arbitrary will of a ruler and which allows for the overthrow of a king who proves himself to be a tyrant. This doctrine is echoed throughout the play, concretely in the statements of Nísida, Leonido and the Grandees (at the beginning of the last act) that a tyrant is by definition not a king and that, such being the case, he may be opposed. It is reflected also in the images associated with the play's antagonists: the King, proclaiming his will absolute, becomes like Satan and the pagan rulers, whereas Leonido is associated with Nature and Christ. Leonido's coronation by the kingdom symbolizes the ultimate repudiation of any arbitrary law which stands in opposition to the precepts of God and Nature.

But Castro is a dramatist and not an ideologist. As such his interest is not the doctrine itself but the existential dilemma tyranny poses to the individual and the kingdom suddenly faced with a situation they are ill-equipped to handle. Castro depicts a kingdom groping for a solution, as each member tries to come to terms with the problem in his own manner. He seems to be anticipating Lope in positing a medieval-type hierarchy in which submission to royal authority is considered a positive social value by its male members. But he diverges from the Lopean construct in that eventually all acknowledge the injustice of the King and call into question his authority. However, until the very end, each male subject, except Leonido, has trouble disassociating active defiance from treason. Thus, the Grandees see the need for action but feel paralyzed before the King's power and even violently protest at first the killing of the King; the old Duke attempts to defend his honor and respect the King's authority at the same time; and Celauro, unable to see the problem in rational terms, revolts impetuously and, as a result, feels guilty and dishonored throughout. Each encounters difficulty reconciling the imperatives of honor and those of moral law, exemplifying what Beysterveldt has called the anti-Christian nature of male honor.

On the other hand, Nísida and Leonido vigorously defy the King with a clear conscience. For the female member of this society there exists no conflict between honor and moral virtue, as her chief concern is her chastity and not her political relationship to the king. Thus a defense of her virtue against the King complies with the demands of both honor and Christian law. Leonido, too, sees no conflict between honor and opposition to the King, particularly after realizing that the King has taken no heed of his warning to reform. Leonido, although concerned with his honor, does not see it endangered by defying the King.[24]

Growing up not in the court but in nature, he is in direct contact with the mandates of natural law (and of Christian law and reason). It is precisely his ability to judge the situation posed by the King's tyranny in terms of these higher laws that allows him to conclude that the most

---

[24] The scene early in Act II in which Leonido proves he will defend his honor if endangered is of great importance in this respect. It serves to prove that Leonido can defy the King *and* consider himself a man of honor at the same time. Castro does not deny the importance of honor. Rather he shows the need to reconcile the claims of honor and those of morality.

appropriate behavior is reasoned defiance. Certain of the justice of his cause, Leonido can confront the King free from the inner doubts that plagued his father. Leonido's defiance never seems simply rebellious. Instead, it is sanctioned by the very laws upon which a Christian kingdom is based. Because of his ability to bridge the human and the divine, Leonido approaches divinity.

A comparison with the theater of Virués offers important insights into the genesis and originality of *El amor constante*. Juliá Martínez sees this work as a clear offshoot of the Valencian neo-Senecan school of drama:

> Reputamos la obra por una de las más antiguas del poeta de Valencia, si no es la primera de las que conocemos, porque en realidad no es más que una acumulación de incidentes y escenas patéticas, a las que tan acostumbrado estaba el público de la época de los pseudoclásicos del siglo XVI.[25]

And he later adds:

> En síntesis, es la obra una manifestación de cierta fantasía juvenil, influida por escenas vistas aplaudir en el teatro por un público que miraba al pasado, y sin que una lectura abundante y meditada pudiera corregir los ímpetus del fervor primero.[26]

Though Juliá helps undermine the «Castro-as-follower-of-Lope» fallacy, his comments invite further discussion of two questions. What exactly in *El amor constante* may be attributed to an imitation of the earlier theater? Where does Castro diverge from the neo-Senecan tradition, revealing his own original vision?

Juliá relates to the earlier theater tradition only the «incidentes y escenas patéticas» in the play. Indeed, certain scenes involving cruelty, bloodshed and madness as well as a certain bombastic rhetoric and devices such as the chorus are all clearly derived from this theater. But Castro's imitation of the plays of Virués in particular touches the very theme and structure of the play. Virués' plays of tyranny involve three character types, all of which serve as a point of departure for Castro: the tyrant king, the subject victimized by the king and the avenger/deliverer. As Juliá himself observed, without relating his insight to the earlier tragedies, the chief theme of Castro's drama is tyranny:

> El título haría suponer que el propósito del autor sería cantar la firmeza de los amores de Nísida y Celauro; éstos, en realidad, quedan en un segundo término, para dejar paso a las tiranías de un monarca que repudia a su esposa...[27]

---

[25] JULIÁ MARTÍNEZ, «Observaciones», I, li.
[26] JULIÁ MARTÍNEZ, «Observaciones», I, liii-liv.
[27] JULIÁ MARTÍNEZ, «Observaciones», I, liii.

Castro shares with Virués the concept of the tyrant as the destroyer of divine and social order. The similarities between Castro's king and Atila, particularly in the third act of *El amor constante,* are too evident to be merely coincidental. While Lope's king will represent God on earth the king of Castro's play, like the kings in the plays of Virués, is allied to the devil.

In the case of the victimized subject we have seen how Menón in *La gran Semíramis* is betrayed by his monarch, feels spiritually defeated when faced with this new reality and finally commits suicide in despair. Celauro, like Menón, undergoes a process of spiritual disintegration when forced to come to terms with the King's injustice. More concretely, we have seen how his mad scene, in which he imagines Nísida in Heaven, is, at least in part, modelled after that of the defeated Assyrian general.

Finally, in Virués' plays the unjust king meets his death at the hands of a character who acts out of motives of both vengeance and divine justice. Here, with certain important differences that we shall soon discuss, is the model for Leonido.

Castro, however, is no mere imitator of his predecessor. Into the familiar pattern set by Virués Castro introduces important new perspectives. In *El amor constante* Castro anticipates Lope by framing the problem of the tyrant within the context of a hierarchically structured, medieval-type society in which duties and obligations are clearly assigned and acknowledged as inherent to one's social role: the king is to rule well, the noble vassal is to obey the king, the woman is to protect her *honor/virtud*. Castro examines tyranny from a new angle: the problem it poses to subjects who have sworn allegiance to their monarch and who yet see that he has violated the mandate of his office. Castro differs from Lope, however, in that while in the later obedience is absolute, in *El amor constante* natural and Christian law stand above that social imperative.

Growing out of this new hierarchical dimension is a second new element, the one which was to blossom most fully in the *Mocedades* and capture the imagination of Corneille: the exploration of the inner struggle of a character caught between the demands of two conflicting codes, be it passion in conflict with duty, or natural/Christian law in conflict with social law. In Castro's work this interiority adds a new dimension to two stock figures of the earlier theater. The king, a blind force of cruelty in Virués, is endowed by Castro with a new consciousness of his wrongdoing, and observes his own moral deterioration with a mixture of horror and acceptance. Celauro, the subject victimized and destroyed by the tyrant, constantly vacillates between rebellion and submission, affirmation and despair. Whereas Menón's disintegration is due to *desengaño* when he discovers that the king has betrayed him, Celauro falls apart because he cannot resolve his own inner conflict. This tragic struggle is what makes Celauro the play's central, though unheroic, protagonist.

Finally, in his reworking of the avenger/deliverer figure, Castro adds to his models the future *comedia* pattern of order restored. In Virués' tragedies the character who proclaims that his act of vengeance is divinely sanctioned can himself offer no hope for any restoration of order. Flaminia is as immoral as Atila and dies along with him; Ninias gives strong signs of continuing the corrupt reign of his mother. Leonido, on the other hand, is a positive saviour figure of the type found in romantic chivalric literature and is not only allowed by God to punish the King but seems himself to be a divine presence. The intervention of this figure assures the restoration of political order and ends the play on a positive celebrative note.

El amor constante is, then, a play poised at the crossroads of the sixteenth-century *tragedia* and the Lopean *comedia*. Though its ideological foundation is that of the sixteenth century and, therefore, different from that espoused by the *comedia,* as a dramatic structure it both looks back to the past and anticipates the future.

CHAPTER III

«*EL CONDE ALARCOS*»

El Conde Alarcos is one of the earliest, if not the first, of Guillén de Castro's plays to be based on a *romance*.[1] Early in his career, while still immersed in the traditions of the neo-Senecan tragedy, Castro began to look to popular ballads as a source for dramatic material. The Spanish neo-Senecan theater had never been strictly classically oriented in either subject matter or dramatic form, and history, legend and fiction, whether ancient or modern, foreign or national, were regarded as appropriate matter for tragedy. In Spain at least two previous dramatists had tapped the immense storehouse of national legends for dramatic purposes: Jerónimo Bermúdez had created a pair of powerful tragedies, *Nise lastimada* and *Nise laureada*, out of the historical legend of Inés de Castro[2] and Juan de la Cueva had already turned to the *Romancero* as a source for some of his tragedies. Castro found in the ballad of the Count Alarcos not an epic celebration of medieval valor (as he later would in the Cid cycle) but a story replete with pathos and tragic power that seemed almost destined for the author who had just written *El amor constante*. Here was a tale which, like that first play, dramatized the tragic conflict between arbitrary royal power and Christian morality. What is more, in the ballad's elaboration of that problem Castro saw elements reminiscent of his own work: a mutual love destroyed by a willful king, a morally problematic king-vassal relationship, and a final condemnation and punishment of the evil monarch.

Castro reworked this material so as to bring it even closer to the pattern of *El amor constante:* Alarcos, like his spiritual brother Celauro, finding himself in a critical moral dilemma precipitated by the demands of the King, goes mad from guilt and grief; the Countess Alarcos con-

[1] BRUERTON, p. 150, dates the play as probably written between 1600 and 1602. JULIÁ MARTÍNEZ writes: «Debió de escribirse muy a principios del siglo XVII o en los últimos años del XVI.» JULIÁ MARTÍNEZ, «Observaciones», II, v.

[2] The legend of Inés de Castro, in which an innocent woman is sacrificed for reasons of state, is strikingly similar to the story of Count Alarcos. One critic has suggested that it may be the source for the ballad. See GUIDO MANCINI, *La romanza del Conde Alarcos* (Pisa: Libreria Goliardica Editrice, 1959).

ceives the Count's child, who is nurtured in the woods and who learns to follow Christian law as his primary ethical guide; and the King is condemned and almost killed by characters who stand outside the central hierarchical structure and who seek vengeance on the King in the name of justice.

However, Castro makes a radical departure from both the ballad source and *El amor constante* by defusing with a happy ending the tragic material that attracted him to the ballad in the first place. This strange mixture of tragedy and comedy was not foreign to the neo-Senecan tradition. Cinthio himself took the first initiative in Italy and in Spain Virués followed the model in his *La infelice Marcela*. What is of chief importance in Castro's play, however, is that even with the deflection of tragedy into comedy there exists throughout *El Conde Alarcos* a strong explicit condemnation of the tyrannical king and a denunciation of those who place a social code, be it politics or honor, over Christian moral law.

The date and origin of the *romance* of Count Alarcos has been a subject of controversy. The versions conserved in *pliegos sueltos* of the early sixteenth century are lengthy *juglaresco* versions which reveal a marked artistic consciousness. Menéndez y Pelayo, following the opinion of earlier Romantic critics, believed these versions to be sixteenth-century reelaborations of a much older ballad of the *tradición oral*. Menéndez Pidal, on the other hand, believed the *juglaresco* versions represent the original *romance:*

> ... el romance pertenece a la primera mitad del siglo XV y... nada hallamos que le ligue a una tradición anterior. Debemos mirarlo como obra de arte muy personal, invención audaz... es bien sorprendente el ver cómo en los medios romancísticos pudo un anónimo juglar mostrarse originalísimo y superior a sus contemporáneos áulicos, Juan de Mena y Santillana, ideando una extraña y poderosa tragedia del honor...[3]

The story of the ballad is as follows.[4] The Infanta Solisa, daughter of the King, in anger and despair confesses to her father that she has been seduced by Count Alarcos. She tells him he had promised to marry her but then broke his word and married another. The angry King, concerned about his honor, asks his daughter's advice on how to remedy the situation. She suggests that the Count kill his wife and marry her secretly. The King so orders the Count who, though first protesting against the injustice, agrees to protect the King's honor and obey. In a long

---

[3] Ramón Menéndez Pidal, *Romancero hispánico* (Madrid: Espasa-Calpe, S. A., 1953), I, xvi.

[4] This version may be found as no. 163 in Marcelino Menéndez y Pelayo, *Antología de poetas líricos castellanos* (Madrid: 1899), vol. VIII; rpt. in Marcelino Menéndez y Pelayo, *Obras completas* (Santander: CSIC, 1945), vol. XXIV. All subsequent ballad quotes in this chapter are from this version.

tearful scene the Count tells his wife of his orders and tells her to prepare for death. Before she is killed she calls for divine retribution upon the King and the Infanta within thirty days. The Count strangles her, returns to court and marries the Infanta, but within thirty days he, the King, and the Infanta die and must account for their actions before the Divine Tribunal.

Menéndez Pidal notes that the originality of the *romance* resides in the development of a problem of personal honor within a political framework:

> [El juglar] No quiere adocenarse narrando, como los demás juglares romancistas, aventuras caballerescas de combates o de amores. Le atraen más los conflictos entre el rey y los nobles adversos, las muertes que por razón de Estado cometen Alfonso XI el Justiciero o Pedro el Cruel, pero él no tratará este conflicto puramente político, como los juglares trataban, sino que lo traslada al terreno del honor familiar. Aspira a una absoluta originalidad.[5]

What stands out is the pathos of the parting of husband and wife:

> El más conmovido patetismo domina toda la segunda mitad del poemita, actuada entre el Conde, que, aunque abrumado por la ternura conyugal, está resuelto a cumplir la inicua sentencia del Rey, y la Condesa, su víctima, que viene a ser la verdadera protagonista... La segunda parte es la parte nuclear de la obra; lo anterior es sólo una preparación.[6]

The King of the *romance* is an unjust, angry monarch, coldly willing to sacrifice an innocent victim to satisfy his honor. When the King first hears of his daughter's dishonor he becomes furious:

> Perdiera el rey en oírlo — el sentido que tenía,
> mas después en sí tornado — con enojo respondía:
> —¡No son estos los consejos, — que vuestra madre os decía!
> —¡Muy mal mirastes, infanta, — do estaba la honra mía!

When he informs the Count of his plan he does so coldly, with little concern for other than his honor:

> Otra cosa os digo, conde, — de que más os pesaría:
> que matéis a la condesa — que cumple a la honra mía:
> echéis fama que ella es muerta — de cierto mal que tenía,
> y tratarse ha el casamiento — como cosa no sabida,
> porque no sea deshonrada — hija que tanto quería.

To the Count's objections the King responds with a chilling nonchalance; according to the monarch, kings have the unquestioned right to dispose of innocent victims for the sake of royal honor:

---

[5] MENÉNDEZ PIDAL, *Romancero hispánico*, I, 358.
[6] MENÉNDEZ PIDAL, *Romancero hispánico*, I, 359.

> —De morir tiene, el buen conde, — por salvar la honra mía,
> pues no mirastes primero — lo que mirar se debía.
> Si no muere la condesa — a vos costará la vida.
> Por la honra de los reyes — muchos sin culpa morían,
> por que muera la condesa — no es mucha maravilla.

Disposing of his subjects at his will seems to be a common prerogative of this uniformly cruel king. We learn that the King had previously executed the countess' brother in much the same way:

> y mataron a mi hermano — el buen conde don García,
> que el rey lo mandó matar — por miedo que dél tenía.

Castro creates a more complex character in his King by modifying the unrelenting cruelty of the ballad.

In this miniature «drama de honor»[7] not only are the King and the Infanta divinely punished for their crime but the Count too stands accountable. Whereas Castro transforms Alarcos into a pathetic victim of royal power, in the ballad he is a more ambivalent figure. To a large degree it is his irresponsible behavior that sets the fateful events in motion. The Count had indeed loved the Infanta and, in a moment of passion, promised to marry her. In fact, the Count still nurtures a love for her; we first find the Count musing over their brief affair:

> si muy bien la quise entonces — agora más la quería;
> mas por mí pueden decir — quien bien ama tarde olvida.

It is only later that the Count realized that his advances to the Infanta might constitute an offense to his king and for that reason he decided not to pursue the issue any farther:

> Por miedo de vos, el rey, — no casé con quien debía,
> no pensé que vuestra Alteza — en ello consentiría.[8]

---

[7] MENÉNDEZ PIDAL, *Romancero hispánico,* I, 360: «El juglar literaliza las exigencias del honor y del sentimiento monárquico con exaltada desmesura, como se hará doscientos años después en ciertos dramas... Todo el romance es calderoniano... Las tremendas leyes del honor, 'a secreto agravio secreta venganza' estaban completamente definidas a comienzos del siglo xv...»

[8] Interestingly enough, Alarcos was the one subject to whom the King would have given his consent:

> pues acá en las nuestras cortes, — hija, mal recaudo había,
> porque en todos los mis reinos — vuestro par igual no había,
> sino era el conde Alarcos, — hijos y mujer tenía.

Here we may see yet another example of what DENIS DE ROUGEMONT sees as part of the cult of passion of the Tristan myth. Like Tristan, Alarcos creates an artificial barrier (here, the supposed objection of the King) in order to keep a passion alive and unfulfilled rather than quench the flame through marriage. See *Love in the Western World,* Book I («The Tristan Myth»).

But by irresponsibly flirting with forbidden passion he had already dishonored the King. The King later makes it clear that the Count was wrong in not giving greater heed to his obligations to his monarch before taking the first fateful step:

> pues no miraste, primero — lo que mirar se debía.

When the King demands that his honor be restored through the murder of the Countess, Alarcos protests the injustice:

> de casar con la infanta — yo, señor, bien casaría;
> mas matar a la condesa, — señor rey, no lo haría,
> porque no debe morir — la que mal no merecía.

But the King reminds him that since he is the cause of his ruler's loss of honor he is responsible for its restoration. He threatens to kill Alarcos, and therefore dishonor his subject, if he does not comply. Alarcos is thus forced to choose between the honor code and a code of ethics: if he follows the dictates of his moral conscience by refusing to obey his King, he will be dishonored in the eyes of the world, but if he acts to protect his honor by killing his wife he will commit a moral crime. The Count chooses to save his worldly honor but he refuses to assume any moral responsibility for the crime about to be committed by his very hands. Ignoring his own exercise of free will in his choice, he seeks to throw the burden of guilt totally upon the King; like many twentieth-century counterparts, he hopes to clear his conscience with the reasoning that he is only following an order he cannot disobey:

> —Yo la mataré, buen rey, — mas no será la culpa mía:
> vos os avendréis con Dios — en fin de vuestra vida,
> y prometo a vuestra Alteza, — a fe de caballería,
> que me tengan por traidor — si lo dicho no cumplía
> de matar a la condesa, — aunque mal no merecía.

With his honor at stake the Count feels he has no choice but to obey. His response anticipates that of many an honorable subject of the later *comedia* tradition who refuses to take a moral stand against the king, arguing that God alone can judge the king's deeds and punish him for any wrongdoing.

In the Count's mind he himself is responsible for the King's dishonor while the King alone stands responsible for the actual murder. The guilt that the Count does feel when he tells the dying Countess «Yo soy el triste culpado — esta culpa toda es mía» is related not to his actual carrying out of the order, but to the careless ignoring of his duties when he passionately made love to the Infanta.

Before killing his wife his attitude towards the royal mandate is one of resignation without protest; though shocked by the injustice he nonetheless defends the King's right to defend his honor:

> demándame por marido — por la fe que me tenía.
> Puédelo muy bien hacer— de razón y de justicia;
> díjomelo el rey su padre — porque de ella lo sabía.
> Otra cosa manda el rey — que toca en el alma mía:
> manda que muráis, condesa, — a la fin de vuestra vida,
> que no puede tener honra — siendo vos, condesa, viva.

At the moment of her death the Countess forgives Alarcos but condemns the King and the Infanta:

> —A vos yo perdono, conde, — por el amor que os tenía;
> mas yo no perdono al rey, — ni a la infanta su hija,
> sino que queden citados — delante la alta justicia,
> que allá vayan a juicio — dentro de los treinta días.

Nonetheless Alarcos too dies within the appointed thirty days to be judged by God:

> Los doce días pasados — la infanta ya moría;
> el rey a los veinte y cinco, — el conde al treinteno día,
> allá fueron a dar cuenta — a la justicia divina.

The *juglar* leaves it to his listener to determine the nature of Alarcos' guilt and his ultimate fate: is Alarcos condemned, and, if so, is it due, at least in part, to his refusal to disobey the King and act ethically? Whether the *juglar* considers Alarcos' claim of non-culpability morally specious remains purposely ambiguous. What is clear, however, is that Guillén de Castro felt he could not reconcile this amoral attitude of the Count with his own desire to portray a sympathetic protagonist. In Castro's reworking of the ballad Count Alarcos not only protests more vehemently but also internalizes his guilt and goes mad from it.

In the first act of his drama Castro changes in important ways the circumstances leading to the tragedy. Whereas in the *romance* the Count had loved the Infanta, Castro presents a perfectly corresponded love between the Count and the Countess, Margarita, from the beginning, thereby bringing *El Conde Alarcos* closer to the pattern of *El amor constante*.

In the very first line of the *comedia* the audience is ironically reminded that the very person who loves the Countess will be the instrument of her death; the hands that now embrace her neck will soon strangle her:

> Vuelve a mi cuello esos lazos,
> del alma alegres despojos. (II, 1a)

As in *El amor constante,* while the Count was absent[9] Margarita bore him a child out of wedlock. Unable to keep the child openly, she entrusted him to the supposedly generous Infanta who promised to protect and nurture him. The news disturbs the Count, for he knows that the Infanta carries an illicit passion for him. Unlike his ballad predecessor, however, he has never repaid her affection. The *comedia* Alarcos is much more attendant to his duties; he tells the Infanta that his respect for the King has not allowed even the possibility of love to cross his mind:

> A quien debo fe y honor,
> pago con honor y fe. (II, 3b)

While in the original *romance* Alarcos' promise to marry the Infanta is a natural extension of his love for her, in the *comedia* he is tricked into giving her his word. The Infanta lies to the Count to the effect that Margarita is having relations with her cousin, the Prince of Hungary,[10] and makes him promise to marry her if she can show the accusation to be true. The Count falls for the ruse and makes the vow requested by the Infanta. Soon, however, the truth is revealed and he asks the King to marry him to Margarita at once.

Her scheme spoiled, the Infanta vows to seek vengeance on the couple. Castro transforms the Infanta of the ballad from an unhappy, wronged woman to a kindred spirit to Medea. The Infanta of the end of the first act becomes another incarnation of the bloodthirsty avenging woman of the neo-Senecan theater. Castro's immediate precedent once again is Virués, who employs this figure in *La cruel Casandra.* The Infanta threatens to kill the child if the two marry and when they decide to carry through their wedding plans she has the child chopped up and served to the couple at their wedding banquet. Here, as in the first act of *El amor constante,* Castro creates a highly-charged situation which threatens to explode violently at any minute. As in the earlier play, the author employs asides and metaphoric language to create a heightened dramatic tension. The ceremonies uniting husband and wife and king and vassal are constantly undercut by the asides and veiled meanings of the Infanta's words until violence breaks forth and destroys the precarious order. In the banquet scene all pay homage to the King in stances of cere-

---

[9] In *El amor constante* Celauro was in prison; in *Alarcos* the Count was off fighting in a war for the King.

[10] The Prince of Hungary is only mentioned in passing in the ballad as the proposed spouse of the Infanta:

> que ya fuérades casada — con el príncipe de Hungría.
> No quesistes escuchar — la embajada que os venía.

In the *comedia* the Prince is in love with the Infanta in the first act. Later, as we shall see, he will represent the voice of protest against royal injustice.

mony, the ceremonial ritual representing an ideal social hierarchy where each accepts his social role and receives honor from it. It is a situation of perfect harmony where king honors subject and subject honors king. The King honors Alarcos by allowing him to eat at his table and in turn Alarcos entrusts himself to the King:

> Rey: Lo que digo ha de ser hoy.
> Conde: Por ser tu gusto lo apruebo.
> Rey: Veréis que sé lo que os debo
> si miráis a lo que os doy.
> A mi mesa y a mi lado
> habéis de comer, que es justo.
> ... ...
> Conde: En todo tu gusto es ley. (II, 11a)

In the ideal society symbolized by ceremony *el gusto* and *lo justo* are united and Alarcos' creed of absolute obedience to the King makes sense:

> El fiel vasallo a su rey
> ha de obedecer en todo. (II, 12a)

As the King honors the Count so the Count pays homage to his lord in the ceremony of washing the monarch's hands:

> Conde: Hoy este oficio he de hacer,
> pues tú me quieres honrar.
> Rey: Sí, que bien puedes lavar
> manos que te han de valer. (II, 11a-b)

But the Infanta refuses to allow the Count to honor her in the same fashion. Bent on destroying this harmonious order, she purposely misinterprets as an affront to her honor the Count's offer to wash her hands:

> ¿En que me lave porfías?
> ¿Alguna mancha me sabes? (II, 11b)

She then turns the ceremony of order and honor into her own perverted, violent ceremony. She offers to wash Margarita's hands, claiming she will gain honor by doing so. Soon, the unifying ceremony is turned inside-out as the Infanta bathes Margarita's hands in the blood of her own son. The scene, which began with harmony undercut by held-in violence and emotion, ends in turmoil and disorder as the Count draws his sword against the Infanta. The explosive ending to the act seems to be clearly modelled after the first act ending of *El amor constante*. Castro will repeat it once again at the end of Act II of *El Conde Alarcos*. With the intrusion of violence *el gusto* and *lo justo* will no longer form a harmonious unit but, rather, each will take its own separate path. The pact of mutual respect and homage between king and vassal will be replaced by threats and imprecations.

Act II contains the heart of the material of the *romance* source. It is in this act that the problem of tyranny begins to become the central concern of the *comedia*. In the first act Castro depicts a king capable of honoring a subject and of maintaining at least the outward semblance of a just and harmonious rule. But in that act Castro also reveals the King's vulnerability to his daughter. He is a weak old man, dependent on the support of the Infanta; when he first greets her he cannot tell whether he is her father or her child:

> Dime padre.
> ... ...
> O hijo, pues tengo en ti
> una hija y una madre,
> y soy, cuando el cuello ciño,
> que es mi arrimo y es mi espejo,
> hijo tierno, padre viejo,
> porque de viejo soy niño. (II, 8b)

A combination of weakness and devotion to his daughter will cause him to surrender his power of judgment to the malevolent Infanta. And, as in *El amor constante,* when he abdicates his responsibility he proves himself to be no longer king.

But weakness only partially describes the faults of this ruler. Castro does not attribute the King's heinous decision to have Margarita killed solely to the Infanta's manipulations; the King himself shows a marked tendency to react in a less than just and prudent manner when he feels his honor or his person are threatened. At the end of the first act we saw how the Count drew his sword against the Infanta in the presence of the King, thereby committing a crime of *lèse-majesté*. However, even in his anger the Count assured the King his personal safety:

> Tu cabeza sola
> está segura en tu casa. (II, 13a)

The King is a man whose sense of justice is easily blinded by fury and by threats against his person. Unable to come to terms with the disorder caused by the murder of the child and by the Count's «rebellion» the King attempts to place the matter out of sight. He imprisons both the Count and the Infanta and in his rage almost kills Margarita as well. Wishing to forget the whole incident, he refuses to listen to any arguments concerning the Count's innocence. His refusal to act as judge and his indiscriminate anger have earned him the title of «tirano» (II, 13b). Both Margarita and the Prince remark that the King's actions are without reason or discrimination; she speaks of «las sinrazones de un hombre / como el Rey» (II, 13a) and he agrees that «muy grandes son» (II, 13a). The King cannot control his rage enough to talk about the problem:

> Y tan fiero se ha mostrado
> desta contraria fortuna,
> que con persona ninguna
> deste negocio ha tratado.   (II, 13b)

When Margarita attempts once again to broach the subject to the King she speaks in terms of «la verdad» and «la razón» (II, 13b), arguing that the Count's spontaneous reaction to the homicide was just and natural and not aimed against the King. Indeed, public opinion criticizes the King, protesting that his sense of justice has been blinded:

> ... cobras renombre
> de injusto y cruel,
> ... ...
> ... no digan, señor,
> que perdona al ofensor
> quien castiga al ofendido.   (II, 14a)

Later, the Prince of Hungary argues that though the Count may have been wrong in drawing his sword, the action was understandable given the extraordinary circumstances:

> Grande fue su atrevimiento,
> pero su culpa no es grande.   (II, 14b)

For the Prince, the good king must prudently weigh the accidentals of each given situation rather than judge in terms of absolutes. The King's rejoinder shows him to be short-sighted and unable to comprehend how human emotions may sometimes supersede the formalized rules of courteous conduct. He can conceive of Alarcos' actions only as a threat to royal power. His words seem particularly off the track when we remember the Count's first-act vow not to harm the King. The King sees the matter differently:

> Mira como no es rigor,
> sino razón la que tengo.
> Tuvo el Conde tantos bríos,
> que en mi casa y a mis ojos,
> con fuego de sus enojos,
> mató tres criados míos.
> No respetó mi corona,
> mas antes la tuvo en poco,
> y aún puso, furioso y loco,
> en peligro mi persona.   (II, 14a)

This incident and the King's reaction to it serve as an important foreshadowing of what is to come. The King proves himself to be more concerned with honor than truth and rashly hastens to protect his personal interests. The seeds of tyranny are already within the King; all that is lacking is the instigation of the Infanta to cause them fully to bloom.

The King finally accedes to Margarita's plea to judge the situation anew and he promises to punish his daughter if she is guilty. When the Infanta appears before him he cannot contain his anger:

>　　INFANTA: Dame las manos.
>　　REY: 　　　　　　　¿Yo? ¿Yo?
>　　　　　　La muerte, dirás mejor. (II, 14b)

He rejects the Infanta's first attempts to excuse her actions:

>　　　　Con la inocencia, el rigor
>　　　　ninguna ley le concede. (II, 15a)

These words ironically condemn beforehand the King's later order to kill the innocent Countess. Speaking here is the voice of the just king, the objective judge who sees that no excuse vindicates the sacrifice of an innocent victim; in his own words, moral law dictates against it.

But the King is too weak to follow his own principles. The Infanta can easily break down his honest determination to act justly by appealing to his sentiments. She reminds him of the special bond between them:

>　　　　como madre te crié,
>　　　　como hija te serví. (II, 15a)

With this, Father begins to replace Judge:

>　　　　¡Oh amor de padre! No llores,
>　　　　y di que algún daño asconde
>　　　　la causa. (II, 15a)

The Infanta lies to the King, telling him that Alarcos has slept with her and dishonored her. The King is crushed under the illusion of his dishonor. He finds himself too confused and weak to know how to defend his honor properly and cedes his responsibility to his daughter:

>　　　　¿Qué ha de hacer un hombre triste,
>　　　　caduco, cansado y viejo?
>　　　　Dame tú misma el consejo,
>　　　　ya que la ofensa me diste. (II, 15b)

She convinces him that killing her would not wipe out the affront and that this could only be accomplished by forcing the Count to murder his own wife and marry the Infanta. The King's principles concerning the persecution of innocents is now put to the test. The loss of honor begins to cloud the King's mind and once again his personal concerns overshadow the cause of justice. Now not only does the King condone the killing of the Count's child but he orders another sacrifice. In his confusion he tellingly states «No soy rey y soy honrado» (II, 16a). Both in ceding his judgment to his daughter and in allowing concerns of honor to supersede those of mercy and justice the King has proven himself to be less than a king. By his own acknowledgment he no longer merits the respect due a legitimate ruler. Such being the case, both Margarita and the Prince of Hungary will later call for his death on the grounds that he has become a tyrant.

When the King summons the Count before him his anger chokes his speech; Castro portrays this through stammering:

> Conde, Con...
> ... ...
> Loco estoy.
> ... ...
> ¡Conde! ... ¿Quién habrá que crea
> que tú, Conde?...
> ... ...
> ¡Ay, triste!
> ¿Que tú, Conde? (II, 16a)

The anger so vividly expressed in broken speech again gives way to a refusal to consider the truth. When the Count admits he promised to marry the Infanta but did not dishonor her, the King puts a stop to any further explanation:

> No tienes modo,
> villano, ya de excusarte
> que quien confiesa esa parte
> no puede negar el todo. (II, 16b)
>
> Calla. (II, 16b)
>
> ¿Que tan mal se corresponde
> a mi autoridad? (II, 17a)

Clearly and cooly he contradicts his indictment of his daughter's crime by proclaiming that for personal reasons a king may break statutory and Christian laws:

> La Condesa muera.
> Traspasa las justas leyes;
> que las honras de los reyes
> las pueden hacer de cera. (II, 17a)

Alarcos objects that what the King orders him to do stands in direct violation of God's law:

> Mira que hay, pues que te obliga
> un cristiano y justo celo,

> Purgatorio, Infierno y Cielo
> y un Dios que premia y castiga. (II, 17b)

The King does not, however, acknowledge the Count's charge of violation of the Christian code. In his anger he does not really listen. The Count's personal and moral objections actually surprise him and he interprets them as an affront to his authority:

> De tu porfía me espanto.
> Este es mi honor y mi gusto. (II, 17b)

Castro's efforts to portray the Count as a helpless victim of arbitrary royal power and malevolent forces rather than as the morally ambivalent figure of the *romance* are again apparent in the author's handling of the King's ultimatum to the nobleman. In the ballad Alarcos must choose between losing his personal honor or committing a crime. In choosing the latter, *his* honor over *another*'s life, he may appear to be a selfish, unsympathetic character to the listener not disposed to accepting honor as an all-important value. Indeed, this may even be the point of view of the *juglar*. The opposition of the ballad Alarcos to the King is nominal. Although saddened, the Count accepts the execution of the King's command as incumbent upon him as an honorable vassal. Hence, he does not seem to be overly disturbed by his participation in the murder. Castro, however, places Alarcos in a less morally complex, though more sympathetic, situation. When the Count begins to raise objections the King delivers a more horrible ultimatum — if he does not kill his wife the King will execute the entire family:

> Lo que digo se ha de hacer,
> pues a mi suerte le plugo,
> o en las manos de un verdugo
> tú, tu hija y tu mujer
> moriréis, pues en mi casa
> juntos os tengo a los tres.
> ... ...
> La palabra me has de dar
> de lo que digo, o morir
> luego los tres. (II, 17b)

Confronted with no real alternative, since he is to lose his wife in any case, Alarcos gives his word that he will kill Margarita. In this light his comment that he is choosing honor over dishonor seems to be intentionally ironic on his part:

> Resistir
> no puedo a tanto pesar.
> ¿Mataré a mi dulce esposa?
> Sí, que en aquesta jornada
> escogió la muerte honrada
> por huir de la afrentosa. (II, 17b-18a)

97

In this play, then, Castro makes use of the brute political power of a king to create a tragic situation. The King forces Alarcos to assume a task for which the Count feels no justification. In the ballad Alarcos also kills his wife against his will but he regards obedience to the King as part of his duties, particularly in the light of his own dishonorable act. A modern audience can accept Castro's play more readily and sympathetically than it can *comedias* in which obedience to an unjust king is shown to be intimately bound to a character's sense of worth and honor. Such is the case of the play *La Estrella de Sevilla* where Don Sancho places blind obedience to the King over all other considerations:

> Mas soy caballero,
> y no he de hacer lo que quiero,
> sino lo que debo hacer.
> Pues ¿qué debo obedecer?
> La ley que fuere primero.
> Mas no hay ley que a aquesto obligue.
> Mas sí hay; que aunque injusto el Rey,
> debo obedecer su ley;
> a él después Dios le castigue. (Act II, scene XIII)

A similar statement appears in Castro's own *El perfecto caballero* when Miguel, the character who deems himself the perfect knight, suppresses his own natural reservations towards the King's orders to kill his own friend. Equating his honor with blind obedience, he declares:

> ¿Si es justicia en el rey, o si es malicia?
> Mas de Abra[h]án imite la obediencia,
> y no mire el vasallo
> si el rey imita a Dios en la justicia;
> y así, aunque yo supiera
> que no la tiene el Rey, lo mismo hiciera. (II, 162a)

In the same manner the concept of divine punishment takes on a different form in Castro's *Alarcos* from that in other *comedias*. In the passages from *La Estrella de Sevilla* and *El perfecto caballero* the subject is most concerned with his own duties; when he questions the justice of the act he decides to leave the problem of moral judgment in the hands of God. Obedience and morality are separate spheres for the vassal concerned with his honor. Hence the archetypical «perfect vassal» never curses the king for unjust acts he is ordered to perform, for he never really feels *forced* to obey but accepts obedience to duty as a creed. However, as in *El amor constante,* Castro is not afraid to have his characters curse and condemn the evil king. Alarcos does not respect or revere the King when confronted with the unjust order. He does not feel that he is upholding his honor; rather he feels trapped. Thus he actively calls down God's punishment on the King:

> Castigue Dios soberano
> los que quieren, por mi mano,
> sacarte sin culpa dél. (II, 18b)

He calls the King «Este injusto, este tirano» (II, 20b) and regards his command as:

> el más cruel pensamiento,
> la más injusta venganza,
> el más injusto rigor. (II, 20b)

Before her death the Countess, in one of the few direct passages from the original ballad, calls for divine punishment as well:

> A vos yo os perdono, Conde,
> por el amor que os tenía;
> pero, pues sin culpa muero,
> para dentro en quince días
> al Rey cito y a la Infanta,
> ante la justa justicia. (II, 21b)

Further condemnation of the King comes from the Prince of Hungary, who comes closest at this point to representing the voice of reason and Christian ethics. In the last scene of the act the King is accompanied by two adulatory Grandees who approve of the King's injustices. All are assembled for the marriage of the Count and the Infanta. Once again Castro violently bursts open a moment of ceremony. While on the outside embracing and kissing seem to unite the King, the Count and the Infanta, the Count's asides of grief and ensuing madness, as well as cross-commentary by others as to the Count's distraught state of mind, undercut the ceremonial unity. The explosion occurs with the entrance of the Prince («Suena dentro ruido», II, 24b) as he bursts into the court hurling accusations and releasing the tension of silence with violent statements. It is a scene repeated from the end of Act I of *El amor constante,* a bravura ending aimed at rousing the excitement of the audience by giving vent to feelings the audience wants to hear screamed out but of which it has been deprived. The Prince questions the King's right to call himself king:

> Si eres, Rey, descendiente de otros reyes,
> ¿ha sido hazaña digna de tu pecho
> romper y traspasar las justas leyes?
> ¿Es hazaña de Rey lo que tú hiciste?
> ¿Hiciéranlo los que andan tras los bueyes? (II, 24b)

And he condemns the Count for breaking Christian law by obeying not a king, for he has lost his title by his behavior, but a mere man:

> Dime, Conde traidor; ¿habrás hallado
> en las leyes de amor o en las de Cristo,
>   que el dar la muerte a quien la muerte has dado
> fue cosa justa? Por querello un hombre
> mataste un ángel. (II, 25a)

The Prince's accusation is yet another echo of the sixteenth-century political philosophy that had formed the ideological backdrop of *El amor constante*. Once again a character explicitly declares on the stage of a Spanish theater that a king who does not rule in accordance with Christian morality can no longer be considered a king and that the laws issued by a tyrant are not to be obeyed in conscience.

Although the Count did not freely choose to kill his wife he nonetheless feels himself guilty. Before killing Margarita he accuses himself: «Infinita / es mi maldad» (II, 22a). Thus, Alarcos does not defend himself before the Prince's accusations, for the Prince merely voices what Alarcos himself has internalized in his own conscience. Frozen with guilt he can only stand and watch as the King orders his men to arrest the Prince:[11]

> Gente llueve;
> remediarle no puedo, estando agora
> como un hombre de mármol o de nieve. (II, 25b)

The Count's only release will be through madness.

Much of Act III chronicles the madness of Count Alarcos and many details of the mad scene are modelled after Ariosto's *Orlando furioso*.[12] Like his predecessor Celauro, Alarcos feels personally responsible for his wife's death. In his madness he expresses the hatred he feels towards the King:

> ninguno vendrá a mis manos
> que se escape de mi furia,
>   hasta que el Rey y la Infanta
> me paguen el mal que han hecho. (II, 34a)

But, again like Celauro, Alarcos has difficulty actually carrying through his intention to punish the King.

Contrary to the ballad and to the tragic tone of the first two acts of the *comedia*, Margarita does not die and the child seemingly killed at the end of the first act is saved by the steward who was to have dismembered him. Mother and child, named Carlos, are now living together in the woods. Carlos is a much less potent version of the young

---

[11] Like Leonido, the Prince protests the unjust use of power when the King sends many men to disarm one enemy: «¡Y tantos contra un hombre!» (II, 25b).

[12] Ariosto is also a source for Castro's *El desengaño dichoso*, written around 1599 according to BRUERTON's calculations.

hero type than Leonido, after whom he seems to be modelled.[13] His strength resides less in his physical attributes than in his moral purity, and he takes no real active part in the drama. Castro uses him to put into moral perspective the anti-Christian actions of the King and the Infanta. In one of many «lesson scenes» in Castro's theater [14] the young boy is taught not the lessons of strength and honor but a code founded on reason and Christian morality:

> MARGARITA: ¿Y [quién tienes] por enemigo?
> CARLOS: Al Rey.
> MARGARITA: Y dime: un buen caballero
> ¿qué cosas ha de tener
> para parecerlo?
> CARLOS: Ser
> buen cristiano lo primero.
> ... ...
> MARGARITA: ¿Si le ofenden?
> CARLOS: Mejorarse.
> MARGARITA: ¿Y qué ha de tener?
> CARLOS: Razón.
> ... ...
> MARGARITA: ¿Y al enemigo?
> CARLOS: Estimalle.
> MARGARITA: ¿Y qué más?
> CARLOS: No serle enemigo.
> MARGARITA: Y, sobre todo, ¿qué importa?
> CARLOS: Que diga siempre verdad. (II, 26a-b)

In Carlos there is hope for a renewed Christian order, as the steward Hortensio comments:

> Gran mujer, si cada día,
> la que tú le das, señora,
> diesen los padres de agora,
> menos infames habría. (II, 26b)

Here there is an implied comparison to the way in which the King brought up his daughter.

The repeated statements of protest against the unjust King and his daughter reach their climax in the last scene of the play when Margarita and the Prince take up arms against them. Margarita cries while pursuing the fleeing King:

> Falso, traidor;
> ya todo el cielo ofendido

---

[13] Carlos is younger than Leonido and has not yet developed physical strength. He runs from the lion although he swears to face it again with valor. He falls in love with his sister Elena in a scene similar to Leonido's awakening to love.

[14] We shall find similar scenes in *El nacimiento de Montesinos* and *El perfecto caballero*.

> pienso que quiere que sea
> instrumento de tu muerte. (II, 37a)

And the Prince, recognizing the King, exclaims:

> ¡Qué buena suerte
> en mi venganza se emplea! (II, 37a)

Their violent, weaponed hands are halted in mid-air by the unexpected arrival of the mad Count who sees to his surprise that his wife is alive. The resolution now becomes like that of a typical Lopean *comedia:* the King recognizes his error and is forgiven by his subjects, the Infanta offers to enter a convent as penance for her sins, there are multiple marriages and Carlos is named heir to the throne.

Although Castro spares the life of the King and restores his authority as ruler, the attitude throughout the play continues to be that of *El amor constante*. The King can be forgiven only because no real crime was ever committed. However there exist throughout the *comedia* repeated condemnations of the unjust King and statements that he may licitly be opposed and, as the last scene suggests, perhaps even killed in the name of justice. *El Conde Alarcos* seems to be less a backing away from the ideological stance of his earlier play than an attempt to experiment with the happy ending for which the Spanish public was perhaps already beginning to clamor.

CHAPTER IV

«EL NACIMIENTO DE MONTESINOS»

The dramatic pattern established in the two plays previously discussed is instantly recognizable in yet a third work, *El nacimiento de Montesinos*. Like *El amor constante* and *El Conde Alarcos* it tells of an act of royal injustice perpetrated against an individual loyal subject, which, before long, takes on broader political implications; soon the problem of tyranny spreads to the whole kingdom and threatens its destruction. The cast of central characters is once again headed by three familiar figures: the unjust king, the wrongly persecuted male vassal and the young hero who serves as both avenger of his father and savior of the kingdom. Similarly, we find comments to the effect that the king's will may be superseded when the welfare of the kingdom is in jeopardy, and a dramatic resolution in which the young hero places his just cause above blind submission to the king and breaks the sacred «ley de palacio» in its defense.

Yet, after the nakedly bold presentation and condemnation of the unjust king found in the first two plays, certain aspects of *El nacimiento de Montesinos* come as a startling surprise. Here, in a work roughly contemporary to, or perhaps even antedating, *El Conde Alarcos*[1] and of much the same dramatic mold in certain structural aspects, Castro seems to have adopted the «orthodox», or Lopean, view of kingship. The tyrannical ruler of the earlier plays becomes transformed here into a weak king, deceived and himself ruled by treacherous counselors. The persecuted vassal no longer openly censors the king but instead echoes the seventeenth-century divine right doctrine, hailing the king as God-like even as he rules in error. In his affirmation of the absolute rights of the king, Grimaltos, like the future Rodrigo of the *Mocedades,* subordinates his personal emotions and interests to a higher social ethic. By so doing, he experiences not the psychological disintegration born of unresolved tensions that we find in Celauro and Alarcos but an inner security and integrity. Indeed, to a large degree *El nacimiento de Montesinos* may be

---

[1] BRUERTON, p. 150, dates it tentatively between 1595 and 1602.

read as a celebration of «perfect» unselfish conduct and, as such, as an important antecedent of *Las mocedades del Cid*. Finally, in line with the «Lopean» norm, while the evil *privados* are punished by the now-familiar young hero, the king himself remains revered and untouched.

In attempting to superimpose on the dramatic vision of his earlier plays a new celebrative view of vertical relationships Castro is in effect wedding to an affirmation of the right of resistance to tyranny its very antipode — the unquestioning glorification of monarchy. As a result, the new celebrative pattern so firmly established by the Lopean *comedia* becomes riddled with ambiguity. *El nacimiento de Montesinos* stands as the first of three plays —*El perfecto caballero* and *Las hazañas del Cid* complete the trio— in which the Lopean celebration of social dynamics appears to be both espoused and undercut at the same time. The opposing dramatic worlds of Virués and Lope, and the political doctrines of natural law and divine right are fused into a tense coexistence in these works.

As early as 1913 the French critic Henri Mérimée sensed in certain works of Castro a vague ambivalence vis-à-vis the established norms of the *comedia*.

> Est-ce donc pour ou contre la morale que Guillén de Castro travaillait? ... car le contenu n'est point toujours en rapport avec l'apparence. En réalité, on pourrait dégager du théâtre de Castro, selon la pièce et selon les dispositions de chacun, aussi bien des leçons de grandeur d'âme que des exemples de mauvaise vie.[2]

And once again we are reminded of the almost cryptic comment of Luciano García Lorenzo that there exist in Castro's theater: «Reticencias, ligerezas e idas acerca del honor y de sus leyes... que, aun siendo de una ortodoxia indiscutible, destacan por la fuerza de sus afirmaciones.»[3]

The basic source of Castro's play can be found in two *romances juglarescos* composed in either the fifteenth or sixteenth century[4] and anthologized in *cancioneros* or circulated in *pliegos sueltos*.[5] As with *El Conde Alarcos* Castro alternates between directly citing the original ballads and giving free rein to his imagination. The narration as found in the ballads is, briefly, the following. Grimaltos, a young page who gains the King's confidence by his virtuous conduct, quickly rises in favor to become governor of the King's territories in León as well as

---

[2] MÉRIMÉE, p. 609.
[3] GARCÍA LORENZO, p. 43.
[4] MENÉNDEZ PIDAL, *Romancero hispánico*, I, 262-263.
[5] The romance «Muchas veces oí decir...» is found both in a *pliego suelto* of the sixteenth century and in the *Silva de varios romances* published in Barcelona in 1592. The romance «Cata Francia, Montesinos» is found in the same *pliego suelto*, in the 1582 Barcelona collection and in the *Cancionero de romances* of 1550. Ballad quotes in this chapter are from MENÉNDEZ Y PELAYO, *Antología*, no. 175 and no. 176.

husband to the King's daughter. Jealous of Grimaltos, the treacherous Tomillas convinces the King that the faithful vassal has plotted against the crown and is planning the overthrow of the King. Convinced of these lies the King exiles Grimaltos and his wife from the kingdom. In their flight from the court the Infanta gives birth to a child in the woods and names him Montesinos. Fifteen years later Montesinos avenges his father's offense by returning to Paris, entering the royal palace and killing Tomillas after catching him cheating the King at a game of chess. The King, realizing the truth, restores Grimaltos to his former position of honor.

The ballad is a straightforward tale of treason and revenge; Montesinos' intervention serves simply to avenge his father's offense and carries with it no further political consequences. Guillén de Castro, however, still intrigued by the political and moral ramifications of personal conduct, once again broadens the scope of the narration in the pattern of his previous plays. Going beyond the problem of personal vengeance he explores the political paradox of reconciling the abstract, absolute principle of obedience to royal authority with the concrete, situational reality of a kingdom endangered by the moral blindness of its leader. In Castro's version of the Montesinos story the King's unjust punishment of Grimaltos is a first but crucial step towards the destruction of the moral fabric of the kingdom and towards his own moral deterioration. Grimaltos' code of honor and absolute obedience prevents him from returning to the kingdom to avenge the wrong done to him by Tomillas. But also, and more insidiously, the very homage Grimaltos renders the King will not allow him to deliver the kingdom and the king he honors from the clutches of traitors. It will take a new generation, headed by Montesinos, to set things aright by redefining the nature of obedience. Paradoxically, only by affirming that the King no longer rules as such when blind to reason will Montesinos be able to restore the King to his full dignity as head of state.

The first act of the *comedia* portrays, as in *El Conde Alarcos,* a harmonious relationship between a loyal vassal and a good king about to be destroyed by petty jealousy and unworthy intrigues. The ballad source compresses the period prior to Grimaltos' exile to a few lines, describing the mutual respect shared by king and vassal in the following manner:

> Miren bien, tomando ejemplo, — do buenos suelen mirar,
> cómo el conde, a quien Grimaltos — en Francia suelen llamar,
> llegó en las cortes del rey — pequeño y de poca edad.
> Fue luego paje del rey — del más secreto lugar;
> porque él era muy discreto, — y de él se podía fiar;
> y después de algunos tiempos, — cuando más entró en edad,
> le mandó ser camarero — y secretario real:
> y después le dio un condado, — por mayor honra le dar;
> y por darle mayor honra — y estado en Francia sin par

> lo hizo gobernador, — que el reino pueda mandar.
> Por su virtud y nobleza, — y grande esfuerzo sin par
> le quiso tomar por hijo, — y con su hija le casar.

Castro begins his play at the point where Grimaltos has already risen to the position of the King's most trusted *privado* and the act will dramatize how his good conduct helps elevate him to even greater honors. The act celebrates the triumph of honor and virtue over treachery as well as the King's prudence and discretion in recognizing the true worth of Grimaltos.

In the opening scene the assembled court celebrates the baptism of the King's granddaughter, the child of his recently deceased son. As in the first scene of *Las mocedades del Cid* this harmonious social ceremony which seems to bring the kingdom together in unity is undercut by voices in disaccord. Here, during the ceremony, Grimaltos and Tomillas argue in hushed tones over their respective right to retrieve a flower fallen from the hands of the Infanta. Grimaltos insults Tomillas and they agree to settle the argument outside the palace after the ceremony, since the «ley de palacio» prohibits fighting in the King's presence. Isabela, Tomillas' sister, counsels her brother against fighting Grimaltos in an honest fashion, arguing that Fortune seems now to favor Grimaltos in the court and will probably continue to do so in battle. She suggests instead that they work to reverse the direction of the Wheel of Fortune by causing the King to doubt Grimaltos' loyalty and turn against him. Their objections to the rapid rise in Fortune of Grimaltos anticipate the similar complaints of the courtiers regarding Rodrigo in the first act of the *Mocedades*.

Isabela's seeming interest in her brother's affairs neatly hides an ulterior motive: she herself loves Grimaltos and is jealous of the attention he bestows on the Infanta. Isabela does not appear in any form in the original *romance* and as conceived by Castro she is a figure who harkens back to both the ferocious women of the neo-Senecan theater and to the character of the Infanta in his own *El Conde Alarcos*. Her literary lineage becomes apparent in lines such as the following:

> ¡Qué de enredos encamino!
> ¡Qué de venganzas prevengo! (I, 420a)

In this play the King carries a passion for her and Isabela expects to be able to exploit his unwise love for her to her advantage.

Brother and sister attempt to convince the King that Grimaltos has been secretly dishonoring him by carrying on an amorous affair with his daughter without the King's knowledge. The King, at this point, however, cannot be so easily deceived. Although old and infatuated by Isabela he remains aware of his weaknesses and is on guard against them. As a dutiful ruler, he attempts to subordinate passion to good judgment, as he indicates in his first soliloquy:

> Amor, quien sigue tu ley,
> ¿qué ejemplo dará o qué leyes
> a su reino y a su grey?
> Pues te atreves a los reyes,
> bien puedes llamarte rey.
>   Pues no bastó mi grandeza,
> respetarás a mis canas.   (I, 414b)

His refusal to allow the force of love to rule in his stead signals him as a wise and just ruler. As the play progresses and his will power wears down he will indeed allow others to usurp the throne and replace him as king while he continues to give the appearance of ruling his kingdom.

When he hears Isabela's accusation against Grimaltos he is torn between believing the woman he loves and the man he has taken into his confidence. The king chooses to act honorably and to examine the case with a clear vision:

> pero debe el que es honrado
> huír los ojos al fuego
> de su amoroso cuidado,
> porque no le deje ciego
> aunque le tenga abrasado.
>   Que ha sido invidia sospecho
> esta acusación cruel
> del Conde; sin duda es fiel,
> que el corazón en mi pecho
> está volviendo por él.   (I, 415b)

In his rejection of the blindness of passion he contrasts sharply with the king of *El amor constante* whom he will begin to imitate in words and deeds beginning in the second act. Here not only does the King protect himself from blindness but he also sharpens his vision and sees clearly into the hearts of the traitors by observing their gestures. He notices Tomillas' wan face as the coward tries to tell his story to the King:

> Pues ¿cómo el color difunto,
> Tomillas?   (I, 416a)

After a few words it becomes apparent from his face that he is lying; the King says in an aside that «En su semblante / vi su engaño» (I, 416a). The King recognizes in Tomillas' story the plotting of a coward without honor and sees in Grimaltos a steady and constant attitude of loyalty. Throughout these scenes there is a deliberate weighing of evidence and a desire on the part of the King not to fall prey to circumstantial evidence.

In a subsequent scene which has no grounding in the Grimaltos ballads we see the King successfully using his power to maintain order in a kingdom beset by petty strife. Reinaldos, Oliveros and Roldán [6] are almost comic characters in the manner in which they are ready to fight each other over any little point of honor. Contrasted to the dignity of Grimaltos these Carolingean heroes are fickle and more concerned with themselves than with the kingdom. Whereas Grimaltos keeps before him the «ley de palacio» and refuses to fight Tomillas within the confines of the palace, Reinaldos and Roldán bicker openly before the King. The first time they are disruptive the King threatens them with exile:

> ¿En mi presencia arrogancia?
> ... ...
> ¡Esta cólera francesa
> pienso desterrar de Francia! (I, 417b)

The second time he threatens to incarcerate them for breaking these laws and embarrasses them publicly by chiding them for their failure to act in accordance with their station:

> De quien sois os enajena
> la cólera que os abrasa;
> sea la cárcel vuestra casa
> y mi desgracia la pena
> del que mis leyes traspasa. (I, 419a)

All of Castro's kings examined so far react similarly to overt threats to the peace of the kingdom. In every case, vassals who break the «ley de palacio» are either punished or threatened with punishment. The reaction of the king is always spontaneous and angry. Castro uses this repeated scene for different purposes. When a just king is involved, as here, the anger takes on a positive shading: the king is attempting to maintain order and suppress strife. In the case of an unjust king, as in *El Conde Alarcos* and, to a degree, in the second act of *El nacimiento de Montesinos,* the king's reaction is like that of an angry Old Testament God, blinded by fury and unable to see beyond the immediate situation to discover the underlying truth. The king's anger indicates justice in the first case, blindness in the second.

Castro uses this scene as an ironic foreshadowing of the main action of the play. With the threat of banishment the audience acquainted with

---

[6] The mention of these heroes clearly identifies the King as Charlemagne; however Castro, following the ballad, merely calls him «el Rey». Clearly, Castro was concerned with a generic king figure and did not want his personal vision of problematic royal authority to be diluted by any associations the audience might have had with the historical-legendary figure of King Charlemagne.

the ballad is reminded that the wrath which now righteously strikes out against the frivolous bickering that threatens to disrupt the peace of the kingdom will soon be blindly directed at the loyal Grimaltos. Later in the play Castro will underline a second irony: while here the King's ire is a reaction to the threat of disorder, in the second act the King's unjust anger at Grimaltos is the first step towards the very disorder which he endeavors to contain here.

Central to Castro's amplification of his source material are the references to *Genesis* used to illuminate the special relationship that exists between the King and Grimaltos. In the first act parallels are established between the King and God, between Grimaltos and Adam, and also between Grimaltos and the loyal angels. Whereas in *Genesis* God exiles Adam from the garden of Eden into the wilderness because of Adam's disobedience and his attempt to usurp divine power, the King of *Montesinos*, lacking omniscience and blinded by passion, does not see that his creation has not sinned, and he wrongly punishes him. Grimaltos is a sinless Adam, and the King a God who unwittingly destroys himself by punishing the noblest of his subjects.

The first use of this Biblical imagery occurs when Isabela accuses the Count of assuming powers not granted him by the King. She claims that although the King has already raised Grimaltos to a position close to his own, the Count aspires even higher in seeking the favors of his monarch's daughter. Isabela presents the King as inhabiting Heaven and as having raised Grimaltos to his own eminence:

> Ese Conde poco fiel
> a quien subiste a tu cielo,
> pues arroja rayos dél. (I, 415a)

She advises the King to clip Grimaltos' wings before he dares fly even higher:

> ... las alas que le diste.
> Porque no vuele tan alto
> cortárselas te conviene. (I, 415b)

The King cannot be convinced by Isabela's lies at this juncture because he cannot imagine a creature of his own making disobeying his laws. He refers to Grimaltos as «mi hechura» (I, 415b), an image that will be expanded in the following scene. When the King sees that Grimaltos carries his loyalty so far as to even report the incident of the Infanta's dropped flower and return the flower to him, the King rejoices and desires to bring Grimaltos even closer to him:

> ¡No en balde te levanté
> casi a igualarte conmigo!
> Estoy por darte a mi lado
> asiento. (I, 418a)

The greatest test of Grimaltos' loyalty comes from the Infanta herself who, yearning to consummate her love, tempts Grimaltos to betray the King's confidence in him. Grimaltos laments his lower social status that bars him from ever hoping to marry the royal princess; though he has been made king-like he dares not presume to be the King's equal. The scene is filled with direct references to *Genesis*. The Infanta, like Satan and Eve, tempts Grimaltos to taste the forbidden fruit, claiming that he need not feel inferior to his lord:

>   Eres, amor,
> señor del mundo absoluto.
> ... ...
>   Soy el fruto
> que te ofrece aquella flor. (I, 420b)

But unlike Adam, Grimaltos heeds the words of his master:

>   ¡Qué dichoso fuera yo
> si me atreviera a cogello!
> ... ...
>   mas como vedado ha sido
> al grande como al pequeño,
> es de mí como su dueño,
> respetado y no cogido. (I, 420b)

The Infanta makes even more explicit the connection between Grimaltos and Adam. She sees their situation as that of Adam rejecting the coaxings of Eve:

>   Si nuestro padre primero [i.e. Adam]
> como tú se resistiera
> por comelle, no perdiera
> la gracia del mundo entero,
> pues no te falta mujer,
> que te obligue. (I, 420b)

In rejecting the advances of the Infanta Grimaltos stands closer to the Cid than does his predecessor, the Count Alarcos. When Alarcos refuses to cede to the Infanta, claiming that he will not offend his king's honor, he experiences no conflict of loyalties because he does not love the Infanta. Grimaltos, on the other hand, feels the pull of amorous passion but rises above his emotions. Like Rodrigo he places duty above love. Depicting his passion as a tempting serpent he arms himself with reason:

> GRIMALTOS: ... [he doesn't lack] Y aun serpiente
>   que me incite y que me tiente.
> INFANTA: Poco astuta debe ser.
>   ¿Quién es ella?

GRIMALTOS: Mi deseo,
    pero tiene a la razón
    por defensa. (I, 420b-421a)

The language used by Grimaltos and the Infanta soon turns to images of God and the fallen angels. The Infanta tempts the Count to raise himself higher than the King has already allowed:

Si él te levanta en sus hombros
para que llegues a mí;
  si al cielo de su privanza
  un Rey a subirte viene,
¿qué temes? (I, 421a)

... ...
¿cómo no vuelas más alto
con las alas que te doy?
  Pues el Rey las da mayores
  a todo cuanto pretendes,
¿cómo agora no las tiendes
al viento de mis favores? (I, 421b)

Grimaltos' response is that he will not imitate Lucifer by trying to usurp the King's powers:

que sería ser Luzbel,
si de su cielo en su ausencia
pretendiese sin licencia
sacar los ángeles dél.
  Cuando más en mí confía
  tengo de preciarme más
  de leal. (I, 421a)

Grimaltos lives by a code of absolute obedience and identifies his personal honor with his adherence to that code. For him an offense to the King's honor is tantamount to a personal affront:

no ha de ofenderse mi honor
ni tan sólo en un cabello;
y pues que le ofende aquello
que ofenda al Rey, mi señor,
  sería inconsiderado,
  sin valor, respeto y ley,
  si pierdo, ofendiendo al Rey,
  la honra que el Rey me ha dado. (I, 422a)

Grimaltos consider his own will merely an extension of the King's. When the King realizes this, he rewards Grimaltos by elevating him to a position even closer to that of the monarch, an act the King sees as imitating God's act of creation:

>   quisiera en esta jornada
>   por igualalle a los dos, [i.e. Grimaltos and the Infanta]
>   que fuera imitar a Dios
>   el hacer algo de nada.
>   ... ...
>   le daré lo que él no quiso,
>   que es la mano de la Infanta. (I, 423b)

Grimaltos will not only be an extension of the King's will but also an extension of his person:

>   es mi gusto que en León
>   represente mi persona. (I, 423b)

Grimaltos' elevation is possible, then, not through revolt but through a submission to and acceptance of the King's will. For him, the only legitimate rise in power is not the audacious flight propelled by his own ambition but an ascension sanctioned by the King himself. This same Stoic-Christian submission to the royal will that makes Grimaltos indifferent to the lust for power will protect him from inner destruction when the King turns against him and strips him of his worldly honors in the next act.

Act I, then, represents a state of perfect social harmony, celebrated time and again in the Lopean *comedia*. This harmony depends on both king and subject accepting the demands of their social roles and rejecting any personal concerns which stand in opposition to their duties. Both the King and Grimaltos refuse to allow love to cloud their reason. In this situation a firm vertical relationship is established: the subject is always subordinate to the king, but this does not preclude his being honored by his monarch. In this relationship the king imitates God and the subject his flawless creation. The result is the flourishing of an earthly Paradise where the subject rises in Fortune and is rewarded with a share in kingly power.

Act II repeats the problem of the first act —here the traitors will once again plot against Grimaltos— with one important difference: while Grimaltos remains constant to his creed the King falls prey to passion. In Castro's adaptation of the myth of Genesis, it is not Adam but God who sins. As the King descends into the darker regions of illicit passion he, like the king of *El amor constante,* abdicates his reason, his judgment and, ultimately, his throne, by allowing others to rule in his stead. His banishment of Grimaltos becomes symbolic of the exile from himself of all those qualities that designate him a legitimate ruler. Grimaltos, for his part, remains unflinchingly loyal to his principles even as he falls from the grace of the King and Fortune. He rejects suggestions that he oppose the now unjust King, as well as the notion that the King has become a tyrant. Instead, he continues to consider his ruler a God. Grimaltos stoically accepts the King's right to take away his privileges, affirming in almost religious language that what the King has bestowed he may also reclaim. This attitude of constancy to his beliefs, regardless of how the King may choose to reward or punish him, approaches the Christian ethic that Calderón was to dramatize in allegorical terms in *El gran teatro del mundo,* and in the lesson that Segismundo learns in *La vida es sueño.* Act II, then, celebrates the code of perfect loyalty that allows for the inner triumph of Grimaltos over adversity. At the same time it will begin to intimate that this set of principles will need to be set aside, at least momentarily, for justice and harmony to be restored to the kingdom and for the King to be saved from himself.

The theme of the Fall from Fortune appears in the original *romances* in connection with Grimaltos:

> mas fortuna que es mudable, — y no puede sosegar,
> quiso serle tan contraria — por su estado le quitar.

As Act II begins we find Grimaltos and his wife five years later in León. Grimaltos has served his King well as governor but in spite of his success he is plagued by dreams and omens of an imminent fall from Fortune:

> pues si a la cumbre he llegado
> del contento, y la fortuna
> no conserva firme estado,
>   recelo que no esté queda
> y que de un bien soberano
> a un gran mal traerme pueda. (I, 425a)

These premonitions are concretized in a symbolic dream, almost directly quoted from the original *romance,* in which the King is portrayed as a persecuted eagle who destroys the very people and city that shelter him from his enemy:

> Soñando, Infanta querida,
> una águila vi volar
> con seis halcones tras ella,
> que persiguiéndola van.
> Ella, por guardarse dellos,
> se retrajo a mi cuidad,
> y una torre, la más alta,
> por asiento fue a tomar;
> por el pico echaba fuego,
> por las alas alquitrán,
> el fuego que della sale
> la tierra quiere abrasar,
> quemábame a mí las barbas
> y a vos, señora, el brial;
> pues un sueño como éste
> ¿qué puede ser sino mal?

> El águila perseguida
> es la persona real;
> los alcones [sic], los traidores
> que el fuego encendido habrán;
> tendránle el pecho abrasado,
> de donde resultará
> que indignado arroje fuego
> y a los dos quiera quemar.[7] (I, 425b-426a)

The dream shows the King irrationally striking against his most faithful followers. The fire that consumes him is both the fire of amorous passion and the fire of anger.[8]

The dream is all too soon realized as Roldán enters announcing that the King, tricked into believing that Isabela is pregnant, has married the treacherous woman. The King, who in the first act was able to see beyond other men and into the hearts and motives of his subjects, is now blinded. This blindness is referred to at various times throughout the act:

> ciego en el alma y loco en el sentido. (I, 426b)

> ... deja a escuras la ley
> sin la luz de la razón. (I, 427b)

> Pon límites a tus rigores,
> y, si lo adviertes mejor,
> verás como no es traidor. (I, 430a)

> Y mira en esta ocasión,
> si acaso lo puedes ver. (I, 430a)

The nature of the blindness is most ironic because of the specific accusation leveled against Grimaltos. Tomillas has set up events to make it appear that Grimaltos now aspires to be king, the very same sin of pride that the King saw Grimaltos incapable of committing in the first act. By keeping the essential nature of the accusation as well as Grimaltos' unflinching loyalty as constants Castro has now reworked the situation of Act I with one major variant: the blindness and confusion of the King.

---

[7] The passage as it appears in the original *romance* is as follows:

> Aunque en sueños no fiemos — no sé a qué parte lo echar,
> que parecía muy cierto — que vi una águila volar,
> siete halcones tras ella — mal aquejándola van,
> y ella por guardarse de ellos — retrújose a mi ciudad;
> encima de una alta torre — allí se fuera a asentar;
> por el pico echaba fuego, — por las alas alquitrán;
> el fuego que de ella sale — la ciudad hace quemar;
> a mí quemaba las barbas — y a vos quemaba el brial.
> ¡Cierto tal sueño como éste — no puede ser sino mal!

The juglar, unlike Castro, does not explain the imagery to the listener and leaves the audience to unravel the meaning of the mystery.

[8] In the ballad the King is not in love and the fire represents only his ire.

The King in the first act begged Love to respect his old age. When he first appears on stage in the second act we see him leaving behind the dignity of his years and aspiring to act as a younger man. Rather than reacting cautiously and prudently to false accusations as a wise old man, he now acts impulsively and worries about his physical strength and virility:

> Verán las gentes villanas
> que en esta edad tengo brío
> escondido entre estas canas. (I, 427b)

His language becomes laden with the ornate artificialities of courtly love rhetoric as he regresses to the behavior of an earlier age. The audience would certainly regard as a humorous breach of decorum lines such as the following in the mouth of a white-haired ancient:

> ¡Ah, mi bien! El agua cese
> de los soles que conquisto,
> del alma sumo interese;
> llover con sol ya se ha visto,
> pero no que el sol lloviese. (I, 428a)

As in *Conde Alarcos* Castro relies on interruptions of the even flow of verse to portray the king's fury: stammering («Y tú, villa... tú villano», I, 428b) and the king's breaking-in to stop explanations, self-righteously shutting out the truth («No me respondas / ... No me repliques»; I, 428b). The King is not only blinded but also deafened to the truth.

Although Grimaltos attempts to defend himself in the face of false accusations, he surrenders himself totally to the King's will, placing his life in his ruler's hands:

> ... tu hechura soy,
> manda deshacer tu hechura. (I, 428b)
>
> que ésta la cabeza es
> que tú mismo levantaste,
>   y como de cosa tuya
> puedes disponer, señor. (I, 428b)

Grimaltos allows that the King has a right to reclaim all he has given him. His language approaches that of the true Christian who, at the moment of death, does not begrudge God the right to take him from the world:

> y todo cuanto me quita
> le debo al Rey mi señor.
>   Quiere cobrar, Dios le guarde,
> sea ansí, pues yo me fundo
> en que lo que presta el mundo
> se paga temprano o tarde.
>   Rapaz y pobre llegué

> a su casa, y cosa es justa
> salir della, pues él gusta,
> de la manera que entré. (I, 431a)

If Grimaltos' words are reminiscent of Christian resignation they are not without dramatic irony. While Grimaltos obeys the King as if he were God, the allusions to irrational Fortune and the obvious manipulation of the King by the traitors underline the distance between the King and God. Grimaltos purposely disregards the all-too-human failings of the King. His obedience knows no exceptions; it denies the existence of the accidental.

A strong contrast to the self-negating Grimaltos may be found in the more volatile, emotional character of Roldán who, like Celauro and Alarcos before him, openly protests what he deems an act of tyranny. When first faced with the King's unjust decision to banish Grimaltos, Roldán too tries to contain his feelings and maintain respect for the King. In an aside he expresses the conflict he feels between his impulse to rebel and his obligation to honor the King:

> ¡Que esto sufro, que esto escucho!
> Reniego de mi paciencia.
> ¡Ah, conservada lealtad,
> ya me tienes de un cabello! (I, 429b)[9]

Seeing, however, that the King cannot be moved even by the Infanta's pleas Roldán speaks out in open anger against the King, calling him «de bronce» and «león» (I, 430a). But he still tries to hold back the full thrust of his anger, as he stops himself from proclaiming a more severe accusation of tyranny:

> Eres tú mi Rey, y eres...
> iba a decirte tirano. (I, 430b)

Grimaltos rebukes Roldán for speaking out for him, and Roldán, like Celauro, feels remorse for having allowed his feelings to supersede his vow of obedience:

> GRIMALTOS: advierte cómo confío
> que es nuestro Rey.
> ROLDÁN: Dices bien. (I, 430b)

But his repentance comes too late. As the King's anger comes to a head he banishes Roldán as well. Roldán's reaction to this order is the exact

---

[9] In a pattern that seems to be a trademark of Castro this scene of held-in asides is followed by a noisy disruption breaking the silence: «Suena ruido» (I, 429b). The particular disturbance here foreshadows the *Mocedades*: it is the Infanta who seeks justice from the King, a scene not in the ballad source. The scene in *Montesinos*, however, lacks the momentum that Ximena's entrance achieves by the use of *romance*.

opposite of that of Grimaltos; he does not submit meekly but rather threatens open rebellion:

¡Oh, reniego!
Dejaré un Rey que está ciego;
iréme a Brava o Anglante;
y aún verá Roldán quien es,
si mira este acero el sol,
pasando al suelo español
y no amparando el francés. (I, 430b)

Another figure carried over from Castro's previous plays is the woman who defies the king. In *El amor constante* it is Nísida who keeps threatening the King with dethronement while Celauro wavers between carrying through his opposition and retreating; in *El Conde Alarcos* Margarita preaches to her son a hatred of the King and herself takes arms against him while Alarcos is compelled to contain his protest; and in *Montesinos* it is the Infanta who speaks out against the King while Grimaltos remains submissive. When her pleas to her father for mercy fall on deaf ears she suggests rebellion to her husband:

Francia se habrá de perder;
amigos tenéis y espada. (I, 431a)

But, as in the first act, Grimaltos resists the temptation offered by his wife; he replies that her plan does not befit a man of honor:

Sois mujer apasionada
y hablastes como mujer. (I, 431a)

The figures of Roldán and the Infanta are not without their ambivalency in these scenes. On the surface it would seem that Castro views their reactions negatively. As in the first act, Castro appears to use Roldán as a model of less than exemplary conduct in order to throw into relief the saintlike submission of Grimaltos; and, again repeating the pattern of the previous act, the Infanta represents a temptation Grimaltos must overcome in order to remain true to his ideals. But the Count's deification of his monarch is placed in an ironic context even as it is celebrated and, given that context, the words and actions of Roldán and the Infanta are not without their justification. As the play develops it becomes apparent that the King no longer rules as such and that blind adoration of him only leads to the perpetuation of further injustices and, ultimately, the destruction of the state. Though Castro tries to steer clear of portraying this King as an out-and-out tyrant, he is either unable or unwilling to renounce fully the validity of the moral and ideological stand of his earlier plays as represented here by these two characters. Indeed, the intervention of Montesinos in the third act will stand midway between the loyalty of Grimaltos and the call for resistance of the others.

Towards the middle of the second act there begins to occur a shifting of emphasis from the private situation of Grimaltos to the public problem of the besieged kingdom. Grimaltos' exile takes on tones not so much of a personal tragedy for the Count as of a misfortune for the state, for while Grimaltos remains spiritually whole both the King and the kingdom begin to disintegrate. The King's language towards the end of the act reveals how his love for the treacherous Isabela causes him to do violence to himself:

> Por ver alegres tus ojos
> me sacara yo los míos. (I, 433a)

His mad passion has him willing to believe half-truths and almost knowingly deceive himself:

> Con todo lo estimo mucho,
> aunque lo digas mintiendo. (I, 433b)

The King is even somewhat aware of the wrongness of his actions. With the passing of the first flush of anger he suspects that love now holds more power over him than reason, but is unwilling and unable to return to his former self. In his soliloquy the audience looks into the heart of a man who contemplates his own self-betrayal and who wills his destruction:

> ¡Ay, Infanta! Dite el ser,
> tratéte con sinrazones;
> pero ¡qué de obligaciones
> atropella una mujer!
>   Mas del pasado desdén
> las causas injustas pruebo,
> pues en el alma te llevo,
> y aun a Grimaltos también. (I, 434a)

In the third act, the play assumes a radical change of focus, passing from the private to the public as the King's personal conduct threatens the political life of the kingdom. In the previous act, the King's surrender to passion carried with it limited and essentially personal implications: by ceding to irrational love the King was betraying himself, failing to act in a manner befitting both a ruler and a man of his years and wisdom. As we have seen, though his unjust anger is directed at Grimaltos, the latter, by remaining faithful to his principles, rises above the immediate situation and affirms his integrity in the face of adversity. Hence, the real victim of the King's wrath is not Grimaltos but the King himself. However in this last act, which takes place some fifteen years later, we learn that with the gradual disintegration of the King's personality comes a similar disintegration of the kingdom; just as traitors control the King's critical faculties so do they guide the state towards destruction.

Enrique, one of Grimaltos' twin sons, describes this new and hopeless situation thus:

> Veo perdida Francia, está mi agüelo [10]
> tan caduco en la edad como en el seso;
> gobierna una mujer, una traidora.
> No asisten en París los doce Pares,
> por esto retirados a sus tierras:
> no hay razón, ni justicia... (I, 447a)

Thus, by the last act *El nacimiento de Montesinos* reaches a familiar impasse: the difficulty of reconciling the abstract principle of absolute loyalty to the monarch with the patent reality that the King has betrayed his office and, in so doing, endangered the welfare of the state. Paradoxically, the very law of perfect conduct that saves Grimaltos from the disintegration faced by Celauro and Alarcos contributes towards this same destruction of the kingdom since it refuses to come to terms with political reality and remains in the world of abstract principles. The mandate of absolute obedience which is intended to maintain order ironically puts the state in jeopardy, since it leaves subjects powerless against a lawless king; Grimaltos cannot save the kingdom and remain absolutely loyal to the King at the same time.

This dramatic impasse is resolved yet again by the intervention of the young son of the persecuted protagonist, a character who continues to be associated with the concepts of divine and natural laws. The character of Montesinos is, of course, central to the *romances* on which Castro based his play. But these earlier ballads limit themselves to a narration of personal revenge; Montesinos, moved by the discovery of his father's affront, seeks permission to exact vengeance from Tomillas:

> Montesinos que lo oyera — los ojos volvió a su padre;
> las rodillas por el suelo — empezóle de rogar
> le quisiese dar licencia, — que en París quiere pasar,
> y tomar sueldo del rey — si se lo quisiere dar,
> por vengarse de Tomillas, — su enemigo mortal;
> que si sueldo del rey toma — todo se puede vengar.

Castro does not eliminate the vengeance motif but, as in the previous plays, superimposes on it that of the son as restorer of moral and political order and saviour of the kingdom.

The association of Montesinos with divine law begins in Act II in the language describing the birth of Grimaltos' sons. Previously, Isabela and Tomillas had sent off their henchman Duardos to kill Grimaltos

---

[10] There seems to be some error here on the part of the copier of the manuscript or of Castro himself, for while Enrique is the King's grandson, at this point he really believes himself to be the King's son. I shall explain this plot complication later.

and the Infanta. But Duardos, seeing the hardships suffered by the couple while fleeing from the kingdom as well as their mutual devotion and their fall from Fortune, is moved to compassion. Not only does he refuse to kill them but he even helps save their newborn twins from an attacking beast. He explains that he was inspired by reason and divine law:

> ... obligóme en la ley
> de la razón la de Dios. (I, 436a)

The birth of the twins is regarded as a divine miracle:

> ... pues Dios
> os dio por milagro dos. (I, 436a)
>
> Yo imagino
> que este suceso es del cielo. (I, 436b)

The reason for this reaction is that Isabela had commanded Duardos to bring her a child whom she would claim to be her child by the King. This false offspring would then be declared heir to the throne. The «miraculous» twin birth, however, allows Duardos to sabotage Isabela's plan by offering to the kingdom as heir the King's own grandson. A second son never appears in the *romance* version of the Montesinos tale; it is purely Castro's own elaboration of the plot. In the play the two sons, Montesinos and Enrique, assume mutually complementary functions: Montesinos, brought up in the natural world, will spontaneously and even violently reject the rules of courtly behavior to right what he instinctively senses to be a wrong, while Enrique, raised in the court, will voice the ideological rationale for opposing the King's will.

Montesinos is a child of nature, a wild child of primitive strength and instincts. Since his function is not to replace the old order but merely to restore that order, Castro does not portray him as the embodiment of right and Christian order, as he does with Leonido, but rather as the destroyer of the evil forces corrupting the kingdom. In spite of the ironies of the play, it is still Grimaltos, and not Montesinos, who is seen as its moral hero. Unlike Grimaltos, who embodies the restraint of passion, Montesinos bursts forth with unbridled anger and emotion, tearing up the countryside, fighting brutally with animals and swearing at his parents when they anger him. Grimaltos attempts to correct these violent excesses and to train him in the courtly code of conduct while stressing the need to avenge affronts. He preaches long lessons to his son on honor,[11] faith, the art of fighting and, especially, vengeance. While

---

[11] Grimaltos' lessons on conduct include a definition of honor in its double guise as *honor* and *honra*. Grimaltos tells his son that to be honorable one must act with honor *(honor)* but that it is also necessary to be esteemed honorable by others *(honra)*.

Grimaltos' own conduct exemplifies the holding in of emotions he tells his son to seek vengeance immediately when his honor is in jeopardy.[12] Like Diego Laínez, Grimaltos puts Montesinos through various tests to see how he reacts to affronts to his honor; when Montesinos proves himself to be quick to seek vengeance Grimaltos approves («Esta cólera bendigo», I, 440b).

The connection between the betrayal of Grimaltos and the imminent destruction of the kingdom literally bursts onto the stage before the eyes of the public by means of a type of scene encountered previously in Castro's plays: the scene of the hunt. It was the hunt which brought the problems of the court into the pastoral world of Leonido in *El amor constante* and here too it introduces Montesinos to a new and larger set of problems and emotions than those of his childhood. Here it is a person who is being hunted — Francelina, the grandchild of the King, whose baptism was celebrated at the very opening of the *comedia*. Francelina is the physical symbol of the kingdom itself —her very name is derived from that of the kingdom, Francia— weak, and persecuted by traitors. She laments the reign of disorder plaguing France:

> los traidores han vencido
> y los leales han muerto. (I, 441b)

Francelina is being pursued by Isabela's henchmen when Montesinos miraculously appears, as if out of nowhere, to save her. The young girl sees this as an act of divine intervention:

> Para mí es cierto que ha sido
> ángel del cielo enviado. (I, 442a)

Her description of Montesinos' physical struggle with the two lackeys suggest that the Wheel of Fortune is beginning to return to a position favorable to the just:

> mas de suerte mata y hiere
> con su ñudoso bastón
> que parece rodeado,
> cuándo abajo, cuándo arriba,
> la fortuna que derriba
> estos hombres de su estado. (I, 442a)

---

[12] Castro makes it clear that Grimaltos has not lost honor by waiting so long to avenge his offense (had honor been at stake the play might have developed differently). It is Tomillas who is without honor because he never properly avenged his own lost honor in the first act. Thus Grimaltos says in Act III (I, 422b): «No afrenta quien tiene afrenta; / y... es cierto que no afrenta / un mentís de un desmentido.» Similarly, when the Infanta tells her son about the offense she makes it clear that Grimaltos still has honor and has only been the victim of treachery: «Privación de estado ha sido / con traición, pero no afrenta» (I, 441a). Had it been a true affront Grimaltos would have had to take care of it immediately.

As in the earlier plays, the young hero's first encounter with a woman from the court awakens a new sensation of love and physical yearning. He finds himself drawn to the court out of these new feelings for Francelina and when he asks his parents for permission to leave home and enter Paris it is to meet the girl once again and serve as her protector. Thus the play suggests that while Montesinos is drawn to the court by his love for Francelina, his primary mission is the deliverance of the besieged kingdom.

It is only after this deliverance motif is stated that the theme of vengeance is superimposed. Montesinos hopes to avenge his father while in Paris, not yet understanding that the problem of Francelina and that of Grimaltos stem from the same cause:

> Licencia, padres, os pido
> pues para esto [i.e. to see and protect Francelina] la quiero;
> mas he de saber primero
> quién decís que os ha ofendido;
> que en olvido no ha quedado
> vuestra ofensa. (I, 449a)

In response to his son's query Grimaltos reveals the treachery of Tomillas. In this scene Castro makes some subtle but important changes from his source. The dramatist cites the beginning lines of the original *romance* verbatim:

> Cata Francia, Montesinos;
> cata París, la ciudad; (I, 449a)

but he develops the rest of the passage quite independently of the ballad in *redondillas* rather than in *romance* meter. In the ballad Grimaltos tells his son of the affront immediately after training him in the use of arms and without Montesinos' probing question, suggesting that all along Grimaltos was preparing the boy to act as his avenger. The Grimaltos of Castro's play seems to be more reluctant to get his son involved with this matter, for he withholds this vital information from him until the last possible moment, that is, until Montesinos himself seeks to know the truth. Even then, Grimaltos does not openly suggest that the boy punish Tomillas. As in the case of Celauro's speech to Leonido, Castro's treatment of the «revelation» scene is purposely ambiguous; just as Celauro wanted Leonido to avenge him but could not reconcile this wish with his desire to act in a Christian manner, so Grimaltos feels a conflict between his desire for vengeance and his vow of obedience to the King's will, since to send Montesinos into Paris under his orders would be tantamount to his own unauthorized return. Not wishing to compromise in any way the «perfection» of Grimaltos, Castro craftily cuts short his speech to Montesinos:

> y pues tu madre es la Infanta,
> pues tan obligado estás...
> ¡No puedo decirte más,
> tengo un ñudo en la garganta! (I, 449b)

The younger generation, however, is less willing to sit back and blindly pay homage to the King. It is Francelina who first states that the King no longer rules as such; though he wears the crown he has ceded his powers to others, and «sólo de Rey tiene el nombre» (I, 445a). Enrique, lamenting a situation in which traitors have banished reason and justice from the land, decides to take matters into his own hands. He seeks out his father and exhorts him to take his rightful place in the court:

> Determinado he venido
> y el cómo traigo trazado
> de que volváis al estado
> de los dos tan merecido. (I, 450b)

Yet Grimaltos refuses to oppose the King's will and retorts, «Si gusta el Rey, mi señor» (I, 450b), to which Enrique replies that the King is in no position to distinguish right from wrong and that loyal subjects must assume the responsibility of protecting the kingdom from tyranny:

> A su corona conviene;
> tiranizada la tiene
> una ingrata y un traidor,
> y han de llevar por mi mano
> castigo sus desatinos. (I, 450b)

The notion that the King's will may and must be cast aside in matters concerning the welfare of the state is further underscored in the final scene of the play. The King's self-destructiveness is symbolized in the chess game he is playing with Tomillas. His inability and unwillingness to judge his situation rationally is revealed in his attitude towards the game; he plays against Tomillas knowing full well that he will lose:

> Perderé si a tal me obligo;
> pero juega, que contigo
> juego yo para perder. (I, 451a)

In his blindness he does not see the false moves made by Tomillas right before his eyes. It is Montesinos who will show the King his errors. The young boy, describing himself as a «jugador milagroso» (I, 451a), asks the King's permission to enter the court and take the King's place in the game. Though he awaits the King's reply, like Leonido he declares that he will enter with or without the King's consent:

> él [i.e. Montesinos] se toma la licencia
> cuando el Rey no se la dé. (I, 451a)

Thus, Montesinos pays homage to the King on one hand while acknowledging his right to place the cause of justice above the royal will. When Montesinos catches Tomillas cheating he takes control of the situation, breaking the «ley de palacio» by striking Tomillas on the head with the chess board and killing him. Again, Montesinos' words at this juncture stand ambivalently between respect and defiance:

> Perdone tu Majestad,
> que así mi mano sangrienta
> da venganzas a una afrenta
> y castiga una maldad. (I, 452a-b)

Tomillas confesses the truth before dying and the King, at first angered by Montesinos' daring liberties, interprets his actions as divinely sanctioned. Grimaltos is restored to his proper place in society and Montesinos is promised to Francelina. Finally, and once again somewhat ambivalently, the King will continue ruling the kingdom, but he will be succeeded by Montesinos.

Throughout *El nacimiento de Montesinos,* then, Guillén de Castro continuously plays off opposing points of view to create a play of ambivalent values. The play may be read as either a bowing to the «Lopean» view of kingship or as a defiance of it. In the *comedia,* though the King is not literally a tyrant, it is through his weakness that tyranny is allowed to reign; though Grimaltos' loyalty is apparently celebrated it is also shown to be potentially dangerous and perhaps even invalid in certain critical circumstances; though Montesinos openly assaults Tomillas and not the King he must defy the King and ignore his authority (even while seeming to defer to it) in order to do so. Similarly Montesinos' intervention may be seen as an act of vengeance directed at Tomillas or as a conscious attempt to restore justice to the kingdom. This ambivalent relationship to the new «establishment» view of kingship (as Maravall would have it) will continue to riddle the next two plays of this study, *El perfecto caballero* and *Las hazañas del Cid.*

CHAPTER V

«EL PERFECTO CABALLERO»

The problem of coming to terms with an unjust ruler that dominates Castro's early plays reappears in a play of what we may term his «middle period», *El perfecto caballero*. Dated by Bruerton as probably written between the years 1610 and 1615, it is contemporary to the *Mocedades del Cid*.[1] If we rely on Bruerton's chronology as well as on textual similarities and details that suggest that the hero of this play, Miguel Centellas, and Rodrigo may have been consciously related in Castro's mind, then we discover a curious complementary but antithetical relationship between the two plays. While in the *Mocedades* Castro dramatizes in celebrative tones Rodrigo's adherence to a demanding code of honor, the hero placing his fame and duty above the more «base» passion of love, in *El perfecto caballero* another aspect of this creed, absolute submission to the monarch, is questioned and seen as morally problematic. The latter *comedia* re-examines the ironic situation of a «perfect knight» who abases himself before an unworthy king (as in the earlier *Nacimiento de Montesinos*) and who is trapped into committing immoral acts in the name of honor (a problem that harkens back in part to *El Conde Alarcos*). Castro's answer to the problem that is posed by the conflict of morality and honor is typically ambiguous: the play will seem both to praise its hero's ideals and to celebrate the assassination of the tyrant by another less idealized, but nonetheless sympathetic, character.

Briefly, the story of *El perfecto caballero* is the following. The setting is the royal court of the kingdom of Naples where the unhappily married King seeks to win the love of Diana. He had been forced to marry the Queen for political reasons: his father had violently deposed the rightful king, grandfather of the present queen, and, to avoid further bloodshed, the Pope intervened and arranged for the present marriage. Though

---

[1] BRUERTON, p. 150, dates the *Mocedades* as written between 1612 (?) and 1618 (?) and then again as between 1612 (?) and 1615 (?). We cannot ignore the possibility that the *Mocedades* may have actually been written first.
Bruerton's dating of *El perfecto caballero* would place the play at least eight and at most twenty years after *Montesinos*.

in the background there are murmurings against the King, the people nonetheless pay him homage. In the court, Ludovico, the Queen's lover since childhood, still seeks her love but is denied satisfaction by her high sense of honor and conjugal duty. Into this situation steps Miguel Centellas, a young Spaniard in search of fortune in the Italian wars, as well as his white-haired father, Don Jaime. Each of the other characters looks to Miguel as a means of resolving his private emotional problem, and each tries to use him, although he attempts to remain true to his own sense of honor and loyalty. The King exploits his power over Miguel to try to force him to abduct Diana and kill Ludovico. Before these crimes can be committed, however, Ludovico, out of frustration, kills the King. The kingdom applauds the assassination and the Queen is restored as rightful ruler of Naples.

An important change from the previous plays is that the King is not a fully legitimate ruler who has betrayed his people and his office. Rather, he is the son of a usurper, whose claim to the throne is somewhat dubious. The reason for this variation is not clear but some speculation is in order. Perhaps Castro had a specific historical model in mind. Or perhaps the political climate had changed so much in Spain that to dramatize the assassination of a legitimate king on stage would have been risky. Not only was the doctrine of regicide falling out of favor among official doctrinaires and politicians —in 1610 the works of Mariana were publicly burned and further publication prohibited in Paris, being cited as the alleged instigator of the assassination of King Henry IV— but the Spanish public itself was becoming accustomed to a more glorified view of monarchy on its theatrical stages. By making the King the descendent of a usurper Castro may have felt himself on safer ground, freer to develop his personal vision of power and obedience. Indeed, seventeenth-century ideologists were little interested in the problem of the *tyranno ex defectu tituli*:

> Quand le régime monarchique héréditaire est stabilisé dans les Etats européens et que la lignée légale et continue de leurs Princes est assurée, il y a un aspect de la tyrannie qui intéresse à peine nos écrivains et qui ne prendra de l'importance qu'à l'apparition du droit naturel révolutionnaire: c'est la tyrannie pour défaut de titre.[2]

Those few theorists who did concern themselves with this matter, such as López Madera and Saavedra Fajardo, opposed the idea of resistance and regicide and claimed that the state must suffer the tyrant, for God placed him on the throne as a cross for the people to bear.[3]

In order to win over the public Castro makes the King not only a usurper —a destroyer of order and social harmony— but establishes

---

[2] MARAVALL, *La Philosophie*, p. 313.
[3] MARAVALL, *La Philosophie*, pp. 314-315.

clearly that this is not a Spanish monarch but an Italian one. Spain is described in the *comedia* as a harmonious kingdom whose rulers are just and whose subjects are obedient. The public will applaud the regicide that ends the act not only because it restores the proper hereditary line of monarchs to the throne and, hence, reestablishes social order, but also because an Italian king has made a mockery of a Spanish hero and his ideals.

Yet even with these safeguards and precautions there is evidence that the thesis of the play was not well received in certain circles. Whether the ending was considered objectionable because it seemed to be politically subversive or merely because it dared to offer an alternative to the «happy ending», it was forced to undergo subsequent alterations. Eduardo Juliá Martínez cites a manuscript copy of *El perfecto caballero* extant in the Biblioteca Nacional of Madrid in which the play is brought to an end in the following more «acceptable», manner: «El Rey entra en la habitación de la Reina, y Ludovico llega luego, con lo que al final el Rey se muestra agradecido y hay un besamanos.»[4]

In the scheme of Castro's play, king and vassal are conceived of in terms of unleashed passion and ascetic self-denial respectively. While the King is presented as a man whose lust is out of control, Miguel Centellas' life undergoes a ritual of purification: his love represents a temptation he must overcome in order to remain true to an ideal of perfect conduct. The contrast is made clear in the play by having both men in love with Diana. While the King pursues her, Miguel puts aside his personal emotions when he senses that they contradict the wishes of his monarch.

The opening scene of the play quickly establishes the violent passion of the King by associating his lust with a runaway horse, a not unfamiliar coincidence in the *comedia*.[5] Diana complains that her horse, suddenly possessed of high spirits, broke the reins and would have thrown her had she not jumped off in time.[6] Her impulse to save herself from this uncontrollable force finds its parallel in her relationship to the King. The connection is immediately made clear to the audience, for as soon as she finishes her lament the King enters, trying to win her favors. He first appears as a gallant lover, professing that he left the hunting party to protect her from the horse. But when she refuses to admit his veiled

---

[4] JULIÁ MARTÍNEZ, «Observaciones», II, ix.
[5] In addition to the beginning of *La vida es sueño* in which the fall occurs *after* the seduction of Rosaura, DONALD R. LARSON has noted that in the plays of Lope «a fall from horseback presages a disastrous plunge into unrestrained sexuality». DONALD R. LARSON, *The Honor Plays of Lope de Vega* (Cambridge: Harvard University Press, 1977), p. 45. See also WEIGER, *Hacia la comedia*, pp. 219-223.
[6] In this scene Diana is seen as related to the goddess Diana, in her dual aspect of goddess of the hunt and goddess of chastity.

advances, reminding him that he is already married, he refers to the horse imagistically, presenting its violence as a model for his own behavior. The following passage strongly suggests a scene of rape:

>¿No viste la furia loca
>de su carrera y no viste
>que al paralle le pusiste
>las espuelas en la boca?
>　¿No le viste al dalle tientos
>mezclar con sangre la espuma,
>y como ligera pluma
>seguir los veloces vientos,
>　y así, por montes y llanos,
>deslumbrando al sol con ellos,
>descomponer tus cabellos
>y no respetar tus manos?
>　Pues ¿tengo en esta ocasión
>donde ciego arderme veo,
>menos fuego en el deseo
>o más vista en la razón?　(II, 129a)

Diana, in turn, employs the same imagery to inform the king that she cannot return his illicit passion:

>　Y tú ¿no me viste a mí
>saltar ligera y dejallo?
>Pues como dejé al caballo
>habré de dejarte a ti,
>... ... ...
>Las riendas, pedazos hechas,
>quiero dejarte en la mano,
>　porque sea en mi favor
>el ejemplo del caballo.　(II, 129a)

As in *El amor constante,* then, it is once again the King's own uncontrolled passion that causes the disruption of order and, as in that same play, this ruler will meet his death by the sword.

The character of Miguel Centellas stands halfway between the figure of the beset loyal vassal (Celauro, Alarcos, Grimaltos) and that of the young hero (Leonido, Carlos, Montesinos) that appear repeatedly in Castro's plays of royal power. He may be seen in this *comedia* as the young hero grown into manhood and faced with the complexities of adult life and the pressures of existence in society. The scene in which he first appears on stage both reveals his heroic dimension and foreshadows his future social problems. The apparently private encounter of Diana and the tyrant is suddenly interrupted by the clash of arms and the appearance of Miguel, not heroically invincible, but on the defensive:

>Suena ruido dentro, y sale Don Jaime Centellas, de barba blanca, y Galindo, criado suyo, como que se retiran, y el viejo sale herido en la cabeza y con mucha sangre que le caiga por la cara. Y salen Don Miguel

Centellas, hijo del viejo y Ludovico, retirándose de muchos [monteros] que los acuchillan. (II, 129b)

Miguel and his father are rescued by the intervention of the King whose very presence causes all involved to lay down their arms. Here both Miguel, who is in principle loyal to his king, and the *monteros*, who at the end of the play will approve of Ludovico's regicidal act, revere the monarch's authority. The Spaniards had been attacked by the *monteros* because Miguel, a foreigner, had dared to kill the boar that they had been so assiduously, but unsuccessfully, hunting. This is the same expedition the King had abandoned in order to pursue Diana, a detail which subtly underscores the contrast between Miguel's heroic compliance to an ideal code of conduct and the King's dereliction of his role. Miguel's description of his feat, narrated in a heroic *romance* meter, clearly links him with Castro's earlier young heroes:

> Corrían un jabalí
> tu gente, y entre unas peñas
> se les reparó, mostrando
> el cansancio y la soberbia.
> Dos perros que le acosaban
> mató la espantosa bestia;
> lanzas y dardos le tiran,
> pero ninguno le acierta.
> Viendo aquello tomé yo,
> con mi natural presteza,
> un dardo, y puse al tiralle
> tanto tino como fuerza.
> Fue de suerte que cosió
> al jabalí con la tierra,
> y quedó blandiendo el asta
> y la cuchilla sangrienta. (II, 131b)

This first appearance strongly foreshadows the latter part of the play. Miguel finds himself in a time and place unpropitious to the heroic role he represents, for just as his admirable physical prowess is not celebrated but rather undercut by the pettiness of the *monteros* so his noble soul will not be allowed later on to shine with its full brilliance as the King will almost taint that nobility by attempting to exploit it for his own base ends.

Castro (like Tirso in *El burlador de Sevilla*) opposes Spain and Naples as contrasted settings in these initial scenes. As a hero, Miguel is the quintessential Spaniard, endowed with special Spanish virtues, in a land supposedly less apt for the full development of heroic potential. When Don Jaime relates the gentlemanly education he has given his son, the Italians marvel, with such comments as «Tierra del cielo es España» (II, 138a) and «Brava nación la española» (II, 138a). When Ludovico later suggests that the tyrant be opposed, Miguel looks to the harmonious relations between king and subjects in Spain for his moral exemplar:

>   Sé que tú le llamas rey,
>   y que todos rey le nombran,
>   y en España sólo el nombre
>   de rey la sangre alborota,
>   y las cabezas humilla,
>   y los corazones postra.   (II, 146a)

Throughout the play Spain and the Spaniards are identified with perfection, harmony and order.

If Spain is a political and moral paradise, Valencia is its capital. Castro, like Tárrega in *El prado de Valencia* and like Castro himself in *Los mal casados de Valencia* and the *Mocedades,* reveals his regional patriotism in his love for Valencia. Miguel sings its praises thus:

>   Yo soy español y tengo
>   por madre a la gran Valencia,
>   ciudad famosa en el mundo
>   por insigne, fuerte y bella.   (II, 130a)

The comic characters Galindo and Merenciana recall with nostalgia their beloved city. Merenciana's words:

>   ¡Ay, patria mía!
>   ¿quién no se muere por vos?   (II, 133a)

suggest Castro's own feelings while in residence in Italy.

These regionalist details in themselves lack the structural importance of the references to Spain, but they do suggest another comparison to Castro. Valencia, it will be remembered, is the land of the Cid, and Galindo, the *gracioso,* does not fail to compare that hero with Miguel:

>   Verás su fama volando,
>   que es un Cid el español,
>   y si la ocasión le llama,
>   no lo dudes que su fama
>   resplandezca como el sol.   (II, 141b)

Important parallels can be found in the ways in which Castro conceives of the two Valencian heroes. Most basic is that both are courtiers who will sacrifice all to duty and honor; Miguel's monologue in the third act in which he weighs the conflicting demands of love and duty finds an exact parallel in that of Rodrigo just before the latter challenges the Count. Miguel's exploits are narrated in *romance* meter, the verse form in which the Cid's deeds were so widely related. When Don Jaime tells of his son's initiation into manhood we are reminded of the opening scene of the *Mocedades*:

> Y a los veinte años, el día
> del Santo Patrón de España,
> después de haber comulgado,
> le ceñí en su altar la espada. (II, 139a)

Finally, there is the important relationship between Miguel and his father which suggests that there is a thematic continuity from the father-son relationships of Castro's earlier plays through to the *Mocedades*. In the early plays the young son assumes the responsibilities of the father when the latter finds himself unable to defend his own cause. In these plays the son's «superiority» is less a matter of his physical vigor than it is of his ability to stand outside the laws of society and make a decisive move against the forces of evil. In *El perfecto caballero* and the *Mocedades* the theme of son defending father takes on a new aspect. In these works both father and son have aged with respect to their earlier counterparts —the son blossoming into gallant early manhood (ready for *mocedades*), and the father facing the frustrating physical decline of old age— and the son must place his superior physical strength at the service of a father who can no longer summon the power to defend himself.

In *El perfecto caballero* we learn that in the encounter between the Spaniards and the *monteros* that preceded Miguel's first appearance on stage the first target of the hunters' anger was Don Jaime. The old man found himself too weak to fight back effectively, forcing Miguel to come to his rescue. In their defense they fight as if they were one person, with Miguel possessing in his youthful vigor the strength lacking in the old man:

> Si los vieras peleando
> como cuando yo los vi,
> el viejo cayendo aquí
> y acullá el mozo matando,
> ser cada uno un león
> hasta quedar desmayado
> el viejo, te hubiera dado,
> con espanto, compasión.
> Cuando el padre desmayaba
> desangrado, parecía
> que a su hijo le infundía
> la fuerza que le faltaba. (II, 134b)

Don Jaime, like Diego Laínez, sees in his son the reflection of his youth and wants to relive his earlier glories through Miguel. Thus, when Miguel goes off to war to seek his fortune, Jaime hurries to join him, though —again like Diego Laínez— hardly able to lift a sword:

> Llegó a mí abiertos los brazos
> y las entrañas abiertas,
> ceñida su vieja espada,

> y esforzando su flaqueza,
> temblando la voz, me dijo:
> «También yo voy a la guerra,
> hijo; acompañarte quiero,
> en tu corazón me lleva.
> ¿No sabes que fui soldado
> en mi mocedad? ¿No piensas
> que de mis pasados bríos
> algunas reliquias quedan?» (II, 131a)

Yet Miguel is not merely the reincarnation of his father but rather his moral superior. He is determined to learn from his father's mistakes. From Miguel's narrative of his life we learn that Don Jaime was an impetuous youth whose actions did not quite measure up to his noble bearing:

> vistió galas, gastó en fiestas
> y aunque dio en sus travesuras
> indicios de su nobleza,
> por no medir cuerdamente
> la inclinación con la fuerza,
> anticiparon sus canas
> y consumieron su hacienda.
> Crecí yo, y creció también
> entre los dos la pobreza. (II, 130a)

As Miguel became older he began to resent the infamy connected with his poverty and set off to seek a new life of honor in the wars, though soon he was to find himself joined once again by his anxious father.

Miguel's narrative reveals the weaker side of Don Jaime's character and so establishes Miguel's claims to being a self-made man. But the old man does not fail to claim his share of the glory in helping to form Miguel's character. In another narration which closely echoes similar passages in *Alarcos* and *Montesinos* Jaime remembers his instructions to his son concerning the conduct of the perfect courtier. As in the earlier plays, they have the flavor of a worldly, courtly catechism, placing most of their emphasis on the rules of honor, though giving a nod to Christian precepts.

The extended discourses on Miguel's history and education serve as a prelude to the central issue of the play: the testing of Miguel's virtue as a perfect «caballero» and the subsequent ironic implications of his blind adherence to his beliefs. Entering society becomes akin to fighting off temptation. The doctrine of absolute obedience to the sovereign becomes the touchstone for his conduct.

In contrast to the well-defined, emotionally uninvolved life of the protagonist, the Italian society to which he is introduced is one of intrigue, of cloaked passions and of emotional despair. Castro has surrounded Miguel with a set of characters desperate for psychological deliverance; each in turn will look to the heroic young Spaniard in the hope of salvation from his emotional stalemate.

Francisco Ruiz Ramón has noted how the construction of this plot recalls the neo-Senecan dramas of Virués:

> La construcción de la intriga, en algunos de sus dramas localizados en una corte italiana, no corresponde del todo al tipo de intriga del drama cortesano del siglo XVII. En una tragicomedia de estructura tan perfecta como *El perfecto caballero* ... La manera como Castro va anudando apretadamente la intriga, aunando en una unidad compleja las intrigas del rey, de la reina y de Ludovico, la aprendió nuestro dramaturgo en su compatriota Virués. Esta obra muestra, con mucha claridad, esa fusión de dos estilos dramáticos que, en mi opinión, define el teatro —una parte de él, a lo menos— de Guillén de Castro.[7]

Indeed, many of the characters and incidents appear to be directly modelled after the *Atila furioso:* a tyrant king, a trick bedroom scene, two sets of lovers, the murder of the king. The complicated blood ties that unite the characters recall Virués' *La cruel Casandra.* But where Virués dotes on gratuitous bloodshed and dehumanizes his characters into mere personifications of vice, Castro reworks the formalized plots of his predecessor and gives them a more human focus. Castro's most sympathetic characters attempt to come to terms with their tragic circumstances and never feel free, as do those of Virués, to act fully on impulse. Perhaps nowhere can this contrast be more clearly seen than in the two Queens in the *Atila furioso* and *El perfecto caballero.* Whereas Virués' Queen is an adulterous woman who plots to meet secretly with her lover in her private chamber, Castro's Queen, like the later Ximena, finds herself caught in a tragic conflict between love and duty.

In a moving scene of the first act the Queen and Ludovico find themselves alone and admit their love for one another. The Queen's declaration is frank but her principles forbid her from carrying through an adulterous affair. She takes pride in the fact that her honor is stronger precisely because it can survive a difficult test:

> ... una mujer,
> cuando no llega a querer,
> no hace mucho su negar.
>   Y es mucho, teniendo amor
> vencelle, pues de ordinario
> el tener fuerte el contrario
> da más honra al vencedor;
>   y así yo, mi Ludovico,
> cuanto más con mi decoro
> encarezco que te adoro,
> mayores honras me aplico. (II, 136b)

[7] FRANCISCO RUIZ RAMÓN, *Historia del teatro español (desde sus orígenes hasta 1900)* (Madrid: Alianza Editorial, 1967), p. 225.

In spite of her highly developed sense of honor and duty the Queen wants Ludovico to remain with her in the court. Thus when he asks to be freed from this difficult situation she begs him to remain and suffer the pangs of an impossible love with her:

> LUDOVICO: pues tan desdichado soy,
> déjame seguir mi estrella.
> Dame licencia, y de mí
> te olvida.
> REINA: ¿Con tanto brío
> me dejas? No, primo mío,
> que habré de morir sin ti. (II, 136b)

Castro's insight into the Queen's heart reveals a woman unconsciously wishing the death of her husband. Though accepting her duty she wants to be saved from it:

> REINA: Si yo la fortuna fuera,
> ¡cómo a servirte aspirara,
> cuántos estados mudara
> y cuántos gustos te diera!
> LUDOVICO: ¿Qué hicieras?
> REINA: Lo que es desvío.
> LUDOVICO: ¿Qué fuera?
> REINA: Dichosa palma.
> LUDOVICO: ¿Y yo qué?
> REINA: Primo del alma,
> Rey del mundo y señor mío. (II, 136b-137a)

At the end of the scene she lets down her guard. Against the warnings of her conscience she desperately reveals her true desires:

> LUDOVICO: No me quieras.
> REINA: Soy mujer.
> LUDOVICO: Déjame.
> REINA: No puedo; ¡ay, Dios!
> LUDOVICO: Me matas.
> REINA: Me desesperas.
> LUDOVICO: ¿Qué me quieres?
> REINA: Que me quieras,
> aunque muramos los dos. (II, 137a)

But this is only a momentary weakening, during which the authentic emotional self breaks through the façade of imposed social conduct. Castro, who in his model for Corneille's Chimène introduced struggle with self to French tragedy, is clearly fascinated with this type of inner conflict, expressed here by the Queen's admission that in spite of her intentions to remain honorable she is still a «mujer». She becomes a figure of tragic nobility as throughout the play she continues to fight off her passion and attempts to fulfill her duties as queen and wife.

If the Queen admits that underneath her social being there still beats the heart of a woman, Ludovico is the only mature male character found so far in Castro's theater who does not see himself in relationship to a fixed political or social role and who feels and acts by his human emotions. While Miguel regards himself above all a «perfecto caballero», Ludovico is a frustrated lover who refuses to define his vital problem in terms of honor or other social conventions. His relationship to the King is not vertical but horizontal; he sees the King not as his sovereign lord but as a rival in love. In a sense, Ludovico, a creature of raw emotions, may be seen as a throwback to the characters of the theater of Virués. Yet he represents a new type of character within the context of Castro's works: one who acts on impulse and yet emerges triumphant. Earlier «emotional» characters —Celauro, Alarcos, Roldán— it will be remembered, were either psychologically devastated, or merely chastised (the case of the semi-comic Roldán) when they began to question the social laws that attempted to strait-jacket their natural impulses and reactions. Though Ludovico shares with such earlier young rebels as Leonido and Montesinos a sense of independence from the social code that prohibits any real opposition to the will of the king, an independence which allows him to take a decisive move against the tyrant without suffering the pangs of doubt and remorse, he stands apart from them in that he is not a particularly exemplary character who promises a return to social order. Rather, he is a problematic character who kills the King not for some higher ideal —be it moral or political— but out of sheer human frustration.

But what are we to make of Ludovico? In action and attitude he often strongly resembles the King and parallels exist between these two men throughout the play. Like his lord, Ludovico will attempt to defile the honor of a woman and is willing to use force to do so:

> ¿Qué haré? Pero si es verdad
> que en tan recíproco amor,
> mi prima, con sólo honor,
> resiste a la voluntad,
>   para acabar de vencello,
> con más fuerza que razón
> buscaré alguna ocasión
> que tenga largo el cabello. (II, 137a) [8]

Later on in the play he decides that he will follow the King's own plans and trick the Queen into sleeping with him, just as the tyrant intends to trick Diana:

---

[8] The allusion is to the literary topos «catching Fortune by the forelock». The parallel between the King and Ludovico is further underlined by their mutual use of this allusion throughout the play. We have already seen the King make reference to it in the opening scene of the runaway horse.

> lo que él procura en mi hermana
> procure yo en su mujer. (II, 163a)

In another scene he bribes the soldiers of the royal army and encourages a seditious attitude towards the King. And finally he kills his ruler outright.

This is hardly noble comportment, particularly when juxtaposed to the idealism of Miguel Centellas. However, a modern audience, steeped in spite of itself in the conventions of Romanticism, would have no trouble in accepting Ludovico as a hero. The real problem is to determine the reaction that Guillén de Castro intended to provoke. In spite of the fact that he is not restrained by the harness of honor or social rote and that as a future practitioner of regicide he is as un-Spanish as possible, Ludovico apparently is not supposed to be condemned. At the end of the play he is not only applauded for killing the tyrant but is also rewarded with the Queen's hand in marriage. One feels that Castro must have derived secret pleasure from finally creating a highly passionate character who could successfully and unproblematically stand up to tyranny. Perhaps it was as if he were avenging all the other unhappy men of his earlier plays forced to suffer unbearably under the yoke of duty. Although functionally Ludovico serves as a type of *deus ex machina,* employed to rescue Miguel from a difficult situation, he is also a creation of great emotional impetus. His contained passions grow without let-up, bursting forth at the end when he can no longer hold them back. If he is not the most exemplary character of the *comedia,* he is nonetheless the most sympathetic to those in the audience who might have become impatient with Miguel's conditioned inability to stand up to the King.

In fact, the only thing that saves Ludovico from the moral condemnation heaped on the King for apparently similar behavior is Castro's obvious sympathy towards him and his hopeless situation. While the King illicitly lusts after Diana, the love between Ludovico and the Queen is meant to be from the beginning and is cruelly interrupted by reasons of state. Also, the intimate scene in Act I between the two lovers, where they admit their love for each other, clearly reveals that if his plan to trick the Queen is dishonest it has been nonetheless encouraged in part by her, insofar as she has indicated to Ludovico a secret wish to transgress the laws of honor.

Into this complex web of emotions enters our idealistic hero, on whom the other characters pin their hopes of deliverance. Miguel will unwittingly serve as the catalyst for the resolution of an emotionally contained but highly charged situation. During the first act he embarks on three new relationships, each with its contradictory demands: with Ludovico, with Diana and with the King.

To Ludovico Miguel is bound by ties of friendship and of obligation for having been helped by him in repulsing the *monteros*. To Diana he is bound by emotional ties of amorous feeling as both fall in love with each other on sight. And finally, the strongest tie of all is to the King whom he has come to serve in the wars and who further obliges him by personally appointing him captain of his army. In a series of asides towards the end of the first act, we see how each of the characters plans to use Miguel to achieve his personal objective:

> Rey: Para lo que agora traza
> mi discurso, el español
> es notable. ¡Ay, bella ingrata!
> Reina: Este español ha de ser,
> si la vista no me engaña,
> medio para echar de mí
> estos celos que me abrasan.
> Ludovico: Pues que me debe la vida
> don Miguel, podré con causa
> de su pecho y de su mano
> fiar la vida del alma.
> Diana: Don Miguel es bien nacido;
> si es que riquezas le faltan
> y tengo riquezas yo,
> lograré mis esperanzas. (II, 140a)

Each then breaks the silence of the asides by asking for a private audience with Miguel. The end of the act sets the theme of the rest of the play: Miguel's attempt to fight temptation and remain true to his ideals in the face of conflicting demands. Don Jaime cautions him not to fall prey to occasions of sin:

> Acuérdate de quién eres.
> ... ...
> No te venzan ocasiones. (II, 140b)

And the act ends with Miguel's determination to act in accordance with his religion of honor:

> Pero en todo pienso hacer
> lo que le debe a su fama
> un perfeto caballero,
> y lo demás Dios lo haga. (II, 140b)

In the second act Miguel's ideals are put to the test in a succession of encounters designed to illustrate his conviction that his honor is inextricably bound to loyalty to the king. In the first three interviews Miguel rejects all suggestions that he «betray» the king. He defines himself as an honorable courtier bound to his oath of loyalty, regardless of the fact that the sovereign is a usurper.

Miguel's first concern in this act is with Diana who has given him very forward indications of her amorous intentions. He enters the stage visibly upset by the conflict aroused by his own erotic longings. He views it as dishonorable to respond to Diana, since to aspire to a woman nobler than he and worthy of a king would be an offense to his liege lord. He considers it his duty to conquer his own impulses:

> Con esto a guardar me obligo
> fe inviolable y buena ley
> a los palacios de un rey
> y a la hermana de un amigo;
> y antes quedaré sin mí
> que les pierda este respeto;
> que el caballero perfeto
> por su honor se vence a sí. (II, 142b)

When he meets with Diana he remains rigidly on guard so as to prevent his feelings from getting out of control (Aside: «Honor, tened»; II, 143b). After she leaves, he acknowledges to himself that his human feelings are a powerful foe:

> ¡Ay, lealtad,
> fuerte contrario tenéis! (II, 144a)[9]

The second test of his knightly «faith» comes in his meeting with Ludovico. His new friend tells him in confidence of his love for the Queen and of their unhappy circumstances. Miguel promises to keep the story confidential but he soon finds himself dangerously compromised when Ludovico hints that out of despair he may kill the King. Miguel cuts off Ludovico, hoping to honor bonds of friendship and loyalty at the same time:

> LUDOVICO: gozaréla, aunque la enoje,
> y para hacella mi esposa
> después...
> MIGUEL: Calla; ese después
> no me digas, por si es cosa
> que pueda más que el secreto. (II, 145b)

He tells Ludovico that he cannot be asked to betray the king who has so generously honored him and his father. To his friend's argument that it is just to kill a tyrant king, Miguel responds:

> Eso a mí
> el juzgallo no me toca. (II, 146a)

---

[9] In this scene once again the code of honor takes on the language of religion. Referring to the firmness and hardness of the diamond Diana has left with him, Miguel comments:

> Y para esforzar mi fe
> pienso que el cielo ha ordenado
> que haya en mi mano quedado
> cosa que ejemplo me dé. (II, 144a)

a doctrine he repeats at the end of the play:

> que el perfeto caballero
> sólo sabe adorar reyes,
> más no dar ni quitar reinos. (II, 167b)

His duty, he maintains, is not to stand in judgment of the King but to carry out his duties in an absolute manner, blinding himself to any reasons that would cause him to waver.

Nor will Miguel oppose the King's will even when the welfare of the kingdom is at stake. In a third important meeting, the Queen reveals to Miguel that the King refuses to fulfill his marital duties, dangerously depriving the kingdom of an heir to the royal throne. The Queen's words show more concern for her people and duties than for her own feelings, thus revealing the rightful preoccupation of a ruler.[10] When she asks Miguel to run away with the noblewoman with whom the King is infatuated (he does not yet know it is Diana) Miguel refuses on the grounds that to do so would be treason to his ruler.

Each of the characters leaves Miguel in despair and yet each acknowledges and admires his firmness and determination to remain honorable. Ludovico still hopes, however, that Miguel will cede to his more human emotions:

> que quizá hará como humano
> lo que negó como amigo. (II, 152b)

The key to Miguel's character is his almost superhuman ability to place honorable action above his more immediate human reactions. This virtue faces its most serious challenges with the dishonorable demands made on him by the King, demands which strain even his extraordinary capacity for repressing his natural feelings. The problem for Miguel is simply how he can remain loyal to his lord —and therefore honorable— when to obey is to commit a dishonorable act.

In his first meeting with the King, Miguel is asked to help him obtain peace of mind by abducting for him the woman who haunts his thoughts. Miguel at first fears —with good reason— that such an action would tarnish his honor, but when the King offers to somehow miraculously protect that precious asset Miguel consents, recalling his duties as a perfect subject:

> Baste, ya callo;
> porque es honra en el vasallo
> no contradecille al rey. (II, 151b)

---

[10] It is to be remembered that had not the father of the present King usurped the throne the Queen would have been the next legal sovereign.

The abduction is never carried through, however, and, after some very complex plot maneuvering, the King allows Miguel to marry Diana. Miguel by now is aware of the King's passion for his betrothed, and he again begins to worry about his honor. He is faced with the dilemma of either compromising his honor by consenting to his wife's infidelity or offending and frustrating the king. His reaction is to openly confront his liege lord with the problem. He asks to be allowed to leave for Spain so as to avoid a difficult situation, though it is never made quite clear whether he intends to take Diana with him or leave her in Naples at the mercy of the King. The latter course would have the advantage of pleasing the King while Miguel would not be present to see the offense to his honor. He tells the King that although he trusts Diana, he is preoccupied with how he could possibly cope with dishonor from such a source as his lord:

> pero como no basta el ser honesta
> la mujer pretendida, cuando agravia
> el pretensor y la venganza obliga,
> viendo que en las personas de los reyes
> no han lugar, sin traiciones, las venganzas,
> tomé por medio huír de los agravios. (II, 161a)

When the King, lying patently, assures the young hero that he is not interested in Diana, the latter promises to remain and serve him in every way possible.

A second test comes when the King unjustly orders Miguel to kill Ludovico in order to avenge his supposedly offended honor. Miguel is visibly upset by the order to kill his friend and his wife's brother, but he is even more shaken to see himself hesitate to obey:

> Cielo, ¿a qué vengo?
> Si es afrenta el dudallo, yo la tengo. (II, 161b)

He nonetheless begins to question the justice of the King's mandate and is grieved by the personal consequences of the deed he is supposed to commit. For the first time human feelings take a strong hold of Miguel and seem to have a chance of prevailing. In a monologue that anticipates that of Rodrigo in the *Mocedades,* he wavers between feeling and duty, but, finally faithful to his creed, he summons up the strength to carry out his duty:

> ¡Yo he de matar de mi querida esposa
> el adorado hermano,
> alma de su valor, vida del mío!
> ¡Terrible confusión! ¡Pena forzosa!
> ¡Pensamiento inhumano!
> Mas de un rey el supremo señorío
> funda en mí su esperanza,
> y es justicia en los reyes la venganza.

> ¿Que ha de morir mi amigo? ¡Oh cruel sentencia!
> ¡Oh riguroso fallo!
> ¿Si es justicia en el rey, o si es malicia?
> Mas de Abra[h]án imite la obediencia,
> y no mire el vasallo
> si el rey imita a Dios en la justicia;
> y así, aunque yo supiera
> que no la tiene el Rey, lo mismo hiciera. (II, 161a-162b)

But on the heels of this «moral» victory Miguel discovers that the monarch plans to besmirch his honor by arranging for a secret rendezvous with Diana that night. Miguel becomes crazed with confusion as he sees his neatly ordered world fall apart, for now he knows the King himself would dishonor him. He desperately wonders how he can protect his honor and not betray the King, but is overwhelmed by the possibility that the two may be mutually exclusive:

> Este sol, en mis ojos eclipsado,
> muerte de un rey señala;
> mas ¡soy yo bueno, aunque mi suerte es mala!
> ¿Qué haré? ¡Afrentado estoy! ¡Saldré de juicio!
> ¿Pondréme un lazo al cuello
> o romperé de la lealtad los lazos?
> ¿Derribaré del templo el edificio,
> pues tengo en el cabello
> de la ocasión la fuerza de los brazos?
> Mas yo muero dudando,
> pues, cuando peno ardiendo, estoy temblando. (II, 162b)

As time passes Miguel takes hold of himself and his momentary emotional outburst gives way to a calmer, more reasoned state of mind. He now hopes to reconcile both loyalty and honor by killing Diana:

> ... veré obligado
> de mi rey y de mi honor,
> si puedo, sin ser traidor,
> dar evidencias de honrado. (II, 164b)

He will not attempt to seek vengeance on the offending tyrant but will merely make a symbolic gesture of protest. When he catches the King entering Diana's room he takes away the royal sword and addresses him in a tone which stands halfway between rebuke and respect:

> pues no consiento ni hallo
> razón, justicia, ni ley,
> que obligue a matar el rey
> sin ser traidor el vasallo;
> y pues es cualquier venganza
> destas infame, en mi esposa
> de tomar venganza honrosa
> sólo me queda esperanza.

> Y así, Rey, quise quitarte
> las armas, porque así puedo
> señalarte que no es miedo
> y es lealtad el no matarte. (II, 166a-b)

When the young courtier discovers that his honor was never really in danger —the other characters had planned to trick the King into sleeping with his own wife by having him believe it was Diana [11]— he repents at having spoken out against him. It little matters to him that the King had every intention of dishonoring him; in atonement Miguel offers his life:

> Si te obligan mis engaños,
> el perderte así el respeto
> me perdona, pues yo soy
> el ofendido, y pues tengo
> ya mi espada y mi cabeza
> a tus pies. (II, 167a)

And even after his unjust execution is ordered by the enraged monarch, Miguel still runs to the aid of the King when he hears his desperate last cry for help:

> Yo te defendiera, Rey;
> mas por tu causa no puedo;
> tú me quitaste la espada. (II, 167b)

Thus, the central thread of the play concerns Miguel's unwavering moral commitment. His is a constant battle to remain pure and true to his doctrine of perfection. In spite of momentary hesitations and threats to his very life and honor he triumphs over temptation.

However, if on one level Castro sets up the young Centellas as an admirable idealist, and as the incarnation of Spanish virtue, he undercuts his heroism with dramatic irony so powerful that one cannot fail to leave this *comedia* without a definite sense of uneasiness about Castro's supposed intention to celebrate Miguel's attitude of unquestioning submission to authority. This irony hinges on the figure of the King and on the manner in which Miguel's «perfect conduct» is juxtaposed to the former's exploitation of that code of conduct for his own ends. From the beginning the tyrant has had designs on Miguel as a means of accomplishing his plans and bolstering his dubiously legal rule. His honoring of the Spaniard, raising him to the rank of captain, and openly praising his virtues, serves insidiously to cement a relationship that would trap

---

[11] According to JULIÁ MARTÍNEZ, «Observaciones», II, ix, Castro's inspiration for this scene is the historical legend of the birth of King Jaime I of Aragón, particularly via the chronicle of the Valencian Béuter. According to the chronicle, King Pedro of Aragón was tricked into sleeping with his wife, believing instead that she was a lady-in-waiting whom the king had desired.

Miguel into service to him. The tyrant understands his power over Miguel and ruthlessly exploits it. In the last scenes of the play, the King becomes both actor and stage director, setting up scenes intended both to distract Miguel's attention from the evil nature of his schemes and to remind him of his sense of duty. The tyrant makes use of lies and melodramatic poses to make a mockery of Miguel's idealism.

In their very first meeting the King craftily performs his role as if on a stage. Pretending not to know that Miguel is in his chamber he sighs aloud and then acts surprised to discover that Miguel has overheard him. He then praises Miguel's virtues, reminding him of how he has honored him in the past, thereby subtly reinforcing the young Spaniard's sense of duty. He then proceeds to describe himself as unjustly rejected by a woman and unable to rule effectively because of this. Miguel sees the woman's resistance as treason:

¡Hay cosa igual!
Pues ¿a un rey? (II, 150b)

In his blind obedience Miguel cannot even imagine the possibility that to respond to the King's advances might compromise her honor and, if she is married, that of her spouse. Ironically, his own sense of honor now puts him on the defensive. Miguel has unknowingly set himself up for the King's unexpected command: the Spaniard is to abduct the woman for the King and then flee, alone, to Spain. Miguel's concern about the consequences of this act to his honor and reputation is met with a royal wave of the hand and the assurance that he will later clear up the confusion and protect Miguel's good name. This alone satisfies the Spaniard and he submits.

In this interplay the King has discovered how far the Spaniard will put himself out for his ruler. He hears for the first time Miguel's affirmation of his code of loyalty and remembers it as a valuable tool for future use.

When Miguel later asks to leave for Spain, the King, who plans to exploit Miguel to dispose of Ludovico, appeals to his sense of loyalty in order to shame him into remaining:

He sido bueno para hacer mercedes,
y ¿no lo soy para esperar servicios?
¿Es digna hazaña de tu heroico pecho,
que con la perfición mide las obras?
La ingratitud fue siempre aborrecible
y más lo son señales evidentes
de cobardía... (II, 160a-b)

And when Miguel hesitates upon hearing the order to kill his friend, the King once again tries to shame him:

> No espero tu respuesta,
> que el rey que duda un sí de su vasallo
> pone duda en su honor. (II, 161b)

Miguel himself touches on the irony of his situation when he tries to summon up the determination to kill Ludovico. He recalls the story of Abraham and finds a curious parallel with his own problem: the perfect courtier is to obey the king as if he were God even if he suspects that the king may not possess God's sense of justice:

> Mas de Abra[h]án imite la obediencia,
> y no mire el vasallo
> si el rey imita a Dios en la justicia. (II, 162a)

Here Miguel is patently attempting to quell a rebelling conscience that is disturbed by the unjust deed he has been ordered to commit. He does so by reciting by rote, as a child would from a catechism, a rule he himself is beginning to question.

At the end of the play the King, frustrated in his desire to seduce Diana, becomes, like the kings of Virués, a creature of blind rage. Equating the contravening of his evil plans with treason, he unreasonably orders the death of both Miguel and Don Jaime. His raised voice and frenzied actions contrast sharply with the calm with which the two Spaniards accept their execution:

> REY: Rabiando muero.
> ¡Parientes, vasallos, [h]ola!
> ¡Ah de mi guarda, corriendo,
> volando! De vuestro rey
> vengad agravios tan ciertos.
> ... ...
> JAIME: Señor, a tus pies estamos;
> no alborotes.
> MIGUEL: Y aunque puedo,
> si mi honor te defendía,
> mi vida no te defiendo.
> Mira en esto mi lealtad. (II, 167a)

In his rage the King unsheathes his dagger to kill his wife for her supposed infidelity, but upon entering her chamber he is killed by Ludovico.

Despite Miguel's repeated assertions that even a tyrant must be honored, Castro assures the audience that the King merits his violent death precisely because he rules tyrannically. Ludovico, upon assassinating the King, cries «eres tirano» (II, 167b). But the first response of the people of Naples is outrage; they clamor for the death of Ludovico: «¡Muera el traidor; muera, muera!» (II, 167b). Ludovico, in turn, argues that the King deserved to die both because he was a usurper and because his laws were in themselves unjust:

> ... Por defender
> la vida a la Reina, he muerto
> al Rey. Ya sabéis, señores,
> que fue vuestro rey su agüelo,
> y el padre deste tirano
> le dio la muerte. Volveos
> a mirar sus tiranías,
> su mal trato y mal ejemplo,
> y co[n]templad en la Reina
> medidos vuestros deseos.
> ¡Viva la Reina, vasallos!
> Señores, suyo es el cetro
> y le debéis la corona
> por razón y por derecho. (II, 167b)

With this, the people support the regicide as a return to natural order:

> ¡Viva la Reina, la Reina
> viva! ¡Viva! Obedecemos
> nuestra natural señora. (II, 167b)

The regicide also has the tacit consent of divine law. Don Jaime comments that «Esto es voluntad del cielo» (II, 167b). And in an earlier scene that recalls *El amor constante,* the King himself had asked for divine punishment if he were asking Miguel to act dishonorably:

> Como rey te prometo y como hidalgo,
> sobre la cruz lo juro desta espada
> y si no lo compliere [i.e. his word not to touch
>   Diana], quiera el cielo
> que me atraviese el pecho con la suya
> el mayor enemigo. (II, 161a)

Thus, *El perfecto caballero* is a play fraught with ambiguities. In terms of political doctrine, Castro seems not completely to have abandoned the principle of the sixteenth-century theory of resistance in a play that in all outward appearances —notably in its title— pretends to be celebrating a divine right theory of monarchy. In terms of characters, while Miguel Centellas is proposed as the audience's object of admiration, it is, ironically, Ludovico who restores order to a kingdom plagued by injustice and tyranny. If in the abstract Miguel and his religion of honor are worthy of esteem, he proves himself to be ill-equipped to deal with the reality of an unworthy ruler; we find Miguel at various times on the verge of committing a moral crime in the name of loyalty. On the other hand, Ludovico cannot be idolized either, for though he delivers the kingdom —and Miguel— from the clutches of evil, his reasons are primarily selfish and only secondarily ideological. Unlike the earlier «saviour» figures whom the audience identifies without difficulty as representatives of natural and divine justice, Ludovico's more human and highly emotional character renders him a much more complex and problematic figure to grasp. In *El perfecto caballero,* then, Castro has created a play of ambivalent values and of unrealized heroes which both celebrates and questions the «Spanish» virtue of submission to authority depicted time and again in the *comedia* of Lope and his followers.

CHAPTER VI

«LAS MOCEDADES DEL CID: COMEDIA SEGUNDA»

In the plays discussed thus far, Guillén de Castro has depicted foreign kingdoms —Hungary, France, Naples— thrown into turmoil by their rulers. The only explicit references to Spain are found in *El perfecto caballero* in which it is praised by Miguel Centellas as a land of harmonious relations between subject and ruler, a sort of earthly political paradise that stands in contrast to the turbulence of the kingdom of Naples. But when Castro finally turns to his own country as the setting for a *comedia* he finds himself drawn to a historical-legendary incident in which a Castilian king brings about political disorder and confusion: the siege of Zamora by King Sancho of Castile. In the light of the previous plays, the attraction of this subject for Castro is not difficult to comprehend, for it offers him the history of an ambitious king who meets his death at the hands of an assassin while carrying out a morally questionable siege of a Christian city.

Yet this history as it exists in chronicle and ballad differs in two extremely important ways from the pattern established in Castro's dramas. In this pattern the character who either kills the king or openly challenges his authority is perceived by both the audience and the other characters of the play as a positive figure who is carrying out the mandates of divine and natural laws. However, although Castro's source material on the theme of the siege of Zamora shows King Sancho to be a morally problematic figure, nowhere is Bellido Dolfos presented as laudable. While in the version found in the *Primera crónica general* the dying King Sancho interprets his murder as an act of Providence, the regicide is universally regarded as an act of treason, and Bellido Dolfos is branded both traitor and coward, even by the king himself. Furthermore, the assassination serves not to restore order, as do similar acts in *El amor constante* and *El perfecto caballero*, but rather leads to further dissension and bloodshed.

Castro's reworking of this material into *Las mocedades del Cid: comedia segunda,* more widely known as *Las hazañas del Cid,*[1] sets in

---

[1] The play is popularly known as *Las hazañas del Cid,* although the Cid

tense juxtaposition the «traditional» view of the assasination of King Sancho as an act of treason with Castro's highly personal interpretation of the claims made in the *Primera crónica general* that the regicide is an act of divine justice. In attempting to justify the regicide on moral grounds without seeming inordinately to exalt either the act itself or its perpetrator, Castro creates a play rich in paradoxes and moral ambivalencies. The *Hazañas* challenges the audience's values and preconceptions by presenting it with a series of incidents that can support any number of conflicting interpretations and which eludes any attempt to reduce a complex historical reality to a simple moral issue of right and wrong.

Castro presents the spectator with the premise that King Sancho's siege is an offense to Heaven and a betrayal of Castile's true mission to expel the Moors. In this light, Bellido Dolfos is introduced as an instrument of divine justice, guided and propelled by Heaven, as if against his will, to punish the king for his wrongdoing. Furthermore, Castro's Bellido is acutely aware of the king's misconduct and of his own divine mission. Yet, in deference to tradition, Castro portrays him not as the pure «saviour» figure of his earliest plays but rather, like Ludovico, as a less than admirable, and even somewhat odious, character. Thus, the audience is pulled between seeing Bellido as a traitor, fully responsible for a crime, and seeing him as a divinely inspired deliverer whose will is manipulated by divine forces. The spectator finds himself both repudiating the regicide and accepting it as divinely sanctioned, and despising Bellido while nonetheless finding him strangely sympathetic.

This ambivalence is further compounded by dramatic irony in the

displays little heroic prowess. Castro, on the title page of his published plays, entitles the two Cid plays thus: *Las mocedades del Cid, primera,* and *Segunda de las hazañas del Cid.* BRUERTON dates the play tentatively between 1610 and 1615 and speculates: «Since the plays had titles originally different, this *comedia* [i.e. *Hazañas*] may have been written first, since in the development of legend in epic and drama the early life of the hero is often treated last.» BRUERTON, pp. 127-128. See JOHN G. WEIGER's introductory study to his edition of *Las hazañas del Cid* (Barcelona: Puvill Editor, 1980) for a discussion of the titles of the two Cid plays. In that same study, Weiger questions Bruerton's assumptions regarding the chronological priority of the *Hazañas*; there is simply no evidence to corroborate Bruerton's claim. Weiger correctly asserts that what is most important is that Castro seemed to conceive of both plays as a single unity. My discussion of the *Hazañas* in this chapter is based on just that premise. Further discussion of the relationships that exist between the two plays can be found in WEIGER, *Hacia la comedia,* pp. 209-214; and in ADRIANA LEWIS GALANES, «*Las mocedades del Cid* de Guillén de Castro: Corteza y meollo», *Hispanófila,* 44 (1972), pp. 13-31. My forthcoming article, «The Cid of Guillén de Castro: The Hero as Moral Exemplar», *Revista de Estudios Hispánicos,* examines how Rodrigo is the moral center of these works. He passes from the saviour of the kingdom in the first play to moral observer in the second. In *Las mocedades del Cid* Rodrigo defeats the Moors and terminates the warfare between Castile and Aragon; in *Las hazañas del Cid,* he seeks to heal the state's inner wounds and bring Castile back to its true mission to save Christendom.

scenes following the death of the king. While the audience is allowed to observe the mysterious workings of Providence, neither *castellanos* nor *zamoranos* understand that superhuman forces are involved. Hence, they are outraged by the murder of their monarch and continue to pay him homage by condemning the regicide as an undiluted act of treason. Here the knowing spectator is torn between admiration for the vassals' loyalty to their king and their refusal to compromise this loyalty by passing judgment on his actions, and the knowledge that this fierce devotion is misguided, based as it is on their inability to see the full complexity of the problem. The worst fears of the audience are confirmed when this lack of vision on the part of the characters leads to Diego Ordóñez's overly self-assured *reto de Zamora,* which ironically and tragically claims the loyal Arias Gonzalo as its victim.

Once again, then, the issue of unquestioning loyalty to the king is examined from an ironic and ambivalent perspective. Castro counters the Lopean notion that punishment of the king is to be left to God with the presentation of a case where honorable men who refuse to pass moral judgment on their sovereign are unable to recognize God's will when it is most manifest. The result of this loyalty is not the restoration of order but further disorder; Spain, rather than fighting the Moorish enemy, continues to turn against itself. Castro stands Lope's celebrative vision of society and its laws on its head and creates a powerful drama that comes close to tragedy.

Accounts of the siege of Zamora long antedate Castro's play. The first extensive written account appears in the *Crónica Najerense* (c. 1160), which was probably based on an early *cantar de gesta* composed near the end of the eleventh century, close to the actual historical events.[2] This, as well as other early Castilian chronicles, such as the *Compostelana,* the *Tudense* and the *Silense,* are sympathetic to King Sancho and not only accuse Bellido Dolfos of treason but also implicate Urraca and the inhabitants of Zamora in the assassination.[3] Later chronicles acquit the *zamoranos* (though they continue to implicate Urraca) and instead build up Bellido as an even greater traitor. According to Reig:

> En primer lugar... los cronistas y juglares eran casi siempre castellanos y no podían sustraerse al rencor contra el asesino de su rey. Pero como para la unidad posterior de los reinos había que suavizar asperezas y ren-

---

[2] For this as well as subsequent information on the chronicles consult CAROLA REIG, *El cantar de Sancho II y cerco de Zamora* (Madrid: Revista de Filología Española, Anejo 37, 1947); and CHARLES F. FRAKER, «Sancho II: Epic and Chronicle», *Romania,* 95 (1974), pp. 467-507.

[3] Most of these chronicles cite a love between Bellido and Urraca which is probably fictitious in origin, and which probably served «para quitar a la hazaña todo tinte heroico», REIG, p. 23.

cores, se acumulan sobre su figura todos los caracteres de la traición, pensada fría y secretamente, para dejar libre de sospecha a los zamoranos.[4]

However, the version of the *Primera crónica general,* based, in all likelihood, on a later *Cantar de Sancho II,* makes some important new changes. As Charles F. Fraker has shown, this poem, unlike other epic *cantares,* seems to betray a strong anti-Castilian bias.[5] It is critical of both King Fernando's decision to divide his kingdom among his children and King Sancho's subsequent shedding of Christian blood in his attempt to wrest Zamora from Urraca, even though he is considered justified in his claim that he has been wronged by his father. The Sancho of this version is a complex figure whose history, according to Fraker, conforms to the medieval pattern of the overreacher, «the man of heroic qualities whose very heroism leads in some way to his fall».[6] In creating his medieval tragedy the chronicle editor takes care to establish the innocence of Urraca. Consequently, Bellido Dolfos is no longer spurred to action, as he was in earlier versions, by Urraca's pleas for help. Rather, he is a somewhat mysterious figure with no clear motivation for his crime. The result is an important new interpretation of the cause of Sancho's death:

> The murder is thus decisively disconnected from the events which precede it. Now, this very curious disposition of the plot cannot but be deliberate; its function is to make it clear that Sancho's death is an act of Providence, a judgment of God. Divinity intervening takes the place of Urraca's revenge on Sancho as in the old poem. In the later *cantar* the dying king is in fact made to admit that his fall was brought about by divine justice...[7]

Reig's study indicates that the version found in the *Primera crónica general,* possibly via the 1541 edition of Florián de Ocampo, served as a direct source of inspiration for Castro's drama.[8] Indeed, the play's negative view of King Fernando, its insistence on the criminal nature of Sancho's decision to wage war on fellow Christians and its view of the role of Providence in the murder of Sancho all seem to corroborate that claim.

Yet Castro makes two important changes from this source, changes that clearly link this work with the earlier plays examined in this study. First, while the chronicle version depicts Sancho as a basically virtuous king who has erred, we see no such virtue in the king of the *Hazañas.* Castro's figure is willful, spiteful and un-Christian, much like the other kings of this author. Second, in developing the rather sketchy figure of Bellido Dolfos from the chronicle Castro attributes some positive quali-

[4] REIG, p. 24.
[5] FRAKER, p. 469.
[6] FRAKER, p. 499.
[7] FRAKER, p. 479.
[8] REIG, pp. 166-170.

ties to him. He is loyal to his native city[9] and is moved to save it from what he sees as tyranny. Bellido is actually divinely inspired and is aware of his mission to punish the king.

But the *Primera crónica general* was not Castro's sole inspiration. Indeed the most popular versions of the history of the siege were to be found in the *romancero*. Such must have been the appeal of the life of the Cid that all *romances* related to it —including those concerned with the siege— were collected by Juan de Escobar and published as the *Romancero del Cid* in 1612. The collection consisted of 102 ballads, both *viejos* and *juglarescos,* and was subsequently reprinted in fifteen separate editions. Numerous studies have often pointed out Castro's debt to the *romancero:* not only does he borrow from it specific details of plot, but he also directly quotes or paraphrases important ballad verses.[10]

Yet, Castro does not slavishly follow either the *romancero* or the chronicle. Rather, he chooses details from one or another source, alters others and invents new ones[11] in order to create a tragic vision of men engaged in a struggle with forces beyond their comprehension. This vision is heightened at every turn by a skillful use of dramatic irony. The playwright exploits the audience's foreknowledge of the plot and makes every effort to alert the spectator to what awaits the characters. This irony is at its most effective when coupled with direct quotes from the *romancero,* creating a heightened sense of expectation and impending doom.

The history of King Sancho and Zamora actually begins in the first *Mocedades* drama in which the young Prince Sancho is portrayed as the impulsive scion of the weak and aging King Fernando. From the beginning the prince is determined to impose his will over that of his father. When the king orders Diego Laínez imprisoned, Sancho rebels: «¡No hará el Rey, si yo no quiero!» (51).[12] In this incident, a preview of his later misconduct, he reveals himself willing to destroy the kingdom to get his way:

¡Ha de perderse Castilla
primero que preso vaya! (52)

---

[9] Both the ballads and the chronicles insist that Bellido is not a native of Zamora. By contradicting this tradition and stressing Bellido's patriotism Castro purposely adds a certain nobility to the traditional figure of the infamous traitor.

[10] For Castro's debt to the *romancero* consult the notes to Víctor Said Armesto, ed., *D. Guillén de Castro. Las mocedades del Cid* (Madrid: Espasa-Calpe, S. A., 1968); ELISA PÉREZ, «Algunos aspectos de la evolución del romancero», *Hispania,* 18 (1935), pp. 151-160; LIDIA SANTELICES, «La originalidad en la segunda parte de *Las mocedades del Cid*», *Anales de la Universidad de Chile,* año 93, 3.ª serie, no. 20 (1935), pp. 169-178; and WILLIAM E. WILSON, *Guillén de Castro* (New York: Twayne Publishers, 1973), pp. 82-87.

[11] For a summary of Castro's changes from the ballads see LIDIA SANTELICES.

[12] All subsequent page references in this chapter are from the above cited edition of Víctor Said Armesto.

Sancho's violent nature is exacerbated by a constant fear of a bloody death revealed to him through an astrological reading:

> Otro miedo el pensamiento
> me aflixe y me atemoriza:
> con un arma arrojadiza
> señala en mi nacimiento
>   que han de matarme, y será
> cosa muy propinqua mía
> la causa. (75-76)

Hoping to prevent the fulfillment of the prophecy, he ventures to interpret its meaning. He is convinced that the assassin will be a member of his family and his mistrust leads him to abuse his brothers and sisters. When Urraca appears on stage carrying a javelin tainted with the blood of a wild boar Sancho interprets this as a forewarning of his murder. In his rage he threatens to kill Urraca:

> ¡Traydora!
> ¡Temo que causa has de ser
> tú de mi muerte! ¡Muger,
> estoy por matarte agora,
>   y asegurar mis enojos! (79)

As a further precaution, he resolves to arm himself against Fate by wearing a protective breastplate.

Like King Basilio of *La vida es sueño*, Sancho believes that man can correctly read the stars and take direct measures to oppose their influence. But Diego Laínez cautions Sancho that astrological readings can be inaccurate and that any prediction should not be taken literally but should serve as a warning to reorder one's life:

> Diego L.:   Mas ninguno la [i.e. la astrología] aprendió
>   con certeza.
> Don Sancho: Luego, di:
>   ¿locura es creella?
> Diego L.:   Sí.
> Don Sancho: ¿Serálo el temella?
> Diego L.:   No. (77)[13]

---

[13] A similar statement is found in Castro's *El caballero bobo* in the following interchange between the ambassador and the duke:

> Embajador: sobrado crédito ha dado
>   el Rey a la Astrología,
>   siendo en alguna opinión
>   mentira, locura y engaño.
> Duque: Los que previenen al daño
>   cuerdos y discretos son,
>   pues el supremo Jüez
>   tiene escritas con estrellas
>   nuestras vidas.
> Embajador: ¿Y leellas
>   sabe alguno?

Urraca mocks Sancho for believing in astrology.

> Mas, tú, ¿crédito has de dar
> a lo que abominan todos? (78)

She warns him to distrust his ability to control the forces that affect his life. As an example, she tells him that although he will wear a breastplate his back will remain exposed:

> Guarda con más prevención
> el coraçon: mira bien
> que por la espalda también
> hay camino al coraçon. (79)

The superimposing of an astrological prediction on the familiar legend establishes tragic irony. Unlike Sancho, the spectator, informed by tradition, understands the true meaning of the prophecy: the «arma arrojadiza» refers to the javelin which Bellido Dolfos will use to kill the king; the «cosa muy propinqua mía» is somewhat more ambiguous [14] but the spectator knows that Sancho's interpretation (i.e. that a member of his family will kill him) is wrong; and Urraca's innocent but sarcastic comment about the breastplate will become a reality when Bellido strikes from behind. With this foreknowledge the spectator sees that Sancho's inaccurate reading of the stars and his misplaced confidence in his ability to decipher their true meaning ensures the fulfillment of the prophecy. The audience will watch in horror as Sancho hands himself over to death, blind to the obvious and deafened to all voices of warning. Precisely by trying to master his destiny Sancho causes his dreaded assassination.

If these early scenes with their emphasis on fateful foreboding and tragic pride suggest Sophoclean tragedy, Castro firmly places the action in a Christian ideological setting, with the result that Sancho will seem to be fated and yet free at the same time. The king's murder will be

> DUQUE: Alguna vez.
> Y, al fin, estas cosas son
> de suerte, si bien se apura,
> que el creellas es locura
> y el temellas discreción. (I, 48b-49a)

[14] It may be taken to mean any or all of the following: (1) Bellido Dolfos, whom the king will make his closest confidant, (2) Urraca, but only indirectly, since, as we shall see, she seems to encourage Bellido, (3) the *venablo* which Sancho will hand over to Bellido as he dismounts his horse and which Bellido uses to assassinate him (this however does not occur in the ballads; there Bellido uses his own weapon). LEAVITT suggests a fourth interpretation: it is the «cierta necesidad» that causes Sancho to dismount. STURGIS E. LEAVITT, «Una comedia sin paralelo: *Las hazañas del Cid*, de Guillén de Castro», in *Homenaje a William L. Fichter. Estudios sobre el teatro antiguo hispánico y otros ensayos*, ed. A. David Kossoff and José Amor y Vázquez (Madrid: Castalia, 1971), p. 431.

interpreted not as the working of a blind Fate but as an act of divine justice, in direct response to Sancho's violation of Christian order. And far from being inexorably condemned, Sancho can at any moment alter the course of his life by judiciously exercising his free will and behaving ethically. From the start, Castro takes care to show that Sancho bears the responsibility for and is deserving of divine punishment. Throughout both *Mocedades* plays his profile is that of a violent and ambitious ruler more preoccupied with the imposition of his will than with the rightful role of the Christian king. Fittingly, his reaction to the prediction is not a heightened awareness of his misconduct, a circumspection which could, as with Segismundo, contravene the inclination of the stars, but an intensification of violence. Ironically, this violence, directed towards his family and aimed at avoiding his own murder, sets in motion the course of events that leads to the act of regicide.

It is in response to Sancho's brutal behavior to his family that his father, Fernando, ponders the unusual decision to divide his kingdom:

> De Don Sancho la braveza,
> que, como sabéys, es tanta
> que casi casi se atreve
> al respeto de mis canas;
> viendo que por puntos crecen
> el desamor, la arrogancia,
> el desprecio, la aspereza
> con que a sus hermanos trata;
> como, en fin, padre, entre todos
> me ha obligado a que reparta
> mis Reynos y mis estados,
> dando a pedaços el alma. (125-126)

While Arias Gonzalo and Peransules support the king's plan, Diego Laínez condemns the decision as detrimental to the welfare of the state, as it will only serve to divide a strong, united kingdom:

> Que es estraña,
> y a toda razón de estado
> haze grande repugnancia.
> Si bien lo adviertes, Señor,
> mal prevalece una casa
> cuyas fuerças, repartidas,
> es tan cierto el quedar flacas.
> ... ...
> Siempre el provecho común
> de la Religión cristiana
> importó más que los hijos. (126-127)

He argues that the division will only aggravate that which it intends to prevent by giving Sancho just cause for waging war against his family:

> ¿Y si el Príncipe don Sancho,
> cuyas bravezas espantan,
> cuyos prodigios admiran,
> advirtiese que le agravias?
> ¿Qué señala, qué promete,
> sino incendios en España?
> Assí que, si bien lo miras,
> la misma, la misma causa
> que a lo que dizes te incita,
> te obliga a que no lo hagas. (126-127)

Diego Laínez's insight into Sancho's character proves correct. When Fernando breaks the news to his son to test his reaction, Sancho threatens more bloodshed, claiming that his cause is righteous:

> ¿Por qué no juntas en mí
> todas las fuerças de España?
> En quitarme lo que es mío,
> ¿no ves, padre, que me agravias?
> ... ...
> Tú, Señor, mil años bivas;
> pero si mueres... ¡mi espada
> juntará lo que me quitas,
> y hará una fuerça de tantas! (130-131)

In a violent crescendo of open hostility and threats, Fernando calls a curse down on his rebellious son:

> ¡Mis maldiciones te caygan
> si mis mandas no obedeces! (131)

An important change of perspective occurs between the two *Mocedades* plays. In the first *comedia* Diego Laínez's comments cast grave doubts on Fernando's wisdom, and, although Arias Gonzalo and Peransules offer good reasons in support of the division, the audience senses that the decision is wrong. The Fernando of the *Mocedades* is indeed a weak king, unable to protect Castile from the threats posed to its welfare by both internal and external forces. In dividing his kingdom he allows his role as caring father to supersede his role as ruler responsible for the political stability and well-being of the state. Paradoxically, in trying to protect his children from Sancho's violence he does the one thing that will precipitate that violence even more; in his misguided attempt to prevent the inevitable, Fernando has, in his own way, wrongly «read the stars». In this context, Sancho's anger at his father's actions has its justification in the first play. Our feelings towards him are ambivalent: though we disapprove of his violence we recognize that his father has wronged him.

Yet, in the *Hazañas* the righteousness of his cause is no longer an issue. When the work begins, Fernando has died and the division is a *fait accompli.* What the king had decreed on his deathbed has passed into law, and, right or wrong, must be upheld.[15] In this new light, Sancho's revolt is regarded as an act of disobedience and a violation of Christian order. The paternal curse of the *Mocedades,* consequently, becomes associated with the workings of divine justice.

The *Hazañas* opens on a note of tragic irony. The play begins in the midst of a battle between the army of King Sancho and that of his brother Alfonso, now king of León. Against offstage battle cries, Sancho and his captain appear on stage. Seeing that his army needs encouragement the king goes off to fight alongside his men, much against the advice of the captain:

> CAPITÁN: ¿Adónde vas, Rey don Sancho?
> D. SANCHO: ¡A morir!
> CAPITÁN: ¡Espera, aguarda! (139)

But the king ignores these words and runs off to battle. This short scene epitomizes the essence of Castro's portrayal of Sancho's situation throughout the drama. The captain is the first of various characters who attempt to alert the king to the consequences of his actions but who cannot prevent him from inviting and almost openly embracing a violent death. The haste of the king in this scene will have a more grave parallel when he later steals away from his army with Bellido Dolfos and finds himself alone with his destiny.

The inability of Sancho's most faithful subjects to save the king from himself is further reflected in the character of the Cid. In contrast to his role of saviour of the state in the first *Mocedades,* the Cid of the *Hazañas* assumes a different and more passive role, that of moral commentator. Rodrigo represents the voice of Christian conscience, much like the *ayo* of Bermúdez's *Nise laureada.* Their remarks concerning the king's conduct serve to place the action of their respective dramas within an ideological perspective. Rodrigo identifies Sancho's disobedience to his father's will with the violation of Christian precepts, and further identifies Fernando's curse with the course of divine justice. This equation is suggested in the *romancero viejo* when Rodrigo warns the king that God punishes disobedient children:

> mas nunca se logran hijos
> que al padre quiebran palabra. — Ni tampoco tuvo dicha

---

[15] WALTER KAUFMANN has noted a similar phenomenon in the *Agamemnon* of Aeschylus: «As soon as Agamemnon is dead, he is seen in a totally new perspective. Those who have lived through the assassination of John Kennedy need no explanation. The man of flesh and blood with his flaws and errors of judgment no longer matters.» WALTER KAUFMANN, *Tragedy and Philosophy* (New York: Doubleday, 1968), p. 221.

en cosa que se ocupaba, — nunca Dios le hizo merced,
ni es razón que se la haga.[16]

In the *Hazañas* the Cid reminds Sancho that in disobeying his father he is calling upon himself Divine Retribution:

> Y apenas murió el buen Rey,
> quando la mano levantas
> (sin mirar que desde el cielo
> con la suya te amenaça). (145)

And he recalls Fernando's curse:

> Acuérdate de que rompes
> a tu padre la palabra,
> y teme el ser desdichado
> si su maldición te alcança. (146)

Rodrigo laments the injury Sancho is criminally inflicting on the state by causing the senseless shedding of Christian blood. The renowned conqueror of the Moors sees Sancho as offending Heaven by diverting energies from the holy warfare against the real enemies of the Christian state:

> «¡Santiago!», dizen todos,
> y todos, «¡España, España!»;
> todo es valor español
> y todo sangre cristiana;
> todo es sangre, todo es fuego;
> aquí mueren y allí matan;
> el peso oprime a la tierra,
> y al cielo ofende la causa. (140)[17]

Although incapable of directly preventing Sancho from attacking Zamora, Rodrigo attempts on his own to carry out the will of Fernando while still remaining loyal to Sancho. Castro uses as a point of departure a detail found in some early ballads[18] in which Rodrigo swears to the dying Fernando not to attack Zamora. Thus, Castro's Rodrigo informs Sancho:

> Con mi lealtad ordinaria
> a defender tu persona
> siguiendo iré tus pisadas;

---

[16] MENÉNDEZ Y PELAYO, *Antología*, no. 40.
[17] Whereas the version found in the *Primera crónica general* clearly condemns Sancho for shedding Christian blood, the only reference to an intra-Christian war in the *romancero* is the following brief allusion:

> Entre dos reyes cristianos — hay muy grande división.

(MENÉNDEZ Y PELAYO, *Antología*, no. 38.)
[18] SAID ARMESTO, p. 147.

> pero vame juramento,
> y no saldrá de mi bayna
> mi espada contra Çamora. (147)

Rodrigo perhaps best represents Castro's ideal of the true «perfecto caballero»: the subject who tempers his allegiance to his lord with moral and ethical considerations. Rodrigo does not hesitate to disobey Sancho when he thinks him wrong even while continuing to pay him homage. Yet, on the other hand, this interpretation of Rodrigo as willing to put conscience above blind obedience is somewhat neutralized by the fact that his vow to Fernando in a way *compels* him, having made a promise, to oppose Sancho. Once more Castro has played off two contradictory visions: Rodrigo may be seen as following the dictates of his conscience and/or as merely caught between allegiances to two kings and attempting to be faithful to both.

Castro's intention to make Rodrigo a morally unblemished character is nowhere more patent than in the scene in which he frees the captive Alfonso after the battle of Golpejares. Here Castro deviates drastically from his ballad sources, which present the decisive action of the Cid as responsible for the capture of Alfonso:

> A Burgos llevaron preso — a Alfonso, del Rey hermano,
> por el gran esfuerzo y fechos — de aquese Cid castellano.[19]

Later, when Sancho orders his men to attack Alfonso again, Rodrigo vociferously protests:

> ¡Deteneos, gente arrojada!
> Tu Magestad se reporte,
> porque no es malicia tanta
> digna de un cristiano pecho. (143)

The Cid's exhortation cannot prevail against the king and the attack is resumed. The Cid is left alone on stage to ponder the king's folly: «—¡Oh, Rey mal aconsejado!», he laments in an aside (148).

The relationship between the paternal curse and the astrological prophecy is made explicit to Sancho by supernatural intervention. In a scene which has no precedent in the previous versions of the Zamora theme, a vision of Don Fernando appears to Sancho to warn him that death awaits him if he continues the siege.[20] This important scene begins with Urraca's call for heavenly aid from her father as she sees Sancho's

---

[19] AGUSTÍN DURÁN, *Romancero general*, vol. X of the *Biblioteca de Autores Españoles* (Madrid: M. Rivadeneyra, 1849), no. 765.

[20] The use of apparitions is a carry-over from the earlier neo-Senecan theater; see HERMENEGILDO, pp. 488-491. Omens of various types are found in nineteen of Castro's works; see L. L. BARRETT, «The Omen in Guillén de Castro's Theater», *Hispania*, 22 (1939), pp. 73-78.

men begin to climb the city walls. Sancho scoffs at her and, like Don Juan Tenorio, openly challenges Heaven:

> ¿Tu padre llamas? ¡Para hazerme guerra
> baxe del cielo, o salga de la tierra! (163)

Immediately a vision of Fernando rises from the earth, holding in its bloodied hand the spear that will kill Sancho. He warns Sancho that his siege is an offense to Heaven:

> Detén, Sancho, la mano, que violenta
> es injusta...
> ... ...
> Quien no obedece al padre ofende al cielo,
> y nunca tierra firme le sustenta. (163)

He then foretells Sancho's death:

> Tu muerte, Rey don Sancho, te revelo,
> cuyo i[n]strumento el cielo soberano
> puso a tus ojos y dejó en mi mano. (163)

Fernando's warning underlines two important concepts. First, Sancho can save himself from his prophesied death by curbing his ambition and asserting his *libre albedrío* (i.e. his choice to be saved). Second, if the prophecy is realized it will not be a senseless act of fate but an act of divine justice, a punishment for the disorder wrought on the kingdom by Sancho's ambition and disobedience.

The warning at first seems to work. Stricken with fear, Sancho hurriedly orders his troops to retreat. For a moment he achieves self-knowledge and recognizes the nature of his crime:

> Ingrato he sido
> a mi padre y a Dios. (164)

Arias Gonzalo sees in this retreat the hand of God:

> ¡Con qué priesa se retira!
> El mismo cielo por tus cosas mira. (164)

Urraca also notes the intervention of Heaven:

> El no perderse Zamora
> milagro del cielo ha sido;
> a mi hermano vi vencido,
> y a su gente vencedora. (166)

But Sancho, forever the impetuous *mancebo,* fails truly to conquer himself. Like a spoiled child he understands his phantom father's warning only as an impediment to his ambition. In a later scene he experiences not the repentance and self-knowledge that would prove him to be a worthy king and would grant him a reprieve from his punishment, but instead the desire both to carry out his will and still avoid punishment. When he communicates his vision to Diego Ordóñez he speaks only of his fear of death and of his ever-burning ambition:

>   Vi que, temblando, la tierra
>   abría el Cielo enojado;
>   vi de mi padre al abrilla,
>   el aspecto soberano,
>   y de un venablo en su mano
>   vi la sangrienta cuchilla,
>   —¡paréceme que a la vista
>   le tengo!— y tras esto veo
>   abraçarse mi deseo
>   por hazer esta conquista. (170-171)

Diego Ordóñez forces Sancho to come to terms with the real motives for his retreat. Not understanding the divine nature of the vision, Ordóñez assumes it is the result of a spell cast by a magician and intended to frighten Sancho away from Zamora. He tells the king that to withdraw solely out of fear is an act of cowardice but that a retreat based on an interior moral conviction will not cause him dishonor:

>   Si es que el cerco se levanta
>   porque pesa en tu conciencia
>   la justísima obediencia
>   de tu padre, cosa es santa.
>   Mas si es por esta visión
>   fantástiga, ciega y vana,
>   a tu valor, cosa es llana,
>   que ofendes...
>   Si es que por hijo obediente
>   lo dexaras, justo fuera;
>   mas si no, poco te estimas,
>   si es que por eso lo dexas. (171)

Diego Ordóñez's reasoning is couched in terms of worldly values: cowardice posing as virtue fools no one and only results in dishonor.[21] But a theological argument is implied as well: man is absolved from sin and subsequently redeemed not by a superficial repentance brought on by a fear of eternal damnation but by the inner realization that one has offended God, coupled with a resolve to mend one's sinful ways. Only the latter course can save Sancho from his doom. But the king is concerned with evading retribution rather than with self-reform, just as in the *Mocedades* he sought to change his destiny by simply arming himself against his assassins. Thus, when Diego Ordóñez suggests that

---

[21] Sancho himself worries whether in his retreat, «pierdo opinión» (171).

the vision of his father may be an illusion, Sancho's momentary repentance is revealed for what it really is. Dismissing supernatural warnings that he is offending Heaven, Sancho returns to his former confidence that he can defy his fate and realize his ambition. In his decision to renew the siege he reveals a fatal incomprehension: a belief that his destiny depends on the arbitrary workings of blind Fate rather than on Divine Providence. Sancho confides in a pre-Christian superstition in a world ordered by Christian principles. Replacing the insight implicit in his words «Ingrato he sido / a mi padre y a Dios» is the concept of pagan Fortune:

> ... si la estrella que sigo
> con venablos me amenaça,
> para poderme igualar
> en las armas al contrario,
> en la mano de ordinario
> un venablo he de llevar.
> Iguales armas tenemos
> la Fortuna y yo... (172) [22]

With this gesture of defiance Sancho rejects Heaven's merciful intervention. As the king embraces the lance, offstage shouts announce the arrival of Bellido Dolfos and the audience of ballad singers and listeners knows that Sancho's doom is sealed as well as they know their own names. Dramatic tension mounts as in ensuing scenes Castro exploits ironic foreknowledge by interpolating well-known *romances* at length and by showing how Sancho disregards further warnings as if fatally drawn towards death.

If Castro's portrayal of Sancho's dilemma conforms to the orthodox Christian doctrine —illustrated so clearly in *comedias* such as *El condenado por desconfiado*— that Heavenly signs can only serve to guide man and not to force his will, and that every man directs his own destiny by exercising his *libre albedrío,* his treatment of Bellido Dolfos seems to suggests just the opposite. Bellido is presented as a natural coward whom Heaven manipulates to serve as an instrument of divine justice. Bellido senses that he is not master of his own will and is constantly surprised to find himself filled with courage. As Leavitt has pointed

---

[22] The problem of Fortune versus Providence was a major theme in medieval literature throughout Europe. For a study of the Christian concept «No hay más Fortuna que Dios» in Spain, see GREEN, *Spain and the Western Tradition,* II, pp. 279-337.
  Both LIDIA SANTELICES and SAID ARMESTO note that in the *Primera crónica general,* chapter 836, it is stated that the king customarily carried a golden lance as a scepter. In purposely altering this detail Castro makes the *venablo* a dramatic symbol of Sancho's defiance of Heaven. It is also a symbol fraught with irony, for the spectator understands that this very weapon will be the instrument by which Sancho will meet his death.

out, Bellido, appears to be possessed by a mysterious «divine frenzy» which inspires or abandons him in direct relationship to King Sancho's actions:

> This frenzy, dependent as it is upon the attitude of the king, does not always sustain the traitor. Whenever the king even remotely considers withdrawing from the siege, the spirit animating Bellido departs and he finds himself in a very desperate situation. In these moments he becomes his real and cowardly self, appreciating fully the danger he is in and reacting to it in a very natural manner.[23]

Given such a situation, Bellido Dolfos stands somewhere between being a divinely inspired saviour and an odious traitor.

Bellido first appears on stage as a messenger, when he brings Urraca news of the Cid's liberation of Sancho from captivity, a scene dramatized earlier in the act. Even then, he is already associated with misfortune, for upon seeing him, Urraca fears the news he may bring, and Arias Gonzalo declares with sarcasm:

> Sí, no lo dudes,
> pues él tan presto se obligó a traellas. (150)

He is characterized here as a coward, fearing Sancho's imminent attack; he tells Urraca:

> Con más causas darás al alma miedo,
> quando sepas que el muro de Çamora
> viene ya amenaçando. (151)

However Bellido undergoes a miraculous metamorphosis after Fernando's premonitory appearance to Sancho. He feels a new surge of patriotism for Zamora and resolves, in spite of possible personally dire consequences, to deliver the city by killing the king:

> ¡Ay, Zamora desdichada!
> ¡Ay, patria amada y querida,
> injustamente perdida
> y dignamente adorada!
> ... ...
> Aunque tenga el fin funesto
> la intención que traygo agora,
> la libertad de Zamora
> gallardamente he dispuesto. (164-165)

---

[23] STURGIS E. LEAVITT, «Divine Justice in *Las Hazañas del Cid*», *Hispania*, 12 (1929), pp. 145-146. For further comments on Castro's unusual treatment of Bellido Dolfos, see MANUEL DELGADO MORALES, «Tiranía y derecho de resistencia en *Las mocedades del Cid*», *Segismundo*, 15 (1981), pp. 173-184. Professor Delgado's study corroborates to a large extent my analysis of Castro's attitude towards King Sancho and Bellido Dolfos.

He discovers in himself an unprecedented valor that surprises even him:

> Mas toda el alma se admira
> del valor que en mí no afloxa.
> ¿Quién me anima? ¿quién me arroja?
> ¿quién me tienta, o quién me inspira? (165)

He senses that he is divinely guided, as that alone can explain the absence of the fear he experienced before committing previous crimes:

> Algún impulso divino
> da fuego a mi pensamiento;
> del cielo soy instrumento,
> aunque malo, peregrino.
> ... ...
> ... Loco estoy
> de ver que covarde soy
> y la muerte no me espanta. (165)

Heaven has also delivered him from the wrath of the *zamoranos* and allowed him safely to cross enemy lines:

> ... el cielo me traxo aquí
> por milagro... (175)

What is most unusual about this vision of Bellido Dolfos, then, is that it is Heaven itself which seems both to inspire him with the requisite patriotic fervor to conceive of the assassination of the king as an act of deliverance, and to endow him with the valor to carry the plan through. Heaven is not merely allowing him to kill the king, it is actually guiding him. Thus, Bellido's surprised consciousness of himself and the audience's traditional consciousness of his tainted identity are used by Guillén de Castro to create utterly new tensions out of the utterly old legend.

Bellido's intended «treachery» is patent to all but King Sancho who is enticed by his offer to win him Zamora. In the last scenes of the first act both Arias Gonzalo and Rodrigo attempt to alert their lord to impending danger but Sancho will be guided only by his ambition. Arias Gonzalo's warning is staged like another voice from Heaven; as Bellido begins to tell the king of his plan to overtake Zamora, the voice of the old man is heard from within the city walls:

> ¡Ah, Rey don Sancho! ¡Ah, Señor!... (177)

This cry instills Bellido with his natural fear, as he senses that the king might change his mind.

The Spanish public, immersed in the tradition of the *romancero*, would, of course, recognize this warning as a variation of the first verse of the famous ballad that begins:

>—¡Rey don Sancho, rey don Sancho, — no digas que no te aviso
> que de dentro de Zamora — un alevoso ha salido:
> llámase Vellido Dolfos, — hijo de Dolfos Vellido,
> cuatro traiciones ha hecho, — y con ésta serán cinco! [24]

Castro plays on the audience's anticipation of the rest of the ballad by interpolating comments on the warning by Rodrigo, Sancho and Bellido. Rodrigo's remarks on the foreboding voice are a variation on yet another ballad;[25] they assume the impersonal and yet solemn tone of the ballad singer:

> Muy grandes bozes se oyeron
> en el Real de don Sancho,
> que las dava un Cavallero
> de Çamora en el andamio. (177-178)

Finally, Arias Gonzalo appears above King Sancho, atop the city walls, a staging that suggests a last Heavenly warning. Again Castro teases the audience with the promise of a familiar ballad; he creates a special tension in the audience by slowly offering his spectators single lines that are recognizable variants of *romance* verses and then releases this tension with a lengthy passage in *romance* meter which clearly imitates the traditional ballad:

---

[24] MENÉNDEZ Y PELAYO, *Antología*, no. 45. «El 45 se cantaba ya en tiempo de Enrique IV, y deriva de la grandiosa gesta del *Cerco de Zamora*. Juan de la Cueva, Lope, Claramonte, Matos Fragoso, Diamante y tantos otros, supieron sacar dramático efecto de este romance, encajándolo en varias de sus obras. Era tal su popularidad, que el antiguo repertorio dramático se lo transporta a situaciones de muy varia índole...» SAID ARMESTO, p. 177.

Lope adapted these verses in the description of the death of King Sancho in *Las almenas de Toro* (1610-1613), a work he dedicated to Guillén de Castro. In this play the events of Zamora are narrated by the character Enrique in a long *relación* in *romance* meter. According to MARSHA H. SWISLOCKI: «Enrique's *relación* begins with a rapid list of his activities upon his arrival at Zamora, an important step establishing him as an eyewitness to the events that take place there... He then reports what happened, paraphrasing two *romances* from the cycle of Zamora: 'Rey don Sancho, rey don Sancho' and 'Ya cabalga Diego Ordóñez'... [In Lope's version of the first of these ballads] the assonance is changed; many of the traditional lines are retained, but many others are entirely new, creating a hybrid version of the *romance*. Probably no ballad was more famous than 'Rey don Sancho', and yet by creating a new version of it Lope permits his audience to listen as though hearing it for the first time (i.e. as though present at its 'birth')... Lope even ties the events at Zamora to what the audience has just seen happen at Toro in the previous act. By mentioning as though it were proverbial the *traición* of Bellido Dolfos at Toro he again gives a sense of the immediacy with which the ballads spring out of events as they occur and stimulate the popular imagination to record them in poetry.» MARSHA H. SWISLOCKI, «Lope, the *Romancero* and the *Comedia*», Unpubl. Diss. Harvard, 1976, pp. 94-95.

[25] SAID ARMESTO, p. 177, cites the source as a *romance* of Pedro Padilla which begins: «Muy grandes voces se oyeron / en el Real de Don Sancho.»

ARIAS:	¡Ah, Rey! ¡Ah, Señor!...
RODRIGO:	Escucha; desde aquí le devisamos.
ARIAS:	De un traydor te guarda...
D. DIEGO:	Entera llega su voz.
D. SANCHO:	¡Cielo santo!
ARIAS:	... que de Çamora ha salido, Bellido de Olfos llamado, traydor, hijo de traydores. El hechizo de sus labios no te engañe, que a su padre y a su misma sangre ingrato, le mató, y echó en un río; testigo bien declarado de quien es. Matarte quiere; toma mi consejo llano; no digas que no te aviso, no acuerdes tarde, don Sancho. (178)

Arias' final words serve to remind the audience of Sancho's ultimate responsibility for his own fate:

> que no puede dar el mundo
> de tan desastrado caso,
> ni a tu descuydo disculpa,
> ni culpa a los çamoranos. (179)

The power of these scenes, then, derives from both the use of *romance* verses and meter and their staging.

On the heels of Arias' cry Rodrigo confronts the king in an attempt to convince him that Arias Gonzalo, and not Bellido, merits his trust. The king will not listen, and a strict code of obedience frustrates Rodrigo from correcting the situation himself:

> ¡Oh, santa obediencia,
> lazo agora de mis manos!... (180)

Angered by the Cid's verbal attacks on Bellido, he orders the Cid banished for one year. Here Castro again departs from his sources. In both the *romance* and chronicles Sancho exiles the Cid for a different reason: he believes that Rodrigo, a childhood friend of Urraca, advised her not to surrender Zamora. In the *Hazañas* this accusation is uttered by Bellido, who wants to discredit the hero:

> Si el favorecer al Cid
> tu hermana Urraca Fernando
> los caducos lo entendieron
> y los niños lo cantaron,
> y el amor entre los dos
> recíproco, aunque pasado,

> tiene fuerça en sus reliquias
> mayor que en los muros altos
> de Çamora... (180-181) [26]

With the banishment of the Cid the king symbolically rejects salvation; Diego Ordóñez sees it as a move towards willful self-destruction:

> Señor, ¿el Cid desterrado
> de tu tierra, que en tus tierras
> es la fuerça de tus braços? (183) [27]

Soon realizing his error, Sancho immediately recalls the Cid from exile, though he still continues to ignore his warning.

The first act ends with a struggle within the king. For a short moment he stops and becomes aware of the danger into which he is heading. «Mucho emprendo» he reflects in a meaningful aside (184), only to return to his folly with stronger resolution («Bellido, yo estoy resuelto»; 184). The final line is a menacing aside by Bellido reminding us once again that the king will most surely meet his death: «Tú has de morir a mis manos» (184).

The opening scene of Act II again reminds the audience that Sancho risks divine retribution. Rodrigo, returning from his brief exile, again laments the shedding of Christian blood and comments:

---

[26] The phenomenon of characters in a play being aware of a ballad tradition which treats events of their own times is also found in Lope's *Las almenas de Toro* in which Bellido comments to Sancho:

> Ya se canta por ahí
> y hasta en la cama se duerme
> el niño con las canciones
> que se han hecho a las almenas
> de Toro, y están llenas
> de tu historia mil naciones.

According to MARSHA H. SWISLOCKI this is a common occurrence in the theater of Lope: «... there is... an awareness on the part of the characters that they have become part of a *romance* tradition that has sprung out of events in which they are still participating. Again we see Lope's interest internalizing dramatically the processes of traditionalization... that the characters themselves should be aware of these processes and express their awareness within the framework of the play is an example of the unique intermingling of poetry and life which is at the heart of Lope's poetics». SWISLOCKI, pp. 92-93.

[27] We have seen a similar passage in *El nacimiento de Montesinos* when the King exiles Grimaltos. Exile by the king of the subject most loyal to him is a repeated motif in Castro's plays and Castro's modification of the circumstances of the Cid's exile follows the pattern set by the earlier works. The Cid responds to Sancho's threat of banishment with verses taken from the *romances* of the episode of the «jura de Santa Gadea» which were originally concerned with his exile from the kingdom of Alfonso VI:

> Rey don Sancho, Rey don Sancho,
> tú me destierras por uno,
> yo me destierro por quatro. (181)

> A Dios pluguiera,
> don Diego, que lo estuviera [i.e. arrepentido]
> de haver al cielo ofendido. (185)

The Conde de Cabra has discovered that King Sancho has slipped away from his encampment and is alone with Bellido. Realizing the danger, the Count, Rodrigo and don Diego seek him out in a last attempt to save him. But it is too late; only the king can save himself. Castro visually underscores the futility of the nobles' efforts through the use of the split stage. As on one side of the stage they search for the king, Sancho and Bellido enter from the other. Seeing them, Bellido draws the king away from the nobles and trembles with fear at the thought of being discovered. Added to the verbal ironies of the play is a visual irony: though the stage gives the impression of physical proximity between the two groupings, they are prevented by Bellido's intervention from discovering each other. Sancho comments:

> Tan lexos estava,
> que apenas la pude ver. (187)

As the nobles leave the stage they grieve for the king in a foreboding, chorus-like apostrophe:

> D. DIEGO: ¡Oh, mancebo mal regido!
> RODRIGO: ¡Oh, Rey mal aconsejado! (187)

The king and Bellido are now alone before the city walls. Bellido, aware of his treachery, wavers and trembles before deciding to strike the king. He despises himself for his fear. Bellido's monologue before throwing the javelin is a coward's grotesque parody of the conflict monologues found in Castro's theater:

> ¡De animoso estoy resuelto!
> Mas... ¿qué yelo, en sangre embuelto,
> por mis venas viene, y va?
>   Ciega el alma ¿con qué espanto,
> en qué inconvenientes piensa?
> Si es un hombre sin defensa
> ¿cómo el ser Rey puede tanto?
>   Pero ya cobro valor;
> ya el yelo en mis venas arde.
> ¡Mataréle! que el covarde
> de lexos mata mejor.
>   Pero... ¿qué miedo, qué laço
> me detiene? ¿En qué despecho
> se acovarda siempre el pecho
> y se encoge siempre el braço? (190)

He achieves the necessary valor only after calling on Heaven to instill in him the strength to carry out his divine mission:

> ¡Cielo, cielo soberano,
> valedme en esta ocasión!
> Esforçar mi coraçón,
> pues castigáys con mi mano. (190)

After killing the king Bellido runs back to Zamora in cowardly fear. According to Leavitt:

> ... Bellido, having accomplished the will of Heaven, loses his divine frenzy and again becomes a cringing human being to whom is eventually meted out punishment in accordance with the standards of mortals who do not comprehend the hidden and terrible ways of Providence.[28]

Death awakens King Sancho to truth. In the throes of death the monarch finally attains true self-knowledge and gives his assent to his assassination:

> Fui hijo inobediente, estuve ciego,
> y el cielo me castiga, a quien le pido
> que entre agua y sangre, me perdone el fuego.
> Sólo instrumento a su justicia he sido;
> que de matar a un Rey atrevimiento
> no tuviera Çamora, ni Bellido. (200)

And later:

> La culpa es mía,
> y de Dios la justicia.[29] (201)

---

[28] LEAVITT, «Divine Justice», p. 145.
[29] In the *Primera crónica general* King Sancho sees that his death is a punishment for his sins: «ca bien beo que muerto so, et matome el traydor de Bellid Adolfo que se auia fecho mi basallo; et bien tengo que esto fue por mis pecados et por las soberuias que fiz a mios hermanos et pase el mandamiento et la jura que fiz a mi padre que non tolliese a ninguno de mios hermanos nada de lo suyo». He also asks Alfonso for forgiveness: «Ruegovos ansi como amigos et a basallos buenos et leales, que digades a mi hermano don Alfonso que me perdone de quanto tuerto le fize et que roguedes a Dios por mi que me aya el alma» (Chapter XXV). The complete chronicle version may be found in REIG.
The following are *romance* renditions of this detail:

> (1) Yo bien sé cuál es la causa,
> Que en tal punto soy llegado
> Por pecados cometidos
> Al inmenso Dios sagrado,
> Y también fue por la jura
> Que a mi padre hube quebrado. (DURÁN, no. 785)
>
> (2) Porque la muerte del Rey
> Permisión de Dios ha sido,
> Porque quebrantó el mandado
> Qu'el Rey su padre le hizo. (DURÁN, no. 790)
>
> (3) Cáusanlo los mis pecados,
> Que contra Dios cometía,
> Y por ir contra la jura
> Que al mi padre yo hacía. (DURÁN, no. 782)

Before he dies he asks his family for forgiveness for his crimes against them.

In this final awakening Sancho understands the human condition: death, the great equalizer, reduces powerful kings to mere mortals, accountable to God for their sins. This lesson is first suggested when the king is forced to dismount in order to relieve himself:

> A cierta necesidad,
> que a los Reyes no perdona,
> me desvío. (189)

It is in this most unexalted and defenseless of positions that Sancho is slain. When Don Diego hears the king's cries of anguish in the woods, Sancho identifies himself to him as merely:

> Un desdichado...
> ... ...
> Un hombre que ha sido... (192)

And later he comprehends that none are exempt from death and final judgment before the Divine Judge:

> no hay segura corona ni tiara.
> Pasóme de un venablo la cuchilla;
> que, sagrado o real, qualquiera pecho,
> es de barro también. (201-202) [30]

Castro offers no easy *comedia* resolution to the death of Sancho. Whether his self-awareness and plea for forgiveness earn him a reprieve from eternal damnation remains unanswered. For Castro, Sancho represents a tragic *exemplum* of a man who, filled with pride and ambition, forgets that he is subject to a higher king and who discovers too late his place in the cosmic order.

Although Guillén de Castro presents the regicide as Heaven's punishment for Sancho's disobedience he does not present the act, as he had in earlier works, as a dramatic solution. Instead, it is a source of greater disorder, provoking further enmity between *castellanos* and *zamoranos*. For the omniscient spectator guided by the dramatist, this

---

Sancho's self accusation is not found in any of the *romances viejos tradicionales*. REIG classifies the first two as *viejos*, but *juglarescos*, and the third as *nuevo* and *erudito*.

[30] A similar message is to be found at the opening of a *romance nuevo*:

> A los muros de Zamora
> Herido está don Sancho
> Que del castigo de Dios
> No hay seguro rey humano.

(REIG, p. 362.)

continued conflict is filled with irony, for while he interprets the assassination as a terrible mystery of Providence, the characters, guided only by their fallible human judgment, can see it only in terms of a violation of human law and can rest only when the demands of that law have been met. The characters' categorical declarations that the king's murder is a crime that cries for justice cannot but be questioned by the audience. Similarly, their staunch allegiance to the king as king cannot but be regarded with ambivalence, particularly when this noble sentiment brings about the seemingly senseless tragedy of the innocent Arias Gonzalo. When Rodrigo proclaims after Sancho's death that «Todo el cielo viene abajo» (199) he could well be describing the reaction of the spectator as he sees himself immersed in a dramatic cosmos where his former beliefs and values are profoundly shaken.

Unlike the characters of *El amor constante* and *El perfecto caballero* who welcome the killing of the king and support the political theories of Mariana, the reaction of those of the *Hazañas* reveals a more «orthodox» stance, as in this important interchange between Bellido and one of Arias' sons:

> BELLIDO: ¿Trayción es poner la mano
> en un rey que fue tirano?
> HIJO 1.º: Nunca es tirano el Señor. (209)

Although Bellido liberates the Zamorans from an unjust siege they react with revulsion to the murder. As he enters the city they cry in unison: «¡Muera el traydor homicida!» (207). Bellido cannot comprehend the apparent ingratitude of those he saved from tyranny:

> ¡Ah, Çamora, cómo en mí
> tu noble opinión estragas,
> pues con prisiones me pagas
> la libertad que te di!
> ¡Por hecho tan valeroso
> atáys tan valientes manos! (210)

But all consider loyalty to the principle of monarchy to be absolute and regicide unjustifiable even if the king proves himself to be unjust. Diego Ordóñez states this position earlier, in response to the dying monarch's statement that neither Bellido nor Zamora are to be considered guilty for his death:

> ... no porque el castigo es justo, es bueno,
> dexa de ser el instrumento malo. (200)

If on one hand we admire the refusal of these loyal subjects to compromise their principles, on the other we recognize that these very principles prevent these men from dealing adequately with this morally problematic issue. Sancho's deathbed plea to recognize the innocence of both Bellido and Zamora goes unheeded as all involved, notably Diego Ordóñez, persist in attempting to apply the reasoning of human justice to a situation they will never fully comprehend.

Error is compounded by further error as the dissimulation of Doña Urraca leads the Castilians to believe that Bellido carried through the explicit mandate of the *zamoranos* in killing the king. Urraca is the most morally insidious character of the *comedia,* for while Bellido believes that he is carrying out the will of Heaven, Urraca acquiesces to the assassination believing that it is treason; while Bellido's motives are pure, Urraca's are self-serving.[31]

Urraca befriends Bellido when he first promises to rescue Zamora. But when Bellido begins to tell her of his plan to kill the king she cuts him short, thereby tacitly giving consent to what she believes to be a crime while feigning ignorance:

> ¡Calla,
> si es trayción; y en mi querella
> escusará el no sabella
> la culpa de no escusalla! (167)

Though hiding the secrets of her heart from those surrounding her she cannot escape from her own conscience. From the moment Bellido leaves Zamora she is filled with apprehension and a vague sense of wrongdoing:

> ¿Qué intención le havrá obligado
> a Bellido? No la entiendo.
>   Y este impensado rigor
> me atemoriça, ¡ay cuytada!
> pues yo soy tan desdichada
> como Bellido es traydor. (170)

When later she sees Bellido fleeing from the pursuing Rodrigo she realizes that she is implicated in Bellido's crime («¡Estoy perdida!», 193). Nonetheless, she refuses to publicize openly her complicity. Rather than punish Bellido she attempts to protect him, and when Rodrigo nears the city walls in pursuit she shames the hero into retreating, thereby assuring Bellido access to the city.[32] When the Zamorans demand the death

---

[31] Though most chronicle and ballad accounts implicate Urraca in some way, one *romance nuevo* makes her guilt absolutely explicit as she herself plans Sancho's death:

> Y non lidiaré con él,
> mas a furto o paladina
> yo haré que le den la muerte
> que muy bien la merecía. (Durán, no. 770)

[32] Her rebuke of the Cid quotes directly lines from the *romance viejo* «¡Afuera, afuera, Rodrigo / el sobervio Castellano!» (Durán, no. 774). However the original

of the traitor she again feigns ignorance and when finally, but grudgingly, persuaded by Arias Gonzalo that Bellido has committed treason, she accedes to his imprisonment but forbids his execution.[33] Though privately acknowledging her guilt, she publicly declares her innocence:

> Cubran de funesto luto
> las murallas de Çamora,
>   y vean el sentimiento
> con que esta desdicha pago,
> mi inocencia, en lo que hago,
> y mi pena, en lo que siento. (209)

It is Bellido Dolfos who comes closest to expressing what is probably Guillén de Castro's view of this morally problematic situation as he complains that he is being sacrificed as a convenient scapegoat for the guilt of others:

> Mas ya, indignos çamoranos
> del nombre antiguo y famoso,
>   ya entiendo vuestra intención
> aunque no me la digáys,
> pues al traidor castigáys
> para lograr la trayción.
>   Mano fui con que tirastes
> la piedra. (210)

Though he is wrong in accusing all of Zamora he has a just complaint against Urraca, who refuses to admit openly that she consented to the assassination. And it is remotely possible that hidden under this rhetoric is the blasphemous thought that Heaven too used Bellido as an instrument for its own providential ends and then cruelly abandoned him to suffer death and infamy as a traitor.

Urraca's sheltering of Bellido effectively implicates the whole city. Diego Ordóñez, the drama's most uncompromising moral judge, argues that all of Zamora is guilty for having welcomed Bellido back into the city. But Rodrigo, less quick to judge a difficult moral question, casts doubt on the validity of such a blanket condemnation. Not sharing the

---

ballad has a different setting; there Urraca chastizes the Cid not when he is pursuing Bellido but when, representing Sancho, he asks her to cede Zamora.

[33] Again the quintessential deceptive politician, she pretends to have the best interest of the city at heart; when Arias Gonzalo suggests that if they do not execute Bellido the city will be implicated in the regicide, she responds:

> Y ¿no será lo más cierto,
> pues la ocasión los obliga,
> dezir que porque no diga
> los cómplices lo hemos muerto,
>   y resultar del suceso
> otra mayor desventura? (208-209)

vengeful wrath of don Diego, Rodrigo remembers that Arias Gonzalo, far from desiring the king's death, tried to prevent it:

> [H]irviendo agora,
> da lugar al enojo, y no al sosiego.
> ... ...
> Que lo fue [i.e. traidor] Arias Gonçalo no lo creo,
> pues aún, lleva su voz el aire vano
> con que quiso estorbar tan mal deseo. (203-204)

Both agree to challenge Zamora to a duel in an attempt to determine guilt, but whereas the overly-confident Diego Ordóñez is certain it will prove Zamora's culpability, the more circumspect Rodrigo refuses to anticipate the outcome. Diego Ordóñez, King Sancho's most unquestioning subject, threatens to continue the disruptive intra-Christian warfare begun by his monarch. On the other hand, Rodrigo, who in the *Mocedades* learned from the leper/Saint Lazarus that «No con sólo pelear / se gana el cielo...» (104), seeks to put an end to the inner strife afflicting Castile. But just as Rodrigo could not halt his king, so he cannot prevail against Diego Ordóñez's blind vengeance.

Diego Ordóñez's challenge to Zamora and the decision of Arias Gonzalo to represent the besieged city precipitate the *comedia*'s final irony: Arias Gonzalo, the most loyal of the inhabitants of Zamora, will be made to sacrifice three of his sons in atonement for Zamora's unwilling participation in King Sancho's death.[34]

Castro's portrait of Arias Gonzalo emphasizes a human warmth and nobility that makes his tragedy the most moving of the drama. According to Lidia Santelices:

> En los romances es más bien un soldado rudo y pundonoroso, el deber prima en él con menos esfuerzo, mientras en Castro su dolor es humano, la lucha es más difícil y desgarradora. El calor de vida, la exquisita ternura, los toques delicados son de nuestro autor.[35]

---

[34] Castro's dramatization of the *reto* episode attempts both to recapture the spirit of the medieval *romance* and to visualize medieval ceremony. The whole scene from verses 1510 through 1625 is written in *romance* meter. Stage directions of the opening of this scene place emphasis on the visual as well as aural elements («... sale arriba Doña Urraca y Arias Gonzalo; y tocan trompas roncas y tambores destemplados y va saliendo el entierro del Rey, y pasando, y entrándose»; 211) as does the later appearance of don Diego («... suena una trompeta, y descúbre[se] en un cavallo a Don Diego Ordóñez de Lara, que viene armado, cubierto de luto, y con una mortaja al hombro, y un Crucifixo en la mano derecha»; 212). Arias Gonzalo's description of the passing funeral procession, verses of Castro's own invention, recalls the tone of many a *romance viejo* in its enumeration of visual details: «Mira en orden las hileras / que vienen de quatro en quatro... Mira a sus pies su corona... mira el agudo venablo...» (211). Don Diego's challenge and Arias Gonzalo's response directly cite many lines from the *romances viejos* (Cfr. DURÁN, nos. 789, 790 and 791).

[35] LIDIA SANTELICES, p. 173. The author also notes that in keeping with this

Arias serves as surrogate father and as chief advisor to Urraca. When the queen laments her brother's siege early in Act I the old man offers his family as the chief defenders of Zamora's independence:

>Defenderánte el muro de Çamora
>estos cinco renuevos arrancados
>de este árbol verde, aunque marchito agora. (149)

Arias clearly distinguishes between defending natural rights and offending the king. In a scene from the first act Sancho confronts him with the argument that loyalty demands complete submission to the king's will. Arias Gonzalo replies that obedience to Fernando takes precedence over Sancho:

>Leyes suyas defiendo, que atropellas
>con tanta fuerça y con injuria tanta;
>¡y los Reyes que son Cristianos Reyes,
>no rompen fueros, ni derogan leyes! (161)

To Sancho's accusation that this is an act of treason, Arias Gonzalo answers that he is defending the cause of «el mismo cielo»:

>¡No soy [i.e. traidor]! ¡Y el mismo cielo
>defiende mi justicia averiguada! (161)

Nonetheless, he proclaims absolute respect for the king's person, establishing early in the drama his opposition to the inevitable assassination which the audience awaits breathlessly:

>Nadie te ha de ofender, Rey soberano.
>... ... ...
>si subes solo, besaré tu mano;
>pero el que te acompañe, por mis braços
>al suelo ha de bolver hecho pedaços. (162)

For the audience the loyalty of this Castilian Nestor is never in doubt.

The opening of the third act adds a note of tragic nobility to the characterization of the old man. Though sensing that death stands ready to claim the lives of his sons he nonetheless nobly accepts the responsibilities of defending the honor of his beloved city. In first addressing his sons, he stoically resigns himself to the possibility that he might lose them:

>A morir, si no a vencer,
>hoy los cinco havemos de ir,
>y yo el primero he de ser. (227)

---

moral celebration of Arias Gonzalo, Castro deletes references in the ballads that suggest that the old man had been the lover of Urraca.

Having awakened early, he awaits the rising of the sun in dreadful anticipation, sensing in nature a foreboding of his own tragedy:

> ¡Oh, lo que tarda en salir
> el Sol! Pero no me espanto;
> teme que lo han de partir
> y por esso tarda tanto. (228)

His anxiety contrasts strongly with the vigorous joy with which his sons anticipate the combat as a test of their valor. An old man and loving father, he offers to sacrifice himself by facing the mature strength of Diego Ordóñez rather than witness the fate of his sons.[36] However, he is eventually dissuaded from being the first to fight by Urraca, who, plagued with fear and grief, asks that Arias Gonzalo remain at her side. Placing duty before his natural paternal desire to protect his sons, the old man reluctantly agrees and, in so doing, is forced to watch his sons die at the hands of Diego Ordóñez, a fate more painful for him than his own death. Moving as these scenes may be in themselves, they carry a greater tragic force for the spectator well versed in the Zamora legend and armed with the foreknowledge of the death of the Arias brothers. For the audience the tragedy that awaits Arias Gonzalo is inevitable, his future grief certain.

The feeling of tragic inevitability that hovers over the Arias family is further heightened by Castro's staging of the combat. The appearance of Diego Ordóñez on the field of combat is announced by a trumpet whose sound instills fear in Arias Gonzalo:

> Una y dos veces replica
> la trompeta... ¡Ah, quién pudiera
> salir! Mis males publica,
> sobradamente me altera...
> ¡Qué daños me pronostica! (234)

Two soldiers, serving as a chorus, comment on the fearful gravity of the ritual about to be enacted. The image of a bloodied rising sun evokes a powerful sense of doom, as does the silence of the crowd:

> SOLDADO 2.º: ¡Hasta el Sol está sangriento!
> ¡Sangriento el día ha de ser!
> SOLDADO 1.º: El mirar la empaliçada
> la sangre al pecho retira...

---

[36] This is but one more metamorphosis of the recurrent theme of a younger son taking over the responsibilities of a weaker father that we have seen in all of the plays of this study. Its treatment in the *Hazañas* comes closest to the *Mocedades* in its contrast of the ages of man: the frustrating weakness of old age, the virility of the mature years, and the unbounded confidence of youth. See PEDRO SALINAS, «La espada y los tiempos de la vida en *Las mocedades del Cid*», in *Ensayos de literatura hispánica* (Madrid: Aguilar, 1958), pp. 151-157.

> SOLDADO 2.º: ¡Y qué de gente la mira
> atónita y admirada!
> Hombres y piedras se imitan
> en el callar.
> SOLDADO 1.º: ¿Quién vio tal?
> A silencio general
> unos a otros se incitan.   (235-236)

The judges, the Counts Nuño and García, echo the sentiments of the soldiers:

> CONDE NUÑO: No vi tan gran suspensión.
> CONDE GARCÍA: No temí tan triste día.   (236)

For Arias Gonzalo, Diego Ordóñez is the specter of death:

> ¡Es la imagen de la muerte!
> ¡Ay, hijos del alma mía!   (238) [37]

The combat itself takes place offstage, its progress related by various observers. This bold dramatic stroke shuns the reproduction of pure spectacle and achieves greater emotional impact by concentrating attention on the reactions of Arias Gonzalo as he watches death claim his sons. These scenes convey the feeling of a ritualistic sacrifice which, once set in motion, follows its own inexorable course. What matters here is not the deaths themselves but the agony of Arias Gonzalo, a grief purified to nobility by his refusal to shed tears publicly. As Urraca begins to cry, Arias Gonzalo stoically cautions:

> ¡Mira que impides, Señora,
> con el llanto la vengança!
> Demás que no hay que llorar
> a quien muere honradamente...
> —La pena que el alma siente [*Aparte*]
> me importa disimular;
> no digan, pues soy honrado,
> que como muger me aflixo.   (243)

Holding back his tears, he heroically exhorts each successive son to fight honorably and to defend the good name of the city.

Set off against the noble resignation of Arias Gonzalo is the arrogance of Diego Ordóñez, the embodiment of an absolute moral and social code. As we have seen in Act II, don Diego cannot accept the ambiguities surrounding Sancho's death. In a play of moral complexities he can only perceive reality as uni-dimensional: Zamora must be guilty and its

---

[37] Diego Ordóñez's victory seems further assured by the fact that by allowing himself to be convinced not to fight first, Arias Gonzalo is forced to send out his youngest son against the experienced Don Diego. For Pedro Arias, just recently knighted, this will be his first and last combat.

punishment sanctioned by Heaven. In the third act he is the personification of blind, self-righteous vengeance. In line with his rhetorically overblown challenge to Zamora he misses no opportunity to insult the Zamorans and exalt his own cause. That don Diego is dangerously overconfident in the justice of his cause is time and again noted by Rodrigo. When the challenger declares that he intends to proclaim his victories not only by touching a stick planted in the ground after each success but also by throwing stakes into the air, a redundant and arrogant gesture, Rodrigo cautions «Esso será si vencieres» (240). After killing Arias Gonzalo's first son he boasts that he is ready to send another to his grave. All are offended by this Castilian version of «hubris», for it goes against all laws of *cortesía*:

> ARIAS: ¡Don Diego! vence matando,
> pero no aflixas diciendo.
> URRACA: ¡Más valiente que piadoso
> y cortés eres, don Diego!
> ... ...
> RODRIGO: advierte, por vida mía,
> que nunca la cortesía
> quitó la fuerça a la espada. (243-244)

Don Diego's exalted world soon comes crashing down around him as a blow from Rodrigo Arias sends his horse fleeing from the field of combat. Pride turns to bitterness as don Diego sees himself defeated and dishonored. He who believed he was fighting to sustain God's law [38] now finds himself the wronged victim of Fortune:

> ¡Ay, cielo! ¡Ah, Fortuna ayrada!
> Si tú contra mí te armas,
> ¿para qué lucidas armas?
> ¿para qué valiente espada? (257)

The outcome of the combat mirrors the complexity of the whole issue. Though Rodrigo Arias succeeds in ejecting don Diego from the combat arena he is also killed by the Castilian. There is no definitive victor and each side can and does claim victory for itself and defeat for the opponent. Sancho's disruption of moral order has created a world of chaos where reality can sustain seemingly opposing interpretations simultaneously: a world where victory is indistinguishable from defeat, where a deliverer is also a traitor, where men are fated and yet free, where the innocent are implicated in guilt and where an accusation can be just and unjust at the same time.[39] Similarly, Arias Gonzalo experiences both grief and pride when he sees his dying son:

---

[38] Before entering combat don Diego commends himself to God: «¡y a Vos, por quien pienso ser instrumento de castigo!» (216).
[39] Similarly, the outcome of the combat can be seen as a sign from God or

> Sólo un muerto vencedor
> heroycamente juntara
> la lástima con la embidia,
> enemigas declaradas. (256)

The judges are forced to come to a compromise decision that paves the way for the restoration of order: Diego Ordóñez is declared official victor while Zamora is cleared from the accusation of guilt. As a final gesture of unified repudiation of the regicide, the tribunal condemns Bellido to death.

The arrival of Alfonso reunites all the forces of the kingdom under a rightful king. For a moment, however, the issue of responsibility for Sancho's death flares up and threatens to divide the kingdom once more. In the «Jura de Santa Gadea» episode Rodrigo offends the king by asking Heaven to strike down Alfonso if he has participated in Sancho's murder. A violent interchange between vassal and king follows and the Cid voluntarily exiles himself. In a number of well known *romances*[40] it is Alfonso who banishes the Cid and the two remain suspicious of each other long after this incident. But Castro chooses to end his play on a note of harmony as Urraca convinces the Cid to return and all swear allegiance to Alfonso.[41] Though no closer to understanding the true significance of the death of its king, the kingdom has decided to pick up the pieces and forge on in unity.

---

as an act of pure chance. The Castilians undertake the *reto* believing that God will allow the just party to win, but nowhere in the course of the combat does anyone comment that God has revealed His will to them.

[40] See Durán, nos. 811, 812 and 814.

[41] With the succession of Alfonso the kingdom returns to its true mission: the conquest and conversion of the Moors. This is symbolized in the figure of Zayda, the Moorish beauty, who falls in love with Alfonso while he is in Moorish territory and who, at the end of the play, converts to Christianity to become María. This romantic subplot is of Castro's invention; he bases it on a passing detail of the *Primera crónica general,* Chap. 847, in which the daughter of Aben Habat, king of Seville, is baptized and later gives her lands to Alfonso. For a further discussion of the importance of these incidents see Weiger's introduction to *Las hazañas del Cid,* pp. 17-18.

CONCLUSION

Guillén de Castro repeatedly portrays kings as the source of social and moral disorder, and his plays implicitly call into question the legitimacy of a social code that places personal honor and submission to the king above reason, morality and the welfare of the Christian state. The result is not an unambiguous celebration of the honor code but a heightened awareness of its moral shortcomings. In the most profound sense —that is, in the system of values that he espouses— Castro cannot be said to be a mere follower of Lope de Vega. From the very outset of his career, Castro reveals a personal vision of kingship and honor that he never abandons, not even when Lope's popularity is at its zenith. When Castro adopts elements of Lope's dramatic system in his later plays, he treats them in a highly problematic and ambiguous fashion.

Throughout his introductory study to Castro's theater Eduardo Juliá Martínez has shown how many characteristics of Castro's «first period» works can be attributed to an imitation of the works of Virués: scenes of cruelty and bloodshed, a certain bombastic rhetoric, scenes of madness, settings in the fantastic kingdom of Hungary, names such as Lotario and Celauro, the character of the vengeful and cruel woman, to mention just a few details. But Virués serves as an inspiration to Castro for more than just the external elements mentioned by Juliá. The whole underlying structure of Castro's plays of unjust power takes its point of departure from the older dramatist, with its emphasis on a trilogy of characters: the unjust king, the male subject caught in a conflictive situation precipitated by an act of royal injustice, and a deliverer/avenger.

Castro's unjust king is a direct literary descendant of Virués' tyrant: a monarch who places his own will over his kingly duties and who exploits his position of power to achieve personal satisfaction. He expects unquestioning submission to his mandates, destroying all those who stand in the way of his gratification. What Castro adds in certain instances to Virués' stock figure is an inner consciousness of his own evil, an awareness of the human weakness that makes him a slave to his emotions. In *El amor constante* the King watches himself descend into a Hell-like state until he finally wishes for his own death; the King of *El nacimiento de Montesinos* realizes the wrong he is committing but finds himself overpowered by love and unable to control himself; in the later *Hazañas del Cid* King Sancho knowingly deafens himself to Heaven's warning in order to satisfy his political ambition. In these three cases this inner awareness adds a tragic dimension to the coldblooded tyrant of the earlier dramatist.

Castro's plays of unjust power are above all studies of individual subjects and of the way they attempt to come to terms with tyranny. As we trace the development of Castro's conception of the central protagonist, a loyal subject unjustly treated by his monarch, we can detect the ways in which Lope's theater merges with the early pattern of *El amor constante*. In Virués' tragedies those subject to the tyrant, whether the faceless masses of the *Atila* or the more individualized Menón of *La gran Semíramis,* emerge not as positive heroes, but as victims of royal power. The case of Menón is of particular importance, for here Virués begins to explore, however superficially, the interior reactions of a loyal subject betrayed by his king. Though King Nino's self-serving exploitation of his position of authority sends Menón's personal fortune plummetting, it is Menón's inner sense of helplessness and impotence that leads to a deeper psychological defeat. Guillén de Castro takes this spiritually defeated character as the model for the central figure of Celauro of *El amor constante* and of Count Alarcos. Both of these protagonists define themselves as subjects loyal to their king when they are suddenly confronted with demands they find both unjust and immoral: Celauro, like Menón, is to cede his beloved to a king already married, and Alarcos is to kill his wife to avenge the supposedly offended honor of the king. Each takes an openly defiant stand against the king but upon experiencing the king's power as greater than his own each undergoes a process of spiritual disintegration. Celauro's inability to justify in his own mind the moral legitimacy of his revolt leads to vacillation, a guilty conscience and a madness that culminates in his death. Alarcos' opposition to the King's violation of Christian law is silenced by the latter's threat to kill the Count's entire family; forced to carry out an act against his conscience, Alarcos, too, goes mad.

However, beginning with *El nacimiento de Montesinos* Castro gives evidence of moving towards Lope in his portrayal of this central protagonist. Both Grimaltos of that play and Miguel Centellas of *El perfecto caballero* believe submission to the king to be an absolute obligation and remain faithful to that principle even when faced with unjust, and even immoral, orders from their sovereign. Like Rodrigo of *Las mocedades del Cid,* the internal conflict between duty and human emotion is resolved with the decision to follow the socially honorable course of action. In making this choice, these characters, in contrast to Celauro and Alarcos, remain spiritually and psychologically whole in the face of crisis. Yet, as Castro ironically suggests, this unquestioning submission gives free rein to tyranny. Finally, *Las hazañas del Cid* brings together the opposing personalities of Rodrigo and Diego Ordóñez. The latter's unwillingness to question his king's actions and his unswerving devotion to King Sancho, even after the monarch's death, lead to continued disorder and further political disunity. Rodrigo, on the other hand, tempers his loyalty with moral questioning. Although Rodrigo cannot rescue Castile from inner strife, his awareness of a higher ethical law singles him out as a moral exemplar.

The resolution of the problem of tyranny in these plays also initially takes its point of departure from Virués. In both *Atila furioso* and *La gran Semíramis* the king meets his death at the hands of an individual who can no longer tolerate the existence of a morally perverse ruler. Such characters, while they act on behalf of moral law, can themselves offer no hope for a restoration of order. Flaminia, herself a woman as immoral as Atila until the point of her conversion, dies along with her victim as a punishment for her sinful life, and Ninias gives signs of beginning a new reign of vice similar to that of his mother. In his earlier plays Guillén de Castro transforms this character into a mythical saviour figure who embodies the spirit of natural and Christian law and in whose action Castro dramatizes the moral superiority of those laws to the arbitrary will of the king. In *El amor constante, El Conde Alarcos* and *El nacimiento de Montesinos* this figure is the young son of the protagonist. Born and raised in the woods, he lives by the laws of nature and judges the king's actions against those laws. Unlike his father, his instinctive ability to judge good from evil allows him to take action effectively against the king when he sees a moral wrong without feeling restrained by respect for the king's social position. It is through his positive intervention, carried out with the absolute conviction of its righteousness, that order is restored to the kingdom. In these works the promise of a new moral order is assured when the young hero is proclaimed the new ruler.

This positive young hero undergoes transformation into a much more problematic and ambivalent character in our later two plays. In *El perfecto caballero* Castro sets against the submissive Miguel Centellas the more emotionally explosive character of Ludovico who, in a moment of rage, kills the usurping tyrant so honored by Miguel. In so doing, Ludovico ironically carries out the mandate of natural law and is hailed as the new king. And in *Las hazañas del Cid* Castro creates a new dramatic tension by setting against the traditional interpretation of Bellido Dolfos as a traitor the startling idea that he acts as an instrument of Divine Justice.

Influenced by the ideological currents of the late sixteenth century,

Castro brings a new political dimension to the pattern set by his predecessor. At the heart of each play we have examined stands the conflict between two opposing views of royal power: the position espoused by natural law theorists that natural and Christian laws stand above the will of the king, and that espoused by the absolutists that the king's will is law. The conflict between resistance and obedience existed not only between these two diverse ideological poles but also within the writings of the proponents of natural law. While these doctrinal works supported disobedience, armed resistance and even regicide, they tempered their position with cautionary warnings that there must exist sound proof that the king is a tyrant before any move against him may be deemed licit, and with the seemingly contradictory affirmation that the state must suffer the tyrant in cases where the public welfare might be endangered by an act of opposition. For these thinkers defiance was a morally problematical issue, a difficult decision of conscience.

Castro's works mirror the complexity of this controversial issue. If in all five plays opposition to the king is seen as justified and sanctioned by the tenets of natural and divine laws, those characters whom we have identified as the «loyal male subject» cannot fully reconcile this point of view with what they feel to be the honorable (i.e. loyal) behavior demanded of a perfect subject. While Castro ultimately sides with the proponents of natural law and Christian morality his chief concern as a dramatist is to explore the vital conflicts that arise both within and among individual subjects when the king turns against his own kingdom. And while Castro looks to the doctrine of natural law to bring these works to a positive conclusion, the works themselves, filled as they are with ambivalencies towards both «imperfect» emotional characters (Celauro, Alarcos, Roldán, Ludovico, Bellido Dolfos) and «perfectos caballeros» (Grimaltos, Miguel Centellas, Diego Ordóñez), must be seen as morally problematic dramas of opposing tensions rather than as vehicles of political propaganda.

BIBLIOGRAPHY

EDITIONS OF THE COMEDIAS OF GUILLÉN DE CASTRO

D. Guillén de Castro. *Las mocedades del Cid.* Edited with an introductory study and notes by Víctor Said Armesto. Madrid: Espasa-Calpe, S. A., 1968.
Obras de don Guillén de Castro y Bellvis. Edited, with an introductory study by Eduardo Juliá Martínez, 3 vols. Madrid: Imprenta de la Revista de Archivos, Bibliotecas y Museos, 1925-1927.

OTHER PRIMARY SOURCES

DURÁN, AGUSTÍN: *Romancero general.* Vols. X and XVI of the *Biblioteca de Autores Españoles.* Madrid: M. Rivadeneyra, 1849, 1851.
MARIANA, JUAN DE: *Del rey y de la institución real.* Translated by Humberto Armella Maza, 2 vols. Madrid: Publicaciones Españolas, 1961.
MENÉNDEZ Y PELAYO, MARCELINO: *Antología de poetas líricos castellanos.* Vol. VIII. Madrid: 1899. Reprinted in: MENÉNDEZ Y PELAYO, MARCELINO: *Obras completas.* Vol. XXIV. Santander: CSIC, 1945.
Poetas dramáticos valencianos. Edited with an introductory study by Eduardo Juliá Martínez. 2 vols. Madrid: Tipografía de la Revista de Archivos, 1929.

SECONDARY SOURCES

ALFARO, ARSENIO: «Observaciones sobre el rey y el sentimiento monárquico en la comedia española de la edad de oro», *Revista Hispánica Moderna,* 34 (1968), pp. 132-139.
ALPERN, H.: «A Note on Guillén de Castro», *Modern Language Notes,* 41 (1926), pp. 391-392.
ARJONA, J. R.: «La introducción del gracioso en el teatro de Lope de Vega», *Hispanic Review,* 7 (1939), pp. 1-21.
— «Two Plays Attributed to Lope de Vega and Guillén de Castro», *Hispanic Review,* 33 (1965), pp. 387-394.
ARRÓNIZ, OTHÓN: *La influencia italiana en el nacimiento de la comedia española.* Madrid: Gredos, 1969.
ATKINSON, W. C.: «Seneca, Virués, Lope de Vega». In *Homenatge a Antoni Rubió i Lluch. Miscellània d'estudis literaris, històrics i lingüístics.* Barcelona, 1936, Vol. I, pp. 111-131.
BARRETT, L. L.: «The Omen in Guillén de Castro's Theater», *Hispania,* 22 (1939), pp. 73-78.
BÉNICHOU, PAUL: «El casamiento del Cid», *Nueva Revista de Filología Hispánica,* 8 (1953), pp. 316-336.

BEYSTERVELDT, A. A. VAN: *Répercussions du souci de la pureté de sang sur la conception de l'honneur dans la «Comedia Nueva» espagnole.* Leiden: E. J. Brill, 1966.
BLEZNICK, DONALD WILLIAM: «Fadrique Furió Ceriol, Political Thinker of Sixteenth Century Spain». Unpubl. Diss. Columbia, 1954.
BRUERTON, COURTNEY: «The Chronology of the *Comedias* of Guillén de Castro», *Hispanic Review,* 12 (1944), pp. 89-151.
CARRASCO URGOITI, MARÍA SOLEDAD: *El problema morisco en Aragón al comienzo del reinado de Felipe II.* Madrid: Castalia, Estudios de Hispanófila, 11, 1969.
CASA, FRANK P.: «Affirmation and Retraction in Golden Age Drama», *Neophilologus,* 61 (1977), pp. 551-564.
CASALDUERO, JOAQUÍN: «Guillén de Castro. Primera comedia de *Las mocedades del Cid*». In his *Estudios sobre el teatro español.* Madrid: Gredos, 1972, pp. 64-87.
CASTRO, AMÉRICO: «Algunas observaciones acerca del concepto del honor en los siglos XVI y XVII», *Revista de Filología Española,* 3 (1916); reprinted in his *Semblanzas y estudios españoles,* Princeton: Princeton University Press, 1956, pp. 319-382.
— *De la edad conflictiva,* 2nd edition. Madrid: Taurus, 1961.
CHARLTON, H. B.: *The Senecan Tradition in Renaissance Tragedy,* 1921; rpt. Manchester: Manchester University Press, 1946.
CORREA, GUSTAVO: «El doble aspecto de la honra en *Peribáñez y el comendador de Ocaña*», *Hispanic Review,* 26 (1958), pp. 188-199.
— «El doble aspecto de la honra en el teatro del siglo XVII», *Hispanic Review,* 26 (1958), pp. 99-107.
CRAPOTTA, JAMES: «The Cid of Guillén de Castro: The Hero as Moral Exemplar», *Revista de Estudios Hispánicos,* forthcoming.
— «The Unity of *La gran Semíramis* of Cristóbal de Virués». In *Creation and Recreation: Experiments in Literary Form in Early Modern Spain.* Ed. Ronald E. Surtz and Nora Weinerth. Newark, Delaware: «Juan de la Cuesta» Hispanic Monographs, 1983, pp. 49-60.
CRAWFORD, J. P. W.: «Influence of Seneca's Tragedies on Ferrera's *Castro* and Bermúdez's *Nise lastimosa* and *Nise laureada*», *Modern Philology,* 12 (1914-1915), pp. 39-54.
DELGADO MORALES, MANUEL: «Tiranía y derecho de resistencia en *Las mocedades del Cid*», *Segismundo,* 15 (1981), pp. 173-184.
DÍEZ BORQUE, JOSÉ MARÍA: *Sociología de la comedia española del siglo XVII.* Madrid: Ediciones Cátedra, 1976.
DUNN, PETER N.: «Honour and the Christian Background in Calderón». In *Critical Essays on the Theater of Calderón.* Ed. Bruce W. Wardropper. New York: New York University Press, 1965, pp. 24-60.
EBERSOLE, A. V.: «La originalidad de *Los malcasados de Valencia* de Guillén de Castro», *Hispania,* 53 (1972), pp. 456-460.
ELLIOTT, J. H.: *Imperial Spain: 1469-1716.* New York: Mentor Books, 1963.
ENTWISTLE, WILLIAM J.: «Honra y duelo», *Romanistisches Jahrbuch,* 3 (1950), pp. 404-420.
FIGGIS, JOHN NEVILLE: *The Divine Right of Kings,* 1896; rpt. with an introduction by G. R. Elton. New York: Harper and Row, 1965.
FIORE, ROBERT L.: *Drama and Ethos: Natural-Law Ethics in Spanish Golden Age Theater.* Lexington, Kentucky: The University Press of Kentucky, 1975.
FLOECK, WILFRIED: «*Las Mocedades del Cid*» *von Guillen de Castro und* «*Le Cid*» *von Corneille. Ein neuer vergleich.* Bonn: Romanischer Seminar der Universitat Bonn, 1969.

FRAKER, CHARLES F.: «Sancho II: Epic and Chronicle», *Romania*, 95 (1974), pp. 467-507.
FROLDI, RINALDO: *Lope de Vega y la formación de la comedia*. Madrid: Anaya, 1973.
FRYE, NORTHROP: *Anatomy of Criticism*. New York: Atheneum Press, 1970.
GALANES, ADRIANA LEWIS: «*Las mocedades del Cid* de Guillén de Castro: Corteza y meollo», *Hispanófila*, 44 (1972), pp. 13-31.
GARCÍA LORENZO, LUCIANO: «Introducción» to *Guillén de Castro. Don Quijote de la Mancha*. Salamanca: Anaya, 1971.
— «Introducción» to *Guillén de Castro. Los malcasados de Valencia*. Madrid: Castalia, 1976.
— «Introducción» to *Guillén de Castro. Las mocedades del Cid*. Madrid: Ediciones Cátedra, 1978.
— *El teatro de Guillén de Castro*. Barcelona: Editorial Planeta, 1976.
— *El tema del Conde Alarcos. Del Romancero a Jacinto Grau*. Madrid: CSIC, 1972.
GILMAN, STEPHEN: «The *Comedia* in the Light of Recent Criticism including the New Criticism», *Bulletin of the Comediantes*, 12 (Spring, 1960), pp. 1-5.
— «The Problem of the Spanish Renaissance», *Folio*, 10 («Studies in the Literature of Spain of the Sixteenth and Seventeenth Centuries», Michael J. Ruggerio, ed., 1977), pp. 37-54.
GÓMEZ-MORIANA, ANTONIO: *Derecho de resistencia y tiranicidio: estudio de una temática en las obras de Lope de Vega*. Santiago de Compostela: Biblioteca Hispánica de Filosofía de Derecho, Porto y Cía., editores, 1968.
GREEN, OTIS H.: «New Documents for the Biography of Guillén de Castro y Bellvis», *Revue Hispanique*, 81, 2ème partie (1933), pp. 248-260.
— *Spain and the Western Tradition*, 4 vols. Madison: University of Wisconsin Press, 1964.
HAMILTON, BERNICE: *Political Thought in Sixteenth-Century Spain*, Oxford: Clarendon Press, 1963.
HAMILTON, T. EARLE: «The Aside in the *comedias* of Alarcón», *Hispania*, 46 (1963), pp. 536-539.
HERMENEGILDO, ALFREDO: *La tragedia en el renacimiento español*. Barcelona: Editorial Planeta, 1973.
HERRERA GARCÍA, MIGUEL: «La monarquía teorética de Lope de Vega», *Fénix*, 1935, pp. 179-224, 305-362.
ISAR, ERBERT E.: «La cuestión del llamado 'senequismo' español», *Hispanófila*, 2 (enero, 1958), pp. 11-30.
JONES, C. A.: «Honor in Spanish Golden Age Drama; Its Relation to Real Life and to Morals», *Bulletin of Hispanic Studies*, 35 (1958), pp. 199-210.
— «Spanish Honour as Historical Phenomenon: Convention and Artistic Motive», *Hispanic Review*, 33 (1965), pp. 32-39.
JONES, SONIA H.: «The Devices of Foreshadowing in Lope de Vega's *Comedia*». Unpubl. Diss. Harvard, 1971.
JULIÁ MARTÍNEZ, EDUARDO: «La métrica en las producciones dramáticas de Guillén de Castro», *Anales de la Universidad de Madrid*, Letras, 3 (1934), pp. 62-71.
— «Sobre *El amor constante* de Guillén de Castro», *Revista de Filología Española*, 30 (1946), pp. 118-123.
KANTOROWICZ, ERNST H.: *The King's Two Bodies. A Study in Mediaeval Political Theology*. Princeton: Princeton University Press, 1957.
KAUFMANN, WALTER: *Tragedy and Philosophy*. New York: Doubleday, 1968.
LA DU, ROBERT R.: «The Dramatic Tradition of Bellido Dolfos», *Hispania*, 46 (1963), pp. 693-699.

- «Eight Lines from *Las mocedades del Cid*», *Romance Notes*, 1 (1959-1960), pp. 46-49.
- «Honor and the King in the *Comedias* of Guillén de Castro», *Hispania*, 45 (1962), pp. 211-217.
- «A Rejoinder to: Matrimony in the Theater of Guillén de Castro», *Bulletin of the Comediantes*, 11 (Fall, 1959), pp. 10-16.

LARSON, DONALD R.: *The Honor Plays of Lope de Vega*. Cambridge: Harvard University Press, 1977.

LEAVITT, STURGIS E.: «Divine Justice in *Las hazañas del Cid*», *Hispania*, 12 (1929), pp. 141-146.
- «Some Aspects of the Grotesque in the Drama of the Siglo de Oro», *Hispania*, 18 (1935), pp. 77-86.
- «Una comedia sin paralelo: *Las hazañas del Cid*, de Guillén de Castro». In *Homenaje a William L. Fichter. Estudios sobre el teatro antiguo hispánico y otros ensayos*. Ed. A. David Kossoff and José Amor y Vázquez. Madrid: Castalia, 1971, pp. 429-438.

LLORÉNS, VICENTE: «La intención del *Quijote*». In his *Literatura, historia, política*. Madrid: Revista de Occidente, 1967, pp. 205-222.
- «Teatro y sociedad: De la tragedia al drama poético en el teatro antiguo español». In his *Aspectos sociales de la literatura española*. Madrid: Castalia, 1974, pp. 21-45.

LYNCH, JOHN: *Spain Under the Habsburgs*. Oxford: Basil Blackwell, 1964.

MANCINI, GUIDO: *La romanza del Conde Alarcos*. Pisa: Libreria Goliardica Editrice, 1959.

MARAÑÓN, GREGORIO: *Antonio Pérez*, 2 vols. Madrid: Espasa-Calpe, S. A., 1958.

MARAVALL, JOSÉ ANTONIO: *Las comunidades de Castilla*, 2nd. edition. Madrid: Revista de Occidente, 1970.
- *La Philosophie politique espagnole au XVIIe siècle*. Translation of *La teoría española del estado en el siglo XVII*. Madrid, 1944, by Louis Cazes and Pierre Mesnard. Paris: Librairie Philosophique J. Vrin, 1955.
- *Teatro y literatura en la sociedad barroca*. Madrid: Seminarios y Ediciones, S. A., 1972.

MARSHALL, PAULINE: *El caballero perfecto de Alonso Gerónimo de Salas Barbadillo*. Boulder: University of Colorado Press, 1949.

MARTÍ GRAJALES, FRANCISCO: «Guillén de Castro. Noticia biográfica». In *Cancionero de la Academia de los Nocturnos de Valencia*. Vol. 3: Apéndice. Valencia, 1906, pp. 119-188.

MATULKA, BARBARA: *The Cid as a Courtly Hero: From the Amadís to Corneille*. New York: Institute of French Studies, Columbia University, 1928.

McBRIDE, CHARLES: «Los objetos materiales como objetos significativos en *Las mocedades del Cid*», *Nueva Revista de Filología Hispánica*, 15 (1961), pp. 448-458.

McCRARY, WILLIAM C.: «Guillén de Castro and the *Mocedades* of Rodrigo: A Study of Tradition and Innovation». In *Romance Studies in Honor of Edward Billings Ham*. Hayward-California: California State College Publications, no. 2, 1967, pp. 89-102.
- «Ritual Action and Form in *La Estrella de Sevilla*». In *Homenaje a William L. Fichter. Estudios sobre el teatro antiguo hispánico y otros ensayos*. Ed. A. David Kossoff and José Amor y Vázquez. Madrid: Castalia, 1971, pp. 505-513.

McCURDY, RAYMOND R.: «Lope de Vega y la pretendida inhabilidad española para la tragedia: resumen crítico». In *Homenaje a William L. Fichter. Estudios sobre el teatro antiguo hispánico y otros ensayos*. Ed. A. David Kossoff and José Amor y Vázquez. Madrid: Castalia, 1971, pp. 525-536.

FRAKER, CHARLES F.: «Sancho II: Epic and Chronicle», *Romania,* 95 (1974), pp. 467-507.
FROLDI, RINALDO: *Lope de Vega y la formación de la comedia.* Madrid: Anaya, 1973.
FRYE, NORTHROP: *Anatomy of Criticism.* New York: Atheneum Press, 1970.
GALANES, ADRIANA LEWIS: «Las mocedades del Cid de Guillén de Castro: Corteza y meollo», *Hispanófila,* 44 (1972), pp. 13-31.
GARCÍA LORENZO, LUCIANO: «Introducción» to *Guillén de Castro. Don Quijote de la Mancha.* Salamanca: Anaya, 1971.
— «Introducción» to *Guillén de Castro. Los malcasados de Valencia.* Madrid: Castalia, 1976.
— «Introducción» to *Guillén de Castro. Las mocedades del Cid.* Madrid: Ediciones Cátedra, 1978.
— *El teatro de Guillén de Castro.* Barcelona: Editorial Planeta, 1976.
— *El tema del Conde Alarcos. Del Romancero a Jacinto Grau.* Madrid: CSIC, 1972.
GILMAN, STEPHEN: «The *Comedia* in the Light of Recent Criticism including the New Criticism», *Bulletin of the Comediantes,* 12 (Spring, 1960), pp. 1-5.
— «The Problem of the Spanish Renaissance», *Folio,* 10 («Studies in the Literature of Spain of the Sixteenth and Seventeenth Centuries», Michael J. Ruggerio, ed., 1977), pp. 37-54.
GÓMEZ-MORIANA, ANTONIO: *Derecho de resistencia y tiranicidio: estudio de una temática en las obras de Lope de Vega.* Santiago de Compostela: Biblioteca Hispánica de Filosofía de Derecho, Porto y Cía., editores, 1968.
GREEN, OTIS H.: «New Documents for the Biography of Guillén de Castro y Bellvis», *Revue Hispanique,* 81, 2ème partie (1933), pp. 248-260.
— *Spain and the Western Tradition,* 4 vols. Madison: University of Wisconsin Press, 1964.
HAMILTON, BERNICE: *Political Thought in Sixteenth-Century Spain,* Oxford: Clarendon Press, 1963.
HAMILTON, T. EARLE: «The Aside in the *comedias* of Alarcón», *Hispania,* 46 (1963), pp. 536-539.
HERMENEGILDO, ALFREDO: *La tragedia en el renacimiento español.* Barcelona: Editorial Planeta, 1973.
HERRERA GARCÍA, MIGUEL: «La monarquía teorética de Lope de Vega», *Fénix,* 1935, pp. 179-224, 305-362.
ISAR, ERBERT E.: «La cuestión del llamado 'senequismo' español», *Hispanófila,* 2 (enero, 1958), pp. 11-30.
JONES, C. A.: «Honor in Spanish Golden Age Drama; Its Relation to Real Life and to Morals», *Bulletin of Hispanic Studies,* 35 (1958), pp. 199-210.
— «Spanish Honour as Historical Phenomenon: Convention and Artistic Motive», *Hispanic Review,* 33 (1965), pp. 32-39.
JONES, SONIA H.: «The Devices of Foreshadowing in Lope de Vega's *Comedia».* Unpubl. Diss. Harvard, 1971.
JULIÁ MARTÍNEZ, EDUARDO: «La métrica en las producciones dramáticas de Guillén de Castro», *Anales de la Universidad de Madrid,* Letras, 3 (1934), pp. 62-71.
— «Sobre *El amor constante* de Guillén de Castro», *Revista de Filología Española,* 30 (1946), pp. 118-123.
KANTOROWICZ, ERNST H.: *The King's Two Bodies. A Study in Mediaeval Political Theology.* Princeton: Princeton University Press, 1957.
KAUFMANN, WALTER: *Tragedy and Philosophy.* New York: Doubleday, 1968.
LA DU, ROBERT R.: «The Dramatic Tradition of Bellido Dolfos», *Hispania,* 46 (1963), pp. 693-699.

— «Eight Lines from *Las mocedades del Cid*», Romance Notes, 1 (1959-1960), pp. 46-49.
— «Honor and the King in the *Comedias* of Guillén de Castro», *Hispania*, 45 (1962), pp. 211-217.
— «A Rejoinder to: Matrimony in the Theater of Guillén de Castro», *Bulletin of the Comediantes*, 11 (Fall, 1959), pp. 10-16.
LARSON, DONALD R.: *The Honor Plays of Lope de Vega*. Cambridge: Harvard University Press, 1977.
LEAVITT, STURGIS E.: «Divine Justice in *Las hazañas del Cid*», *Hispania*, 12 (1929), pp. 141-146.
— «Some Aspects of the Grotesque in the Drama of the Siglo de Oro», *Hispania*, 18 (1935), pp. 77-86.
— «Una comedia sin paralelo: *Las hazañas del Cid*, de Guillén de Castro». In *Homenaje a William L. Fichter. Estudios sobre el teatro antiguo hispánico y otros ensayos*. Ed. A. David Kossoff and José Amor y Vázquez. Madrid: Castalia, 1971, pp. 429-438.
LLORÉNS, VICENTE: «La intención del *Quijote*». In his *Literatura, historia, política*. Madrid: Revista de Occidente, 1967, pp. 205-222.
— «Teatro y sociedad: De la tragedia al drama poético en el teatro antiguo español». In his *Aspectos sociales de la literatura española*. Madrid: Castalia, 1974, pp. 21-45.
LYNCH, JOHN: *Spain Under the Habsburgs*. Oxford: Basil Blackwell, 1964.
MANCINI, GUIDO: *La romanza del Conde Alarcos*. Pisa: Libreria Goliardica Editrice, 1959.
MARAÑÓN, GREGORIO: *Antonio Pérez*, 2 vols. Madrid: Espasa-Calpe, S. A., 1958.
MARAVALL, JOSÉ ANTONIO: *Las comunidades de Castilla*, 2nd. edition. Madrid: Revista de Occidente, 1970.
— *La Philosophie politique espagnole au XVIIe siècle*. Translation of *La teoría española del estado en el siglo XVII*. Madrid, 1944, by Louis Cazes and Pierre Mesnard. Paris: Librairie Philosophique J. Vrin, 1955.
— *Teatro y literatura en la sociedad barroca*. Madrid: Seminarios y Ediciones, S. A., 1972.
MARSHALL, PAULINE: *El caballero perfecto de Alonso Gerónimo de Salas Barbadillo*. Boulder: University of Colorado Press, 1949.
MARTÍ GRAJALES, FRANCISCO: «Guillén de Castro. Noticia biográfica». In *Cancionero de la Academia de los Nocturnos de Valencia*. Vol. 3: Apéndice. Valencia, 1906, pp. 119-188.
MATULKA, BARBARA: *The Cid as a Courtly Hero: From the Amadís to Corneille*. New York: Institute of French Studies, Columbia University, 1928.
MCBRIDE, CHARLES: «Los objetos materiales como objetos significativos en *Las mocedades del Cid*», *Nueva Revista de Filología Hispánica*, 15 (1961), pp. 448-458.
MCCRARY, WILLIAM C.: «Guillén de Castro and the *Mocedades* of Rodrigo: A Study of Tradition and Innovation». In *Romance Studies in Honor of Edward Billings Ham*. Hayward-California: California State College Publications, no. 2, 1967, pp. 89-102.
— «Ritual Action and Form in *La Estrella de Sevilla*». In *Homenaje a William L. Fichter. Estudios sobre el teatro antiguo hispánico y otros ensayos*. Ed. A. David Kossoff and José Amor y Vázquez. Madrid: Castalia, 1971, pp. 505-513.
MCCURDY, RAYMOND R.: «Lope de Vega y la pretendida inhabilidad española para la tragedia: resumen crítico». In *Homenaje a William L. Fichter. Estudios sobre el teatro antiguo hispánico y otros ensayos*. Ed. A. David Kossoff and José Amor y Vázquez. Madrid: Castalia, 1971, pp. 525-536.

MENÉNDEZ PIDAL, RAMÓN: «Del honor en el teatro español». In his *De Cervantes y Lope de Vega*. Madrid: Espasa-Calpe, S. A., 1940, pp. 145-173.
— *La España del Cid*, 2 vols. Madrid: Editorial Plutarco, S. A., 1929.
— *Romancero hispánico*, 2 vols. Madrid: Espasa-Calpe, S. A., 1953.
MÉRIMÉE, HENRI: *L'Art dramatique à Valencia, depuis les origines jusqu'au commencement du XVIIe siècle*. Toulouse: Edouard Privat, Editeur, 1913.
— «Pour la biographie de don Guillén de Castro», *Revue des Langues Romanes*, 50 (1907), pp. 311-322.
— *Spectacles et comédiens à Valencia (1580-1613)*. Toulouse: Edouard Privat, Editeur, 1913.
MONTESINOS, JOSÉ F.: «Observaciones y notas» to Lope de Vega. *La corona merecida*. Madrid: Teatro Antiguo Español, textos y estudios, V, 1923.
MOORE, JEROME AARON: *The Romancero in the Chronicle-Legend Plays of Lope de Vega*. Philadelphia, 1940.
MORBY, EDWIN S.: «Some Observations on *Tragedia* and *Tragicomedia* in Lope», *Hispanic Review*, 11 (1943), pp. 185-209.
NORTHUP, GEORGE TYLER: *Three Plays by Calderón*. New York: D. C. Heath and Company, 1926.
ORTIGOZA VIEYRA, CARLOS: *Los móviles de la «comedia»*. México, 1954.
PAPPANASTOS, GEORGIA: «The Heroic Ideal in Guillén de Castro's First Play», *Kentucky Romance Quarterly*, 23 (1976), pp. 421-437.
— «Verbal Subtlety in Castro's *El amor constante*», *Bulletin of the Comediantes*, 28 (1976), pp. 17-22.
PARKER, A. A.: «The Approach to the Spanish Drama of the Golden Age», *The Tulane Drama Review*, 4 (1959), pp. 43-59.
PÉREZ, ELISA: «Algunos aspectos de la evolución del romancero», *Hispania*, 18 (1935), pp. 151-160.
PRADES, JUANA DE JOSÉ: *Teoría sobre los personajes de la comedia nueva*. Madrid: CSIC, 1963.
PRIOR, MOODY E.: *The Drama of Power: Studies in Shakespeare's History Plays*. Illinois: Northwestern University Press, 1973.
RANK, OTTO: «The Myth of the Birth of the Hero», 1914; rpt. in *The Myth of the Birth of the Hero and Other Writings*. Ed. Philip Freund. New York: Vintage Books, 1959, pp. 1-96.
REGLÁ, JOAN: *Aproximació a la història del País Valencià*. Valencia: L'Estel, 1968.
REICHENBERGER, ARNOLD G.: «The Uniqueness of the *Comedia*», *Hispanic Review*, 27 (1959), pp. 303-316.
REIG, CAROLA: *El cantar de Sancho II y cerco de Zamora*. Madrid: Revista de Filología Española, Anejo 37, 1947.
RENNERT, HUGO A.: «Introducción» to Guillén de Castro. *Ingratitud por amor*. Philadelphia: Ginn and Company, 1899.
ROCA FRANQUESA, JOSÉ MARÍA: «Un dramaturgo de la edad de oro: Guillén de Castro. Notas a un sector de su teatro», *Revista de Filología Española*, 28 (1944), pp. 378-427.
ROUGEMONT, DENIS DE: *Love in the Western World*, 1940; rpt. New York: Harper and Row, 1956.
RUIZ RAMÓN, FRANCISCO: *Historia del teatro español (desde sus orígenes hasta 1900)*. Madrid: Alianza Editorial, 1967.
SALINAS, PEDRO: «La espada y los tiempos de la vida en *Las mocedades del Cid*». In his *Ensayos de literatura hispánica*. Madrid: Aguilar, 1958, pp. 151-157.
SÁNCHEZ AGESTA, LUIS: *El concepto del estado en el pensamiento español del siglo XVI*. Madrid: Marisal, 1959.
SANTELICES, LIDIA: «La originalidad en la segunda parte de *Las mocedades del Cid*

(Guillén de Castro)», *Anales de la Universidad de Chile,* Santiago de Chile, año 93, 3.ª serie, no. 20 (1935), pp. 169-178.
SARGENT, CECILIA VENNARD: *A Study of the Dramatic Works of Cristóbal de Virúes.* New York: Hispanic Institute in the United States, 1930.
SEBOLD, RUSSELL P.: «Un David español, o 'Galán Divino': El Cid Contrrareformista de Guillén de Castro». In. *Homage to John M. Hill. In Memoriam.* Ed. Walter Poesse. Indiana: Indiana University Press, 1968, pp. 217-242.
SCHEVILL, RUDOLF: *The Dramatic Art of Lope de Vega, Together with La dama boba.* Berkeley: University of California Press, 1918.
SPITZER, LEO: «'Soy quien soy'», *Nueva Revista de Filología Hispánica,* 1 (1947), pp. 113-127.
SWISLOCKI, MARSHA H.: «Lope, the *Romancero* and the *Comedia».* Unpubl. Diss. Harvard, 1976.
TILLYARD, E. M. W.: *Shakespeare's History Plays.* London: Chatto and Windus, 1964.
WARDROPPER, BRUCE W.: «Fuenteovejuna: *el gusto* and *lo justo», Studies in Philology,* 53 (1956), pp. 159-171.
WATSON, ANTHONY: *Juan de la Cueva and the Portuguese Succession.* London: Tamesis Books Ltd., 1971.
WEIGER, JOHN G.: «Another Look at the Biography of Guillén de Castro», *Bulletin of the Comediantes,* 10 (Spring, 1958), pp. 3-5.
— *Cristóbal de Virués.* Boston: Twayne Publishers, 1978.
— «Forced Marriage in Castro's Theater», *Bulletin of the Comediantes,* 15 (Fall, 1963), pp. 1-4.
— «Guillén de Castro: Apostilla cronológica», *Segismundo,* 14 (1978-80), pp. 103-122.
— *Hacia la comedia: De los valencianos a Lope.* Madrid: Cupsa Editorial, 1978.
— «Introducción» to *Las hazañas del Cid,* Barcelona: Puvill-Editor, 1980.
— «Matrimony in the Theater of Guillén de Castro», *Bulletin of the Comediantes,* 10 (Fall, 1958), pp. 1-3.
— «The Relationship of Honor, Fama and Death in the Valencian Drama of the Golden Age». Unpubl. Diss. Indiana, 1966.
— «Los silencios de *Las mocedades del Cid», Hispanófila,* 23 (enero, 1965), pp. 1-7.
— «Sobre la originalidad e independencia de Guillén de Castro», *Hispanófila,* 31 (septiembre, 1967), pp. 1-15.
— *The Valencian Dramatists of Spain's Golden Age.* Boston: Twayne Publishers, 1976.
WILSON, WILLIAM E.: *Guillén de Castro.* New York: Twayne Publishers, 1973.
— «Guillén de Castro and the Codification of Honor», *Bulletin of the Comediantes,* 19 (Spring, 1967), pp. 24-27.
— «Two Notes on Guillén de Castro», *Hispanic Review,* 18 (1950), pp. 63-66.
— «Two Recurring Themes in Castro's Plays», *Bulletin of the Comediantes,* 9 (Fall, 1957), pp. 25-27.
YOUNG, RICHARD A.: *La figura del rey y la institución real en la comedia lopesca.* Madrid: José Porrúa Turanzas, S. A., 1979.